Turning the Tables on Apologetics

Princeton Theological Monograph Series
K. C. Hanson, Charles M. Collier, D. Christopher Spinks,
and Robin A. Parry, Series Editors

Recent volumes in the series:

Steven C. van den Heuvel
*Bonhoeffer's Christocentric Theology and Fundamental
Debates in Environmental Ethics*

Andrew R. Hay
God's Shining Forth: A Trinitarian Theology of Divine Light

Peter Schmiechen
*Gift and Promise:
An Evangelical Theology of the Lord's Supper*

Hank Voss
*The Priesthood of All Believers and the Missio Dei:
A Canonical, Catholic, and Contextual Perspective*

Alexandra S. Radcliff
*The Claim of Humanity in Christ: Salvation and
Sanctification in the Theology of T. F. and J. B. Torrance*

Yaroslav Viazovski
*Image and Hope:
John Calvin and Karl Barth on Body, Soul, and Life Everlasting*

Anna C. Miller
*Corinthian Democracy:
Democratic Discourse in 1 Corinthians*

Thomas Christian Currie
*The Only Sacrament Left to Us: The Threefold
Word of God in the Theology and Ecclesiology of Karl Barth*

Turning the Tables on Apologetics

*Helmut Thielicke's Reformation
of Christian Conversation*

JEFFERY L. HAMM

◆PICKWICK *Publications* · Eugene, Oregon

TURNING THE TABLES ON APOLOGETICS
Helmut Thielicke's Reformation of Christian Conversation

Princeton Theological Monograph Series 231

Copyright © 2018 Jeffery L. Hamm. All rights reserved. Except for brief quotations in critical publications or reviews, no part of this book may be reproduced in any manner without prior written permission from the publisher. Write: Permissions, Wipf and Stock Publishers, 199 W. 8th Ave., Suite 3, Eugene, OR 97401.

Pickwick Publications
An Imprint of Wipf and Stock Publishers
199 W. 8th Ave., Suite 3
Eugene, OR 97401

www.wipfandstock.com

PAPERBACK ISBN: 978-1-5326-4522-8
HARDCOVER ISBN: 978-1-5326-4523-5
EBOOK ISBN: 978-1-5326-4524-2

Cataloguing-in-Publication data:

Names: Hamm, Jeffery L., author.

Title: Turning the tables on apologetics : Helmut Thielicke's reformation of Christian conversation / Jeffery L. Hamm.

Description: Eugene, OR: Pickwick Publications, 2018. | Princeton Theological Monograph Series 231 | Includes bibliographical references and index.

Identifiers: ISBN 978-1-5326-4522-8 (paperback) | ISBN 978-1-5326-4523-5 (hardcover) | ISBN 978-1-5326-4524-2 (ebook)

Subjects: LCSH: Thielicke, Helmut, 1908–1986—Criticism and interpretation. | Van Til, Cornelius, 1895–1987—Criticism and interpretation. | Apologetics. | Apologetics—History—20th century.

Classification: BX8080 T475 H36 2018 (print). | BX8080 (ebook).

Manufactured in the U.S.A. 04/03/18

Unless otherwise noted, Scripture quotations are from the ESV® Bible (The Holy Bible, English Standard Version®), copyright © 2001 by Crossway, a publishing ministry of Good News Publishers. Used by permission. All rights reserved.

To Kelly

A faithful companion in my pilgrimage on this earth

Lord, I believe; help thou mine unbelief
(Mark 9:24; KJV)

Contents

Tables | viii
Acknowledgments | ix
Abbreviations and Shortened Titles | xi
Introduction | xiii

1. A Theology for Apologetics | 1
2. A Confession for Apologetics | 34
3. The Rejection of Traditional Apologetics | 60
4. An Apologetic of the Cross | 90
5. The Apologetic Method of Christ's Conversations | 127
6. The Apologetic Venture of Faith | 173
7. The Advance of Christian Apologetics | 196
8. Conclusion | 210

Bibliography | 215

Tables

Table 1. Thielicke's Translation of Van Til | 209

Acknowledgments

This book is a revision of my PhD thesis written at King's College, University of Aberdeen, Scotland. It would not exist without the help and support of many whom deserve acknowledgment. Gratitude should be expressed to my *Doktorvater*, Philip Ziegler, who took me in as a stranger and wanderer between universities. His pastoral care, which I shall never forget, carried over into my research, even that which extended beyond the boundary of this project, yet into which he unreservedly invested himself. I remain amazed at his command of historical and modern theology, which made the task of the ignorant even manageable. Indeed, from our early supervisory sessions, he could see into my project vital elements that I did not comprehend until the very end. He is the icon of a scholar and a gentleman, from whom I have learned responsible God-talk.

I shall always be thankful for my true neighbors, Warren and Sallie Williamson, without whom this project, and much else in my life, would have been simply impossible. Words fail. Not to be forgotten is Warren's sister, Carol, who thoughtfully introduced me to a German theologian when needed, and supplied the first three volumes of Thielicke.

Dr. Michael Calvert, *the* Thielicke scholar, also deserves credit. Though I was unknown to him, he took my random phone call to inquire about the feasibility of this project, and faithfully supported it to the end. Most of all, I give thanks for and to my undeserved family, whose lives and love are a refuge in the stress and storm of my very existence.

Abbreviations and Shortened Titles

Adventure	*Faith: The Great Adventure*
Believe	*How to Believe Again*
Between	*Between God and Satan*
CD	Karl Barth, *Church Dogmatics*
Chips	*Being a Christian When the Chips Are Down*
Conversations	*Between Heaven and Earth: Conversations with American Christians*
Creed	*I Believe: The Christian Creed*
Death	*Death and Life*
Depths	*Out of the Depths*
Diary	*African Diary*
Ethics	*Theological Ethics*
Fragen	*Fragen des Christentums an die Moderne Welt*
Freedom	*The Freedom of the Christian Man: A Christian Confrontation with Secular Gods*
God's World	*Man in God's World*
How Modern?	*How Modern Should Theology Be?*
Human	*Being Human . . . Becoming Human: An Essay in Christian Anthropology*
Letters	*The Faith Letters*
LW	*Luther's Works*
Meaning	*Christ and the Meaning of Life: A Book of Sermons and Meditations*
Modern Thought	*Modern Faith and Thought*

Mount	*Life Can Begin Again: Sermons on the Sermon on the Mount*
Mythology	*The Restatement of New Testament Mythology*
Nihilism	*Nihilism: Its Origin and Nature—With a Christian Answer*
Notes	*Notes from a Wayfarer*
Prayer	*The Prayer that Spans the World: Sermons on the Lord's Prayer*
Question	*The Hidden Question of God*
Sex	*The Ethics of Sex*
Silence	*The Silence of God*
Trouble	*The Trouble with the Church*
Voyage	*Voyage to the Far East*
WA	*Luthers Werke (Weimarer Ausgabe)*
Waiting	*The Waiting Father: Sermons on the Parables of Jesus*
World Began	*How the World Began: Man in the First Chapters of the Bible*
Zwischen	*Zwischen Gott und Satan: Die Versuchung Jesu und die Versuchlichkeit des Menschen*

Introduction

DURING THE APOCALYPTIC REIGN of the Third Reich, the "Führer's Deputy" notified the young chair of theology at the University of Heidelberg,[1] Helmut Thielicke (AD 1908–86), that he was dismissed from the faculty and no longer employable as a theologian anywhere in Germany. Thielicke's "bad reputation" as an outspoken critic of National Socialism had become well known through his lectures and other venues,[2] not the least of which was his own doctoral dissertation.[3] He recalls, the project "—which was an attempt to construct something like a reformed theology of history—stemmed to a large degree from my protest against this questionable form of natural theology."[4] Since it "was diametrically opposed to the Nazi understanding of life and history, it was later one of the reasons for my dismissal in 1940."[5]

To eradicate his political resistance, the Nazis interned Thielicke in a small town in southern Germany and forbade him to write, speak, or travel. From this location, however, he managed to do all three. Diplomats smuggled his secret books across the Swiss border via briefcase. Friends then published them anonymously and distributed them to German troops both at the front and in prisoner-of-war camps.[6] During the Allied air raids, Thielicke lectured weekly to some three thousand who made their way through the

---

1. Thielicke, *Notes*, 114.

2. The title of Thielicke's speech, "Christ or Antichrist," delivered to the Rhineland-Westphalia Parish Congress gives a slight sense of his criticism.

3. Referring to Thielicke's second doctorate (*History and Existence*; translation mine and for the below titles), supervised by Paul Althaus (see *Notes*, 72–79). Thielicke wrote a prior PhD under Eugen Herrigel (*Relationship between the Ethical and Esthetic*; see *Notes*, 61). The dissertation for the second work was so extensive that the faculty allowed it to stand as his *habilitation* thesis (a postdoctoral degree that qualifies one to teach at a German university). Nonetheless, Thielicke resumed postdoctoral studies—to supplement his systematic work—in historical theology (*Reason and Revelation*; see *Notes*, 79–81).

4. *Notes*, 75.

5. Ibid., 77.

6. Thielicke, *God's World*, 11; see *Notes*, 79.

ruins and rubble to gather in the Stuttgart Cathedral Church.[7] After the venerable *Stiftskirche* was destroyed, the newspapers cryptically announced the continuation of the lectures—not even referencing Thielicke's name—with the small print notice: "Thursday, 8 P.M. T."[8] Not least, Thielicke traveled to Freiburg where he joined a conspiracy group plotting to overthrow Hitler.[9] Following the failed assassination attempt of July 1944, the Gestapo arrested most of those involved, but not Thielicke. Years later he learned the reason why they had never apprehended him. A surviving collaborator informed Thielicke that while imprisoned, "the Gestapo had confronted him with a list of the people present at the main meeting of November 17, 1942, one name of which was illegible. It was mine."[10]

After the war, Thielicke eventually became the first rector of the newly formed theological faculty at the University of Hamburg. At the offer of the local bishop, and with the conviction that preaching precedes theology, he began to fill the pulpit of Hamburg's largest church, the Great Church of St. Michael. On the Sundays that he preached, the three thousand seat sanctuary filled to capacity as early as an hour before the start of the service, creating such a traffic problem around the Gothic sanctuary that police assistance was required to prevent gridlock in the inner city.[11] Without modern marketing techniques, advertisement or any high-powered propaganda, his sermons, addressed to those "for whom 'God' is still an open question,"[12]

---

7. *God's World*, 8–9; see *Notes*, 151–52.

8. *God's World*, 9; see *Notes*, 163. After a few meetings in the new location, the town church of Bad Cannstadt, the bombers destroyed it also. At the sound of the air-raid siren, Thielicke immediately gave the benediction and the audience evacuated to the bomb shelters. As Thielicke was the last to leave, he only found a bunker by the light of the bombers' flares. After the attack, Thielicke learned of its dreadful result, "Two of my hearers, one of them the organist who had just been playing, were killed" (*God's World*, 10; see *Notes*, 186–87).

9. Among this circle of resisters were Carl Goerdeler, who was intended to become the first German Chancellor of the post-Nazi government; and Dietrich Bonhoeffer, the group's contact to the international church, especially the bishop of Chichester. Their famous roles in the conspiracy, and consequent executions, need no introduction. Thielicke's unsung contribution was to help draft a document, following the lines of Christian ethics, "on the comprehensive reorganization of political, economic, and cultural life after the war" (*Notes*, 174). Thielicke later published the document (*In the Zero Hour*; translation mine).

10. *Notes*, 178.

11. Doberstein reports the capacity of the St. Michael's Church as "four thousand," which still could not meet the demanding response, requiring an additional service "again during the week with a repetition of the same sermon" (Thielicke, *Waiting*, 7).

12. *Believe*, 7. About his preaching, Clyde Fant maintains that "Helmut Thielicke may well rank as one of the greatest preachers in the history of the Christian faith. His philosophy of preaching has made a profound impact both in Europe and America, and

attracted the attention of the atheists, nihilists, and skeptics from a cross-section of society in non-churchgoing Hamburg; a phenomenon all the more remarkable for such a notoriously secular city. The spectacle even caused the national media to inquire curiously into the excitement, which ended with a 1955 cover article of *Der Spiegel*, beaming a photo of Thielicke's face from every kiosk in Germany.[13] Indeed a vital figure for post Second World War Germany, Thielicke's celebrity as a theologian gained for him invitations to address audiences from the Bundestag to the White House.[14]

No small part of Thielicke's success was due to an apologetic venture that guided his theological work. In a rare moment of reflection on this project, he divulges:

> Perhaps this may even be the particular goal that hovers before the author and his work—that it must take over the task of previous apologetics in a *new way* and perhaps contribute in a small way to transplanting the task of Christian discussion to a different and *theologically genuine level.*[15]

Traditional apologetics of Thielicke's time—methodologies founded on philosophical and scientific assumptions—lies entombed in the sublevel of unrealistic, that is, natural theology. Thielicke's objective, therefore, is to commandeer the mission of apologetics in order to develop a new approach which operates on the high ground of actual, or Reformational, theology. In sum, the audacious goal of Thielicke's theological calling is nothing less than to help usher the Protestant Reformation of apologetics. Though a guest professor at Drew University and lecturer at prestigious divinity schools such as Union, Chicago, and Princeton, of whose sermons, lectures, and theological works over thirty volumes have been translated into English, scholars have given surprisingly little attention to his theology, and almost none to his apologetic.[16] At this crucial moment in the

---

virtually all of his sermons are masterpieces (*Christian Preaching*, 226).

13. "Pulpit and Lectern" (translation mine), *Spiegel*, 34–39; see *Notes*, 285–87.

14. Thielicke's June 17, 1962 "secular" speech to the Bundestag regarding national identity in a democracy, broadcast on television and radio, resulted in a book analyzing its sociological effect on the Germans (Othmer, *Democracy or Fatherland*; translation mine). While Thielicke was lecturing in Washington D.C., the first lady who knew his books invited him to the White House. After their long theological discussion, Mrs. Carter announced, "Now Jimmy wants to see you!" She then took Thielicke to the Oval Office to speak with the President (*Notes*, 362–63).

15. *God's World*, 217; italics added.

16. Substantial interest in Thielicke's thought has been limited mostly to doctoral dissertations, focusing mainly on his anthropology, ethics, or homiletics. The only work addressing Thielicke's apologetic is Speier's published dissertation (*Initiator*) which

secular age,[17] the deficiency presents the urgent and unavoidable challenge of attempting to introduce it.

The purpose of this book is to explore whether Thielicke achieves his goal of reforming apologetics in order to accomplish the task, as he explains, in a "new way" and at a "theologically genuine level." This is done in view of what Thielicke perceives as the three problematic characteristics of traditional apologetics, specifically, that it speaks from a position of rational certainty instead of a realistic position of *Anfechtung*; seeks to demonstrate the faith according to the allegedly neutral epistemological standards of autonomous humanity; and functions in a defensive answer-giving mode rather than an offensive counterquestion role which challenges a hearer's unbelief.[18] The research follows the course that Thielicke steers away from these faulty features where he discovers, or rather rediscovers, a "new way" of persuasion, that is, a table-turning method modeled after Christ's conversations. This new apologetic operates on the "theologically genuine level" of an *Anfechtung* "theology of the cross." The counterquestion approach integrates the counterdemonstrationism of the cross which renounces the supposedly neutral systems of empiricism and rationalism. Simply stated, the method is controlled by its own message.

We argue that Thielicke's self-described agenda to recover the task of apologetics holds and provides the interpretive framework for his entire theological enterprise. This argument turns around the above three characteristics of traditional apologetics which he sees as troublesome, each of which is addressed specifically in particular chapters. Thielicke's response to the first feature is treated in the initial two chapters. Chapter 1 introduces Thielicke's theology for apologetics that he identifies as a theology of *Anfechtung* which I carefully translate as *faith-crisis*, the antithesis of faith. Following Luther, Thielicke believes that *Anfechtung* is what makes the apologist and is crucial for the task of Christian conversation. For until one is in the hell of *faith-crisis* one cannot see what is truly real and come to the truth. Chapter 2 examines a confession for apologetics that expresses its *Anfechtung* theology; the "Nevertheless" of faith recorded in Psalm 73. This countercausative confession of God's existence against all appearances to the contrary is what overcomes *faith-crisis* and emerges as the fundamental presupposition for

---

remains in German. He devotes much attention to Thielicke's biography (ibid., 19–88), after which he coordinates the topic in the scope of Thielicke's preaching, dogmatics, and ethics. Regarding Thielicke's goal to reform apologetics, Speier confirms that "the concept of 'apologetics,' which had become problematic in the 20th century, underwent an entirely new interpretation through him" (ibid., 11; translation mine).

17. Taylor maps this era on history's timeline (*Secular Age*).
18. *God's World*, 216–18.

the task of apologetics. Closer examination of the confession shows that the presuppositional "Nevertheless" repudiates a postsuppositional "Therefore" of rational certainty. The second fault of traditional apologetics is covered in chapter 4, to which Thielicke responds with an apologetic of the cross. The approach is committed to the counterdemonstrationism of the message of the cross, and is thus both counterempirical and counterintuitive (1 Cor 1:22–23). For the ability to perceive God, over and against the empirical and rational which seemingly contradicts his existence, is a function of faith. The third feature of traditional apologetics is considered in chapter 5, which Thielicke addresses by advocating apologetics' offensive role to counter-question unbelief. His counterquestion method follows the negative table-turning approach of Jesus' conversations. The presuppositional approach, which pushes the *faith-crisis* antithesis of the hearer's worldview, appeals to the *imago Dei* within the hearer that one seeks to suppress and thus focuses on the region in which the Holy Spirit performs the miracle of regeneration.

The remaining chapters of the book serve to augment the triadic structure. Chapter 3 reviews Thielicke's perspective on the history of apologetics and its failure. He repeatedly points to the Logos Apologists to illustrate the destructive characteristics of traditional methods. The survey then shows how both the philosophical proofs of classical apologetics and evidential apologetics of the scientific age fail, in Thielicke's judgment, because they do not witness to transcendence. Chapter 6 highlights the positive side of the Law-Gospel dialectic, contained within Thielicke's apologetic, which equalizes his negative table-turning strategy. This venture of faith incorporates aspects of Pascal's "Wager" and Kierkegaard's leap. Thielicke persuades those open to truth to gamble on God or leap into belief in order to discover whether God exists and who he is.

Chapter 7 investigates the relevant question whether Thielicke's reformation of traditional apologetics even could be used to advance contemporary Reformed apologetics. To draw attention to the significance of Thielicke's contribution, we compare and contrast Thielicke to Cornelius Van Til (1895–1987), the founding professor of apologetics at Westminster Theological Seminary in Philadelphia, Pennsylvania. The choice of this conversation partner, rather than any other apologist, is due to the fact that Van Til is commonly considered as the pioneer of presuppositionalism.[19] Even

---

19. A *presupposition* is a first principle or operating assumption about reality. Van Til takes presuppositions into account and maintains, e.g., "the existence of this God is the presupposition of all possible predication" (*Apologetics*, 39). His approach seeks to challenge the unbelieving presuppositions of a skeptic's worldview and thereby argue for God indirectly. Van Til did not christen his method by the term *presuppositionalism*, rather it was coined by a critic (*Defense*, x, 241n10). Instead he referred initially to his

Van Til's critics acknowledge that he is "without doubt, the leading exponent of presuppositionalism" to the extent that "Van Tillianism [sic] is almost a synonym for presuppositionalism."[20] Since the approach, accordingly, "has become the majority report today among Reformed theologians,"[21] many acclaim Van Til as the Protestant reformer of apologetics, at least in the English speaking world.

When reading Thielicke, however, one cannot but notice that his "new way" of apologetics is virtually identical to that of Van Til, albeit in its own unique idiom. One might even think that Thielicke's apologetic engagement at a "theologically genuine level" represents a reinvigoration, that is, reformation, of Van Til. Indeed, no one less in stature than K. Scott Oliphint, heir to Van Til's chair, recognizes the need and therefore endeavors "to translate much of what is *meant* in Van Til's writings from their often philosophical and technical contexts to a more basic biblical and theological context."[22] Van Til—though I am personally indebted to him as a Van Tilian myself—is admittedly known to be "philosophical" and "technical." What a Reformed apologetic consequently needs is a "biblical" and "theological" translation. Could a friendly conversation partner be found where least expected, outside of the Van Tilian, moreover, Calvinistic tradition that might assist the translation? Specifically, could the unique idiom of Thielicke's apologetic reformation—relentless in its biblical and theological form and force—supplement the necessary task particularly along the lines for which Oliphint calls in order to "take a Reformed apologetic and move it forward"?[23]

This book clearly displays that Thielicke's reformation of traditional apologetics stands on its own weight and merits attention for its own worth,

---

apologetic as *transcendental*, a more helpful description, but abandoned the Kantian buzzword when accused of philosophical Idealism. Unfortunately, the confusing label *presuppositionalism* is the name by which his method is most popularly known.

20. Sproul et al., *Classical Apologetics*, 183.

21. Ibid., 183.

22. Oliphint, *Covenantal Apologetics*, 26; see 28–30, 38, 139, 198, 222. Frame confirms that Van Til's work is "in need of translation" (*Apologetics to the Glory*, xii). Although, as Frame himself acknowledges, some Van Tilians consider his work a revision (ibid., xi, xii).

23. Oliphint, *Covenantal Apologetics*, 26. Bosserman brilliantly clarifies Van Til's claim that only the ontological Trinity solves the ancient problem of philosophy, i.e., the one and the many—the very core of his apologetic—and is thus the transcendental precondition of predication (*Trinity and Vindication*). Indeed, Oliphint is appreciative for the fine-tuning of Van Til's sometimes ambiguous thought, which as he states is "moving it forward" (ibid., xiii). Yet Bosserman's refinement of Van Til's project, applied to the "*dissolution*" of the one-many problem (ibid., 85), leaves Van Til untranslated in his "philosophical and technical contexts" which sets the former's work on a different course than that of this project.

any reference to Van Til notwithstanding. Nonetheless, the question remains whether and to what extent Thielicke's contribution could help reform contemporary presuppositional apologetics. Footnotes explore the question from this introduction through chapter 6 and provide over 6,000 words of analysis. Chapter 7 then retrieves the content and summarizes the most substantial contributions in order to help advance Reformed apologetics.

A Theology for Apologetics

AMONG THIELICKE'S EARLY WORKS is an untranslated collection of essays bound together under the rubric *Theologie der Anfechtung*,[1] the label which he employs to categorize his theological methodology. The foreword to the volume explains the trademark title and thus provides the lens through which Thielicke views the entire theological landscape, and it would be important to note that especially prominent in this scene is his apologetic.

Etymologically, the term *apologetics* is derived from the Greek word *apologia*, a combination of the preposition *apo* (from) and root *logos* (word), which literally means a "word from." The lexicon defines it as a "speech of defense."[2] A classic example from antiquity of such an *apologia* is Plato's dialogue, *The Apology*, a retelling of the defense of his famous teacher, Socrates, against the accusation of marketing strange gods. In Scripture, the word is employed by the Apostle Peter in the exhortation to his readers, Gentile believers slandered unjustly, "but in your hearts honor Christ the Lord as holy, always being prepared to make a defense [*apologia*] to anyone who asks you for a reason for the hope that is in you" (1 Pet 3:15).[3] From this mandate has arisen the modern theological discipline of *apologetics*, which deals with the reasoned defense of the faith.[4] Traditionally, theologians saw

---

1. This methodologically illuminating volume is that to which Thielicke continually points throughout his career (*God's World*, 181n9; *Sex*, 279n22; "Temptation," 232n9; *Ethics* 1:94n2; *Evangelical Faith*, 1:94n17; 2:15n7; 336n7; 339n10). Indeed, *Theologie Anfechtung* is also that to which *Spiegel* points to identify Thielicke's theology. In its feature article on his popularity as a Hamburg preacher, the work is noted when describing the pulpit theatrics Thielicke avoided not only in his practice, but also researched in his "theory" ("Pulpit and Lectern," 34).

2. Bauer et al., *Greek-English Lexicon*, 96.

3. All scriptural quotations are from the English Standard Version (ESV) unless otherwise noted. The word is also used to describe the trials of the Apostle Paul, who not surprisingly reasons, "Brothers and fathers, hear the defense [*apologia*] that I now make before you" (Acts 22:1; see 24:10; 25:8, 16; 26:2, 24). The description of Paul's apologetic manner is that of winsome "persuasion" (Acts 18:4; 19:8, 26; 26:28; 28:23–24).

4. *The Oxford Dictionary of the Christian Church* defines apologetics as "the defense of the Christian faith on intellectual grounds" (73). Thielicke, however, shows that the

1

the subject as the prolegomena to or preparation for systematic theology, which categorizes the orthodox doctrines of theology proper, Christology, soteriology, anthropology, ecclesiology, and eschatology.

In Thielicke's *Theologie der Anfechtung*, however, he never sees apologetics in distinction from his theology but rather as its destiny. He explains, "In this respect it is not about apologetics, but rather theology—of course a form of theology which in a particular way forces itself upon the author as his fate."[5] Elsewhere Thielicke boldly asserts that "all theology which pursues the genuine goal of ungenuine apologetics has a character of a 'theology of *Anfechtung*.'"[6] To this, theology's mission statement, Thielicke adds, "Theologians to a high degree have the task of representatively carrying the intellectual and spiritual conflict on behalf of their contemporaries. Here, if we are not afraid of an overloaded term, is the *apologetic* task of theology."[7] According to Thielicke, the primary task of theology, reflecting its true goal, is apologetic.[8] This apologetic purpose of theology then eliminates the false dichotomy between theology and apologetics as it is traditionally known. Instead, for Thielicke, they are one and the same.[9] Theology is apologetics

---

task of apologetics is offensive rather than defensive. Instead of proposing "to give Christian answers to human questions . . . it attacks the world with *its* questions and forces it to face them" (*God's World*, 217). Accordingly, we may state provisionally that apologetics is the art of Christian persuasion which attacks unbelief by counterquestioning, i.e., turning the tables on, its autonomous presuppositions; see ch. 5.

5. *Theologie Anfechtung*, iv; translation mine. Again, in referring to "apologetics," Thielicke is rejecting the traditional methods controlled by philosophical and scientific assumptions. This becomes clearer in the following quotes, and particularly perspicuous in chapters 3–6.

6. *God's World*, 218.

7. *Modern Thought*, 9. This statement, made over three and a half decades after the first "apologetics" quotation at n5, reveals the unwavering consistency of Thielicke's theology.

8. Reviewing Thielicke's *Evangelical Faith*, Pless agrees that "the weight of the work is tilted toward issues of prolegomena and, to a degree, apologetics" ("Helmut Thielicke [1908–1986]," 289). Although critical of its content, Klann concedes that Thielicke's systematics is an attempt to meet "apologetically" rational inquiries about the Christian faith ("Helmut Thielicke Appraised," 162).

9. Concerning Thielicke's apologetic, Speier explains, "That this theme hitherto was not taken up is hardly surprising, for Thielicke's overriding interest in apologetics was never made an explicit theme. So it appears at first glance that the formulation of the question raised here touches only a marginal dogmatic theme. However, on closer examination it becomes clear how much Thielicke's apologetic understanding is a systematic correlation with his total theology. One could even successfully hypothesize, on the basis of this observation, that Thielicke's theology is only understandable when one has considered his apologetic approach" (*Initiator*, 16; translation mine).

and apologetics is theology. Consequently, to understand Thielicke's apologetic reformation, it is critical to comprehend his theology of *Anfechtung*.[10]

Anfechtung in Luther

Anfechtung, as Thielicke employs it, is a German term borrowed originally from Martin Luther (1483–1546). Within the American edition of *Luther's Works*, the word is rendered as "temptation," "trial," "affliction," "assaults," as well as "tribulation."[11] In *The Theology of Martin Luther*, written by Thielicke's *Doktorvater*, Erlangen professor Paul Althaus, the translator notes about *Anfechtung*: "This word has been translated in various ways, e.g., trials, temptations, assault, perplexity, doubt."[12] Finally he settles on "temptation," as per his explanation: "the theology of faith is and remains, however, the theology of temptation {*Theologie der Anfechtung*}."[13] David Scaer, in his helpful essay, "The Concept of *Anfechtung* in Luther's Thought," states that *Anfechtung*, and its Latin counterpart *tentatio*, could be listed among those unique words that "defy adequate translation" and consequently suggests since the reformer's concept of *Anfechtung* is so multifaceted, "it is best left untranslated."[14] Recently a work of Oswald Bayer—Thielicke's eventual successor as professor of theology at the University of Tübingen[15]—was published in English by the title, *Theology the Lutheran Way*. The translators also acknowledge the staggering linguistic challenge presented by the

---

10. Just as Thielicke considers theology as apologetics, so too he considers preaching as apologetics. Yet it must be stressed, though one sees his approach predominantly in the lectern and pulpit, he also engaged in personal apologetics. For example, he recalls one such encounter on board ship with an old sailor, a self-described freethinker, who insisted that the theologian drink whiskey with him. After their midnight conversation, Thielicke left the rough sea-dog "with the curious feeling of having achieved a minimum of missionary success with a maximum of alcohol consumption" (*Voyage*, 119). Thielicke's engagement in personal persuasion is also seen in his conversation with Ludwig Feuerbach which he models as his "new way" of apologetics ("Critical Appraisal: The End and New Beginning of Apologetics," *Modern Thought*, 449–57; see ch. 5).

11. Scaer, "Concept of *Anfechtung*," 15.

12. Althaus, *Theology Luther*, 33n21.

13. Ibid., 34.

14. Scaer, 15. This seems to be common practice. Trueman employs the German term "for the sake of brevity and conformity with convention" (*Luther*, 118).

15. Thielicke occupied this post in Tübingen from the end of the war in 1945 to 1954—during which time he also served as rector of the university and president of the Conference of the University Rectors of Germany—until he was called to become the first rector of the theological faculty and its chair of theology at the University of Hamburg (*Notes*, 199–265).

word *Anfechtung*, yet do not take Scaer's good-humored path of "theological and literary cowardice."[16] Instead, after citing a few common options for translation, the duo offer their own dynamic definition, "The word *Anfechtung* is difficult to render into English. It can mean trial, testing, temptation, challenge, or attack. The precise meaning it has in a given place will depend on the context. Usually we have translated it as spiritual attack."[17] Their innovative rendering of *Anfechtung* as "spiritual attack" is attractive, but there is still more to be considered. For in an encyclopedia article on *Anfechtung*, authored by Thielicke himself, the word is also translated by the entry "Temptation." The editor, however, hastens to note that "the English word 'temptation' is not quite adequate as a translation of the German word *Anfechtung*" and defensively insists that this "article deals largely with Luther's ideas on this subject and uses the word 'temptation' in its more deeply theological sense."[18] Naturally, the question is: What is the deeper theological meaning that Luther has in mind by his use of the word *Anfechtung*?

Psalm 119

The first occurrence of *Anfechtung*, at least in its Latin garb *tentatio*, is found in the 1539 Wittenberg edition of the reformer's writings, specifically the preface to volume one. Luther mentions "three rules" which "point out to you a correct way of studying theology . . . amply presented throughout the whole Psalm [119]. They are *Oratio, Meditatio, Tentatio*."[19] It is vitally significant to note, that in these three terms, Luther encapsulates his whole understanding of and approach to theology. Given their theological predominance, he highlights them within the preface, not only by capitalizing them, but by writing them in Latin in the middle of the German text. Their importance is all the more magnified when viewed through the referential lens of Psalm 119, which in the context of Luther's battle with Rome brings them into still sharper focus. For this psalm dedicated to the Word of God, employing no less than eight different terms for the Word of God, that is, law, statutes, precepts, commandments, testimonies, etc., literally becomes

---

16. Scaer, 15.
17. Bayer, *Theology Lutheran Way*, 239n280.
18. "Temptation," 2327.
19. *LW* 34:285. Bayer notes that this is the only place in all of Luther's writings where the famous formula emerges: "The reference to it in WA 48:276: 'Meditatio, Tentatio, Oratio make a theologian' is not a second occurrence, but merely 'an excerpt from Luther's preface'" (*Theology Lutheran Way*, 225n126).

Luther's fight song against the Pope as it "was to be sung and read daily in worship."[20]

Against this background, Bayer summarizes the significance of the third rule, *tentatio*: "In this particular context, 'temptation' or 'spiritual attack' (*Anfechtung*) becomes the specific focus for understanding 'prayer' and 'mediation,' which are key themes of the psalm anyway."[21] His invaluable insight into the prominent role of *Anfechtung* in Luther's theology has not gone unnoticed. His editors state:

> Bayer's important contribution here is to stress the role of *tentatio*. He says that we only properly understand what God does through *oratio* and *meditatio* if we view it through the lens of *tentatio*. In other words, prayer and meditation, prayer and engagement with God's word, must be seen in the context of spiritual attack, which includes trial, doubt, and testing.[22]

This observation is critical to help grasp Thielicke's understanding of the prominence of *Anfechtung* in Luther's theology, for whenever he refers to the reformer regarding what it is that makes a theologian, he never once mentions the first two rules. He simply states, "This is what Luther meant when he said that '*tentatio facit theologum*' ([*Anfechtung*] makes the theologian)."[23]

Third Rule: *Tentatio*

Overlooking Luther's comments on the first two rules that make a theologian, prayer and meditation, the reformer writes in the preface:

> There is *tentatio*, *Anfechtung*. This is the touchstone which teaches you not only to know and understand, but also to experience how right, how true, how sweet, how lovely, how mighty, how comforting God's Word is, wisdom beyond all wisdom.
>
> Thus you see how David, in the Psalm mentioned, complains so often about all kinds of enemies, arrogant princes or tyrants, false spirits and factions whom he must tolerate because he meditates, that is, because he is occupied with God's Word (as has been said) in all manner of ways. For as soon as God's Word takes root and grows in you, the devil will harry you and

---

20. Luther, in Bayer, *Theology Lutheran Way*, 39–40.
21. Bayer, *Theology Lutheran Way*, 42.
22. Silcock and Mattes, in Bayer, *Theology Lutheran Way*, xi.
23. *Nihilism*, 176; see *Modern Thought*, 7.

make a real doctor of you, and by his assaults [*Anfechtungen*] will teach you to seek and love God's Word. I myself . . . am deeply indebted to my papists that through the devil's raging they have beaten, oppressed, and distressed me so much. That is to say, they have made a fairly good theologian of me, which I would not have become otherwise.[24]

A cursory exposition of this vital passage helps gather the "more deeply theological sense" of the meaning of *Anfechtung* in Luther's use of the term.

Outward Appearance—Inward Struggle

As is evident, Luther applies the interpretation of Psalm 119 to his own existential situation. Surrounding Luther, he sees "all kinds of enemies." On the one side, there are "arrogant princes or tyrants"—those German nobility allied with the Pope in Rome—and on the other side, "false spirits and factions"—the radical reformers. This outward focus on the political and religious world brings upon him "assaults" (*Anfechtungen*). So the outward appearance of reality that questions his faith in God triggers within Luther's soul a most agonizing spiritual struggle. Its symptoms are "something deeper than despair on account of sin, as are the trials and spiritual attack (*Anfechtung*) spoken of in . . . Psa. 22: 'My God, my God, why have you forsaken me?'"[25] The inner despair hurls the believer into the deepest spiritual crisis. Basically, for Luther then, what is at stake in the subject of *Anfechtung* is nothing less than the veracity of the first commandment, in other words, the reality of God. *Anfechtung* raises the question of whether God exists and is in control of this world or not. "*Anfechtungen* in Luther's thought," Scaer explains, "appear as contradiction."[26] As a result, "In the *Anfechtungen* the Christian is placed on the boundary line between faith and unbelief."[27]

In this situation of *Anfechtung*, as the passage shows, two different dimensions are involved—the outer realm of the world and the inner realm of the soul. This two-dimensional aspect here would then exclude from the theological meaning of *Anfechtung* any interpretation of it as mere sexual desire or bodily pain. Scaer reminds, "Luther suffered headaches and woke up in drenching sweats, but he also suffered from the *Anfechtungen* even when there were no physical maladies."[28] Thielicke adds, "Neither can

---

24. *LW* 34:286–87.
25. Luther, in Bayer, *Theology Lutheran Way*, 245n339.
26. Scaer, 16.
27. Ibid., 19.
28. Ibid., 21.

temptation be properly understood as merely psychological phenomenon, for it need not at all be marked by recognizable emotional disturbances (e.g., shock, fear, anxiety, or despair)."[29] Instead, inward *Anfechtung* cannot be isolated from outer contradiction. For it involves the two dimensions of what is inwardly a soul-searching struggle accompanying genuine faith and outwardly the appearance of reality which contradicts faith. Once again, in Luther's life situation, both realms intersect.

Experiential Knowledge

Another characteristic of *Anfechtung* shown in the preface is that it is a source of theological knowledge. Luther states, *Anfechtung* is "the touchstone which teaches you . . . to know and understand" by which knowledge he was qualified to be "a fairly good theologian." Yet about this theological education, one must take care to note that the knowledge to which Luther refers is not merely an intellectual assent reached purely by academic scholarship; rather, it is an experiential knowledge. *Anfechtung*, he states in the preface, "teaches you not only to know and understand, but also to experience." This reference to experience reflects Luther's extremely dim view of unaided human reason to which he refers as "the Devil's whore" and nicknames "Frau Hulda."[30] Reason was responsible for the perversion of the Gospel by the Scholastics, who attempted to harmonize it with Aristotelian philosophy. Since speculation lacks the *terra firma* of experience, Luther does not withhold from it any strong words: "All speculative theologians who deal only with ideas and have learned everything from books and nothing from experience, and who want to judge divine things on the basis of philosophy and human reason are of the devil."[31] Of course, the experience in view here is not a "pure experience that could only be the principle of a vague openness and incompleteness. What makes the theologian a theologian is not experience as such, but the experience of scripture."[32] Thielicke expounds on this vital point:

> In this context Luther thinks that temptation [*Anfechtung*] fulfills a most necessary function in the Christian life: it places faith in proper relation to the two poles within which it must operate. Faith is both: flight *from* God (inasmuch as he is the author of the Law) and *to* God (inasmuch as he is the author of

---

29. *Temptation*, 2327.
30. *LW* 40:174–75; see ch. 4.
31. In Bayer, *Theology Lutheran Way*, 46.
32. Bayer, *Theology Lutheran Way*, 63.

the Gospel) . . . Through temptation God initiates the flight from God to God . . . Temptation thus becomes the opposite pole of the Gospel.[33]

Anfechtung, functioning as the Law and driving one to the Gospel, leads then to the profound experience of the Word which Luther describes: "To experience how right, how true, how sweet, how lovely, how mighty, how comforting God's Word is." It is this experience of Scripture, initiated through *Anfechtung*, which provides a corrective to Scholastic theology.

Theology of the Cross

Finally, perhaps the most distinctive feature of *Anfechtung* theology is that it is totally counterintuitive, as detected in the preface by such statements as, "I myself . . . am deeply indebted to my papists that through the devil's raging they have beaten, oppressed, and distressed me so much." The paradox in this confession is truly baffling. For human nature is such that it would attempt to avoid the beatings, oppression, and distress that Luther associates with his experiences of *Anfechtungen*, yet he admits his genuine gratitude for them, knowing that they provide a real opportunity for faith to grow, and that through them, faith becomes "never stronger and more glorious."[34] As evidenced here, *Anfechtung* counteracts human reason, and runs in complete defiance to all worldly wisdom. Noetically, it operates in complete isolation from the philosophies of the world. This paradox, as shown above, is underscored in that the most basic characteristic of *Anfechtung* is its contradiction of all experiential appearance; historical, existential, and epistemic. In other words, explains Althaus, "Luther's understanding of *Anfechtung* as an essential characteristic of Christian existence is part of his theology of the cross."[35]

Luther's theology of the cross, to which Althaus refers, is found in the reformer's famous 1518 *Heidelberg Disputation*, particularly theses 19–21:

19. That person does not deserve to be called a theologian who looks upon the invisible things of God as though they were clearly perceptible in those things which have actually happened (Rom. 1:20).

20. He deserves to be called a theologian, however, who comprehends the visible and manifest things of God seen through suffering and the cross.

33. *Temptation*, 2328.
34. Luther, in *Temptation*, 2327–28.
35. Althaus, *Theology Luther*, 33.

21. A theologian of glory calls evil good and good evil. A theologian of the cross calls the thing what it actually is.[36]

The proofs of the theses provide insightful explanation of their interconnected propositions, but especially noteworthy to this discussion is that of article 20:

> Because men misused the knowledge of God through works, God wished again to be recognized in suffering, and to condemn wisdom concerning invisible things by means of wisdom concerning visible things, so that those who did not honor God as manifested in his works should honor him as he is hidden in his suffering. As the Apostle says in I Cor. 1 (:21), 'For since, in the wisdom of God, the world did not know God through wisdom, it pleased God through the folly of what we preach to save those who believe.' Now it is not sufficient for anyone, and it does him no good to recognize God in his glory and majesty, unless he recognizes him in the humility and shame of the cross. Thus God destroys the wisdom of the wise, as Isa. (45:15) says, 'Truly, thou art a God who hidest thyself.'[37]

Thielicke provides his own commentary of these theses:

> What the OT people of God experienced as God's absence . . . reappears in acute form in the NT theology of the cross. The cross represents God's extreme absence. It is a scandal to the Jew and folly to the Greek (1 Corinthians 1:23; Romans 9:32). There is here no theology of glory which can depict God at the heart of reality. There is instead a theology of the cross in which God is concealed.[38]

And with Luther's theology of the cross in mind, Thielicke muses over his own theological resume and lists the sole qualification that would indicate how the world should consider him; "Therefore, the author would not like to be another and remain just as he is—a theologian of *Anfechtung* and not a theologian of 'glory.' For all theology of the cross believes against *Anfechtung*."[39] For Thielicke, then, an apologetic of *Anfechtung* is elemental to an apologetic of the cross (see chapter 4).

---

36. *Heidelberg Disputation, Luther's Basic Theological Writings*, 31.

37. *Heidelberg Disputation*, 43–44.

38. *Evangelical Faith*, 1:229–30. Here Thielicke refers the reader to "Luther at the Heidelberg Disputation" (1:230n5; see 2:33n20; 2:59n90).

39. *Theologie Anfechtung*, iv; translation mine. As a theologian of *Anfechtung* is a theologian of the cross, Thielicke happily repeats, "We are theologians of the cross and

Anfechtung in Thielicke

The brief review of Luther's comments on *Anfechtung* from the preface to his 1539 collection indeed reveals a multi-faceted concept. Especially important for our purpose, though, is his understanding of *Anfechtung* as an essential element of Christian experience, "particularly the inner suffering to which a Christian is subjected in hours of trial and doubt,"[40] which points to the deeper theological meaning that Thielicke has in mind by his use of the term. Unfortunately, this connotation would be totally lost upon English speakers simply because of the inadequate translation of *Anfechtung* rendered by the unhappy and most commonly used choice of *temptation*. For in contemporary secular culture, the word temptation is probably not taken in the theological sense causing one to think of a spiritually anguishing experience which subjects one to doubt the reality of God. Regrettably, for moderns and post-moderns, the existence of God is not usually the question. More than likely, the word temptation is merely taken in its moral sense, perhaps just evoking the idea glamorized in a low budget movie of the seduction of a priest to illicit sex.[41] Nonetheless, the deeper theological meaning of *Anfechtung* is unambiguously clear throughout Thielicke's theological works, lectures, and sermons. A brief pilgrimage through this literary land bypasses any confusion and arrives precisely at Thielicke's idea of *Anfechtung*, enroute to which we are gladly led to a more sufficient definition.

Faith at Failure

The survey would begin most reasonably with Thielicke's *Theologie der Anfechtung*. Returning to the foreword, which also preliminarily previews all of his dogmatic work, Thielicke writes, "But the faith always faces *Anfechtung*, as certain it always believes against appearance, as certain as it is always besieged, and as certain as it never gets beyond the petition: Lord, I believe; help thou my unbelief."[42] In this description of *Anfechtung* that

---

not of glory" (*Evangelical Faith*, 2:33).

40. *Temptation*, 2327.

41. See *Temptation: Confessions of a Marriage Counselor*, written and directed by Tyler Perry (Tyler Perry Studios, 2013), DVD.

42. *Theologie Anfechtung*, iii; translation mine (Der Glaube aber ist immer angefochten, so gewiss er immer gegen den Augenschein glaubt, so gewiss er immer bedrängt ist und so gewiss er nie über die Bitte hinauskommt: Ich glaube, lieber Herr, hilf meinem Unglauben). Since *angefochten* is the perfect past participle of *anfechten*, the verb form of *Anfechtung*, I have chosen to translate it provisionally as "faces *Anfechtung*,"

ever accompanies faith, the theologian describes, as already seen in Luther, the fabricated "appearance" of reality that contradicts what one believes and contests faith. Thielicke illustrates the spiritual challenge with the request that is readily recognizable as that unique plea of the father of the demoniac recorded in the Gospel of Mark (9:24). Given the text's early introduction in Thielicke's thought, this petition is extremely influential in helping to shape his view and that from which he is never able to never escape.[43] Its theological moment for Thielicke would naturally warrant consideration of the context to gain the fullest sense of the meaning of the father's plea.

Arriving from the glory of the transfiguration, the Nazarene reenters the ruined realm of the demonic. The scene is of a disputation between the disciples, scribes, and a few bystanders. Out of the confusion of the crowd emerges the vexed dad of a demon possessed boy who brings his son to Jesus for exorcising. For the destructive power of the evil spirit, not simply a chronic neural disorder, throws the lad into near fatal seizures of epilepsy. In Christ's absence, the disciples try to heal the boy, but only in vain. Now the disillusioned father doubts Jesus' ability to deliver at all, and only after another brutal convulsion does he discouragingly appeal to Jesus for help, "If you can." At that point, Jesus counters the father's words where they are most laden with doubt and challenges, "'If you can'! All things are possible for one who believes" (Mark 9:23). To which the father utters the plea that so marks Thielicke. In the strictest sense, the petition manifests the father's unbelief, which he willingly confesses. William Lane adds:

> His cry expresses humanity and distress at being asked to manifest radical faith when unbelief is the form of human existence. At the same time that he affirms his faith, he associates himself with the rebuke addressed to the disciples: this generation is always unbelieving. The ambivalence in his confession is a natural expression of anxiety in the earnest desire to see his son released, but it is also a candid plea for help at that point where his faith is ready to fail.[44]

The cry reveals that the man is on the edge of failing faith, and it is exactly at this *Anfechtung* borderline between belief and unbelief, Thielicke asserts,

---

instead of as "tempted," "tested," "tried," "afflicted," "assaulted," or "attacked," etc. The rationale is twofold, to retain the deeper theological sense of the word and to make the subject more easily identifiable for the English reader.

43. Thielicke's sermon on the father's plea, "What Does It Mean to Believe?" introduces his homiletical series on the Apostles' Creed (*Creed*, xii, 2–14; see *World Began*, 117, 286; *Ethics*, 1:94; *Between*, 61, 86; *Evangelical Faith*, 2:381; *Letters*, 135, 140).

44. Lane, *Mark*, 334.

that faith "certainly never gets beyond."⁴⁵ Keeping this idea of "failing faith" in mind, itself an illuminating facet in Luther's concept of *Anfechtung*, we shall resume our survey of Thielicke's corpus in search for its definition.

"Death of God"

Of Thielicke's theological works, that which most extensively exposits the meaning of *Anfechtung* is his three volume dogmatics, *The Evangelical Faith*. In as early as the opening book of the trilogy, and no later than the third page of text, he resounds the above theme previewed in the preface to *Theologie der Anfechtung* with the same tune: "Faith by nature always faces *Anfechtung*."⁴⁶ The note can still be heard echoing at the end of his dogmatics, "Since faith is not once and for all a habit of implanted belief, but it rather always faces *Anfechtung*."⁴⁷ After the introductory glance at *Anfechtung*, the theologian moves toward a more substantial treatment which he takes up later, but only after setting the theological context. In the first half of volume one, Thielicke helps the reader "orient" his or her theological compass in order to structure the dialogue between Cartesian and Non-Cartesian theology.⁴⁸ He then engages the secular age in the second half, as suggested by the subtitle, the "Situation and Task of Theology in the Generation of the Supposed Death of God."

---

45. *Theologie Anfechtung*, iii; translation mine. Yet, with that stated, Thielicke is not too egocentric to wonder about the father, "May it not be that he perhaps was the profoundest believer of them all?" After which Thielicke presses from the pulpit, " . . . far more believing perhaps than many a church Christian who swallows all the dogmas of the catechism whole and rattles them off at the drop of a hat?" (*Creed*, 11).

46. *Evangelical Faith*, 1:25; translation mine, cf. *Evangelische Glaube*, 1:6.

47. *Evangelical Faith*, 3:205; translation mine, cf. *Evangelische Glaube*, 3:271. And yet closer to the end, Thielicke claims, "One can say in Luther's sense that there is no faith without *Anfechtung*" (*Evangelical Faith*, 3:333; translation mine, cf. *Evangelische Glaube*, 3:445).

48. The first half introduces the reader to "The State of Theological Discussion: Orientation of Our Theological Thinking" (*Evangelical Faith*, 1:21–218). In his approach to theology, Thielicke rejects the popular distinctions of "conservative" and "modern" not only as inadequate, but moreover as misleading. Instead he prefers to classify theology around the pivotal epistemological method of René Descartes. This "Cartesian" orientation is based on the emancipated modern self, condensed into the phrase, "I think, therefore I am." In contrast, a "Non-Cartesian" orientation which begins with revelation might be summarized by J. G. Hamann's inversion, "He is, therefore I think" (*Modern Thought*, 51). The psalmist encapsulates the epistemological methodology in a favorite verse to which Thielicke constantly refers, "In Thy light shall we see light" (Ps 36:9; KJV).

In describing this section, Thielicke borrows from the popular "God is dead" catchphrase of atheistic philosophy so influenced by Friedrich Nietzsche (1844–1900) in order to describe the secular environment in which modern theology finds itself. With this subtitle framing the textual portrait, it becomes obvious that Nietzsche is an epic figure that molds not only this volume of Thielicke's dogmatics, but is one to whom the theologian tirelessly refers throughout his corpus and most engagingly in his sermons.[49] Indeed, in reviewing the historical attack against God made by the "death of God" theologians, Thielicke assigns "prototypical" significance to Nietzsche's parable of "The Madman."[50]

The atheistic fairy tale recounts how in the broad daylight of bright morning this lunatic lights a lantern and repeatedly yells in the town square, "I'm looking for God!"[51] At this comic sight the unbelieving bystanders jeer and mock, "Has he been lost, then?"[52] The madman glaringly answers— with the infamous phrase—"God is dead! God remains dead! And we have killed him!"[53] Crazed, he then invades several sanctuaries and holds funeral services for God. When questioned by authorities, he only mutters, "What then are these churches now if not the tombs and sepulchers of God?"[54] Interestingly, in the parable one does not find the usual and respectable atheistic reasoning about the end of an illusion, enlightenment, or freedom. Instead of breaking dawn that the "death of God" supposedly brings, there is only gloom, darkness, and the shocking horror of nihilism.

---

49. *Evangelical Faith*, 1:31–32, 97, 232–35; 2:32, 47, 74, 124, 151, 384; 3:215, 349, 392; *Waiting*, 12, 31, 37–38, 42, 69, 144, 183, 187; *World Began*, 27, 175, 277; *Nihilism*, 26, 99, 110, 127, 149, 159, 164, 179n1; *Meaning*, 129; *Silence*, 13, 60; *Depths*, 26; *Freedom*, 28, 55, 59, 62, 100, 104, 113; *Mount*, 61, 85, 102, 129; *God's World*, 15, 17, 18, 19, 21, 38, 39, 143, 163; *Sex*, 36; *Prayer*, 45, 73, 86, 115; *Ethics*, 2:9n5, 28, 36, 168; *Creed*, 98, 122; *How Modern?* 78; *Death*, xxiii, 19, 23–27, 59n3, 64; *Believe*, 63, 109, 211; *Diary*, 98; *Human*, 126–27, 132, 175, 209–10, 218, 229, 244, 364, 377, 385, 444; *Faith*, 20, 81, 111; *Modern Thought*, 16, 18–21, 39, 42, 73 106, 114, 255, 293, 302, 315, 426, 436–38, 517, 549; *Notes*, 111. These few instances do not include the endless references to "God is dead" or "death of God"; see Thielicke's sermon, "What is the 'Death of God' All About?" (*Believe*, 207–20).

50. *Evangelical Faith*, 1:232. Thielicke traces the "History of the Idea of the Death of God" (Ibid., 1:232–64) from Jean Paul through Wetzel and Jacobsen to Nietzsche with references to the 1960's American theologians such as Altizer, Hamilton and van Buren, however, he intentionally focuses on the classical loci of Jean Paul and Nietzsche throughout his works.

51. Nietzsche, "Madman," 119.

52. Ibid.

53. Ibid., 120.

54. Ibid.

The logical conclusion at which Nietzsche's atheism arrives was first intimated in its modern version by Jean Paul (1763–1825), another favorite among "death of God" theologians for Thielicke.[55] In his "Dream of a World Without God,"[56] Jean Paul dreams of himself falling asleep on a hillside and awakening in a church graveyard, the cemetery of the cosmos in which there is no God. A mournful Christ confesses that he has been mistaken, that he has misled people into a false religion and lulled them into a false security. Having vainly traversed the wasted universe in search of God, he summarizes his discovery in reply to the dead children's question, "Jesus, have we no Father?"[57] He answers with streaming tears, "We are orphans all, both I and ye. We have no Father." From the terrifying dream Jean Paul awakes, but what is only a nightmare for him becomes, after Nietzsche, waking consciousness for modernity.

In view of this "death of God" theology overshadowing half of the first volume of his dogmatics, we can already discern an additional reason why *Anfechtung* is given such prominence in Thielicke's theology. He is consciously dialoging with his contemporary culture. Of course, as we know, the primary reason Thielicke is a theologian of *Anfechtung* is simply because as a neo-Lutheran he is drastically impacted by the reformer's triadic formula. That the priority of the three rules, however, is here given to *Anfechtung*—although not at the expense of the other two—in addition to the interpretive paradigm suggested by Bayer, is because Thielicke is a citizen of modernity, the supposed "God is Dead" age, or simply the age of institutional and cultural *Anfechtung*. Nevertheless, in this early glimpse within his dogmatics, the reader sees a most enlightening facet of *Anfechtung* that helps one to arrive at a definition: "God is dead," and in the indefatigable attention given to this "silence of God" theme, a certain term emerges in the spotlight that brings his meaning of *Anfechtung* into perfect clarity: *crisis*.

Crisis of John the Baptist

The term, *crisis*, is also used to describe an assault of *Anfechtung* recorded in this second volume of his dogmatics. Here Thielicke returns to one of his favorite examples, that of John the Baptist.[58] As John is wasting away in

---

55. *Evangelical Faith*, 1:236–44, 270, 398; 2:135, 167, 234, 425; 3:399, 407; *Nihilism*, 16, 30, 129–32, 139; *Silence*, 20; *Mount*, epigraph; *Creed*, 4–6, 112, 179; *How Modern?* 12, 68; *Believe*, 10, 212; *Modern Thought*, 36, 419, 458.

56. Jean Paul, *Wit, Wisdom, Philosophy*, 195–200.

57. Ibid., 197.

58. *Evangelical Faith*, 2:332–35; see 3:342; *Silence*, 28; *Mount*, 18; *Believe*, 80–81, 182–93; *Adventure*, 108–15.

prison on death row, he cannot reconcile the contradiction in his apocalyptic expectations of the coming of the Christ with his own existential situation. Evident from sermon titles like, "Who Warned You to Flee the Coming Wrath?" (Matt 3:7), the Baptizer expects the Christ's advent to usher nuclear incineration and restore international justice. Yet the Nazarene seems totally content simply to remain incognito while merely challenging the attitudes of a few social outcastes.

Thielicke introduces John's dilemma: "The doubt plagued disciple in the prison cell" sends messengers to Jesus to ask,[59] "Are you the one who is to come, or shall we look for another?" (Matt 11:3). The shocking question on the part of the forerunner, he theologizes, "finds expression in that he asks in *Anfechtung*."[60] It should also not escape one's notice that this *Anfechtung* arises from the fact that John is suffering "under the silence of God."[61] From the pulpit, Thielicke illustrates the Baptizer's confusion, "How long are you going to keep us in suspense? If you are Christ, say so! Let a voice from heaven say that you are! Don't you notice that your silence upsets us?"[62] Thielicke imagines the contradiction between faith and experience as John perceives it, "If this Nazarene has the power to shake the foundations of the world in God's name, then he must ultimately be able also to destroy the prison walls behind which his witness languishes."[63] Furthermore, "If he lets his witness, his best friend, fall prey to the executioner's blade, without being able to halt the mills of this shameful justice, then that is a flagrant contradiction of all the claims he ever made."[64] As Thielicke makes abundantly clear, however, John's anxiety is not merely about his own survival. Rather, the issue involves his role as the forerunner of the Messiah, for if the herald of the Christ who announces the arrival of the eschatological kingdom were to perish, then what would that imply of the Messiah's reign? His omnipotent power to establish an everlasting kingdom? In other words, if the forerunner of Christ does not survive, then neither will faith in Christ survive. Everything believed about Him by the Old Testament patriarchs and prophets would have been in vain. All of redemptive history that was to be fulfilled in Him, would end as an illusion. Thielicke vividly expresses John's sinking despair, "'I would gladly die in this hole,' John the Baptist may have said to himself, 'if only the faith that still supports me in this darkness

---

59. *Believe*, 188.
60. *Evangelical Faith*, 2:333; translation mine, cf. *Evangelische Glaube*, 2:408–9.
61. *Believe*, 81.
62. Ibid., 81.
63. Ibid., 185.
64. Ibid., 185–86.

wouldn't die with me.'"[65] The realization of this, according to Thielicke, plunges John into a "mental *crisis*."[66] So in the search for a definition of *Anfechtung*, the reader should note that here in one of Thielicke's frequently employed examples, the "silence of God" experience of *Anfechtung* throws one into anguishing psychological *crisis*.

Concluding this glance at his systematics, the reader should see the last volume where Thielicke relentlessly returns to the *Anfechtung* "silence of God." Discussing the absence of God within the Old Testament that culminates in the New Testament theology of the cross, Thielicke writes, "Only the most serious *crisis* is also the fulfillment of that which is prefigured in shadowy outline in the old covenant to the extent that only the one who obeys and trusts overcomes the *Anfechtung* of the hiddenness of God."[67] Again, the *Anfechtung* experience of a dead, hidden, or silent God catapults one into "crisis."

Crisis of Faith

One sees this notion of *crisis* throughout Thielicke's sermons, particularly in a significant collection concerning his apologetic. *How to Believe Again* starts with "A Word to the Reader" where in the context of the "hiddenness" of God, Thielicke explains how to persuade someone "for whom 'God' is an open question."[68] In describing a characteristic of his apologetic influenced by Pascal's "Wager" (see chapter 6), Thielicke explains the background of the conversation between Blaise Pascal (1623–62) and his dialogue partner, "a man who cannot believe and yet does not consider himself ready simply to lay his faith aside."[69] Convinced that the brilliant mathematician would have rationale reasons for belief, he approaches Pascal with the "God question." Thielicke continues to diagnose the man's condition, "We now presume that his *crisis of faith* arises from the same diseased area that affected his intellectual brethren."[70] For Thielicke, the *Anfechtung* challenge of the hidden God traffics in crises of faith.

In the same vital apologetic volume, Thielicke showcases another case of *Anfechtung* in his sermon, unsurprisingly entitled, "How Crises

---

65. *Believe*, 186.

66. Ibid., 186; italics added.

67. *Evangelical Faith*, 3:166; italics and translation mine, cf. *Evangelische Glaube*, 3:222.

68. *Believe*, 7.

69. Ibid., 11.

70. Ibid., 16; italics added.

in Faith Arise."⁷¹ The biblical text recounts the narrative of Peter walking on the surface of the storm-tossed Sea of Galilee. The disciples, on a nocturnal voyage across the massive inland lake, observe a mysterious figure approaching them on the water. After determining that it is not an apparition, but is in fact Jesus, Peter impulsively yearns to meet him. Confident of Christ's authority and power over nature, the apostle ventures out of the boat and glides across the waves. Unfortunately, though, after beginning to reason about wind velocity and wave amplitude, Peter finds himself submerging. At this, the Lord queries, "O you of little faith, why did you doubt?" (Matt 14:31). Thielicke summarizes the event: "Peter's faith has deserted him."⁷² After applying the text to the moments in which his hearer is "immersed in anxiety" during one's "night of distress,"⁷³ the preacher asserts that if there is no "savior-figure who takes me up in his arms and pulls me back from the abyss" then the picture of Peter sinking beneath the waves "remains just a symbolic representation of the *crisis* I am in."⁷⁴ Without a Lord to rescue one from the atheistic abyss of nothingness, the hidden-God *Anfechtung* experienced during times of distress leaves one in a "crisis of faith."

The paradigmatic example of a "crisis of faith" which unquestionably defines Thielicke's notion of *Anfechtung* is that text which is referenced not only throughout his sermons, but from the very beginning of his systematics to the last page of his modern theology textbook for at least eighty times in the English translations of his works: the 73rd Psalm.⁷⁵ Its significance becomes clear a mere three pages into *The Evangelical Faith* at the first mention of *Anfechtung* seen above. Thielicke emphasizes his conviction that "there can be no timeless or supratemporal theology (*theologia perennis*)."⁷⁶

71. Ibid., 64–76.

72. Ibid., 75.

73. Ibid., 64, 65.

74. Ibid., 65; italics added.

75. The reader finds it in Thielicke's dogmatics and modern theology (*Evangelical Faith*, 1:25, 95, 120, 228, 356, 391, 402; 2: 12, 33, 37, 74, 82, 84, 186, 188, 192, 195, 197, 219, 238; 3:23, 29, 76, 152, 168, 172, 181n11, 333, 353, 362, 402, 410, 418, 433; *Modern Thought*, 35, 37, 38, 380, 511, 563). One also sees it in his sermons and other works (*World Began*, 88, 183, 246, 258; *Meaning*, 15; *Depths*, 79, 89; *Freedom*, 199; *God's World*, 138, 140; *Mount*, 139, 140; *Sex*, 220; *Conversations*, 4, 96, 189; *Ethics*, 1:xvii, 312n5; 2:96, 190, 322; *Creed*; 8, 9, 19, 59, 203, 209; *How Modern?* 50, 69, 72; *Believe*, 165, 176–77, 191, 213, 216; *Letters*, 33–34; *Living with Death*, 187; *Human*, 323, 441, 462, 469; *Adventure*, 75, 80, 134).

76. *Evangelical Faith*, 1:23. Thielicke restates this conviction in *Modern Thought*, "That theological statements arise by way of attack explains why there are no timeless theological statements and no perennial theology. Theology arises out of a challenge

Yet he assures, "there is a sphere of unchanging primal models of *Anfechtung* (that is why we can understand directly *Anfechtungen* such as those of Psalm 73)."[77] So though theology is always in flux to address the ever new contemporary ideology, and though different times produce various forms of *Anfechtung* which demand new points of preaching and appropriation for each generation, the constant and primary example of a "crisis of faith" that people in all eras can understand directly is Psalm 73.

Thielicke endlessly returns to the psalm to dogmatize over this perpetual and universal example of *Anfechtung*, as illustrated in all three volumes of his systematics:

> Reality always seems to stand opposed to God's rule and hence to God's existence. Long before the modern idea ever arose of self-resting finitude—and this idea is only a form of the experience of absence—what the believer could see always seemed to be determined by forces and laws that resisted God's control. How else could the wicked prosper unpunished while the righteous were plagued every day and had to watch them triumph (Psalm 73)?[78]

> If the Wisdom literature and sayings influenced by it often link their summons to fear of the Lord and obedience with the promise of a reward . . . the afflictions described in . . . Psalm 73 present us with a rationally insoluble problem, namely, that of reconciling the divine overruling of history with the complete absence of any such relation, and hence of bringing it out of its obscurity (Psalm 73:12, 16).[79]

> Here, too, frontier experience is the shadow-side of the faith which follows or precedes it. It is this on the basis of biblical (not religious) encounters with God. For the promise that God will be my God and grant me salvation brings fear of such experiences—the suffering of the innocent and triumph of the wicked (Psalm 73:3-11), in short, the apparent contradiction between what happens in the world and the promises of salvation.[80]

---

and is thus always related to its historical time and place" (7). Yandell asks cheekily "whether it is a perennial truth that there is no perennial theology, and, if so, how Thielicke could, on his grounds, know this" ("Thielicke, Helmut," 370).

77. *Evangelical Faith*, 1:25; translation mine, cf. *Evangelische Glaube*, 1:6.

78. *Evangelical Faith*, 1:228.

79. Ibid., 2:12.

80. Ibid., 3:333.

How the psalmist overcomes this *Anfechtung* is the subject of chapter 2. For now, we should just note that Thielicke contextualizes the man's existential crisis when preaching on "Overcoming Anxiety," such as that caused by his audience's fear of nuclear holocaust during the Cold War:[81]

> In Psalm 73 we have set before us the utter predicament of a man who no longer discerns the leadings of God, a man who, like Job, saw the terrible and senseless inversion of reward and punishment and therefore was plunged into care and anxiety in the face of this unpredictable world. Isn't the devil in ultimate control after all? The psalmist was almost at the point of drawing this conclusion. And he forbore doing so only because it would condemn all the children of God and turn their faith into nothing but a satanic delusion. Only this caused him to recoil from this ultimate desperate conclusion.[82]

In still another sermon pointing to Psalm 73, Thielicke explains more about the man's *Anfechtung*. When preaching on the "fire of doubt and temptation" sparked in response to the "silence of God" during the believer's suffering,[83] the psalmist's observing scoffer poses the sneering question, "Where is your God now?" to which there is "no rebuttal from heaven."[84] Here the theologian discloses, "Then it is that *faith*—which is the theme posed by our Lord in this chapter—comes to *crisis*."[85] This "faith" coming to "crisis" is the heart of Thielicke's *Anfechtung*, which the primary model of Psalm 73 timelessly illustrates.

The translator of Thielicke's systematic works, Geoffrey W. Bromiley,[86] most often employs "temptation" or one of the predictable options for *Anfechtung* throughout Thielicke's dogmatics. When writing an encyclopedia article on the *Anfechtung* apologist, however, he describes the thrust of Thielicke's theological approach using a term this survey highlights: "As a preacher Thielicke addressed the deep questions of life that emerge in days

---

81. This sermon (*Mount*, 122–46) was part of a series delivered at the St. Mark's Church in Stuttgart during the worst of the post-war years, 1946–48. Thielicke remembers, "For in more than one respect that time had in it something that was profoundly typical of man's *Anfechtung*, temptation, despair, and need" (ibid., xv). The "atom bomb" is an application of this particular sermon (ibid., 141, 145) and is referenced throughout the series (ibid., 33, 123, 139, 164).

82. Ibid., 139.

83. *How Modern?* 70.

84. Ibid., 72.

85. Ibid., 72; italics added.

86. In addition to the three volumes of *Evangelical Faith*, Bromiley also translated *Silence*, *Depths*, *Question*, *Death*, *Human*, and *Modern Thought*.

of *crisis*."[87] So in summary, pulling all of these instances together beginning with the faith-failing plea of the demoniac's father, to the "God is dead" theology of modernity which runs parallel to "silent" and "hidden" God experiences of all ages, to the sermonic examples of psychological crisis and crises of faith, we would define Thielicke's use of *Anfechtung* as *faith-crisis*.[88] This means that *faith-crisis* then is the antithesis of faith which Thielicke describes interestingly as "its alter ego."[89]

Philosophy of Doubt

With the crux of Thielicke's *Anfechtung* understood as *faith-crisis*, his theology can be further delineated by negative contrast. In the illuminating foreword to *Theologie der Anfechtung*, Thielicke emphatically states what it is not:

> This book is not named 'Theology of *Anfechtung*' for nothing and not: 'Philosophy of Doubt.' The difference is more than a nuance. It is of fundamental and qualitative weight. Already from the start, the theme should deliver the explanation, that we not regard those encounters as controversies of faith with its misunderstandings, i.e., with its misunderstandings invading from the outside, but rather as an encounter of faith with itself as a faith that faces *faith-crisis*.[90]

A theology of *faith-crisis* should not be mistaken for a philosophy of doubt. For it is not an epistemological theory hypothesized in order to analyze rational uncertainty. It is not a thought experiment to overcome skepticism. It should furthermore not only be distinguished from any philosophy,

---

87. Bromiley, "Thielicke, Helmut," 682; italics added). To one's relief, he admits that "readers may often find Thielicke wordy, repetitive, and provocative, and at times obscure" (ibid.).

88. Roberts confirms this definition when he asserts that Thielicke "articulated, in his mature systematic theology, an *Evangelical Faith* for a modern context characterized by a *crisis of faith*" ("Helmut Thielicke," 321; italics added). Though writing in the context of the 20th century's "crisis" or "dialectical" theology, Thielicke's *Anfechtung* is to be distinguished from the former which he addresses in the polemically entitled section, "The Answer and Crisis of Dialectical Theology" (*Modern Thought*, 546–63).

89. *Evangelical Faith*, 1:228. "The *antithesis* of faith," Thielicke stresses, ". . . takes on the character of *Anfechtung*" (ibid., 2:51; italics and translation mine, cf. *Evangelische Glaube*, 2:61–62). Likewise, "temptation [*Anfechtung*]," he explains, "thus becomes the opposite pole of the Gospel" (*Temptation*, 2328). However, in functioning like the Law, *Anfechtung* is "not to be regarded as the opposite of *faith*, but rather as its God-willed opportunity" (ibid., 2328).

90. *Theologie Anfechtung*, iii; translation mine.

but from the cognitive phenomenon of doubt as well. In his encyclopedia article on *Anfechtung*, Thielicke insists:

> Temptation [*Anfechtung*] must not be confused with the intellectual phenomenon of doubt. It is rather a spiritual experience which threatens our faith. It defies rational analysis because the 'wisdom of this world' (i.e., our human rationality itself) constantly jeopardizes our faith and is the very opposite of the 'foolishness of the cross' on which faith thrives (1 Cor. 1:18ff.; 2:6ff.).[91]

Faith-crisis is not a skeptical psychological state. It is a spiritual experience or condition that challenges faith. The theologian continues to clarify: "Doubt is not identical with temptation; it is merely one of its accompanying symptoms. One might say that it is the rational facet or mask of temptation."[92] Doubt is not duplicate *Anfechtung*; rather, it is the intellectual camouflage of *faith-crisis*. To dispute with doubt assuming that one is eradicating *faith-crisis* is to mistake the pseudo-problem for the real problem. The actual dilemma for faith is not the lack of rational certainty, but the threat of *faith-crisis*. One can develop a philosophy of doubt and still not secure faith from *Anfechtung*. Therein, in Thielicke's view, is the history of modern theology.

Descartes' Philosophical Doubt

When Thielicke surveys the history of thought over the last centuries, one discovers the reason for which he so urgently raises the subject of doubt. As he summarizes the course, "If I were to reduce the common theme to a short formula I would say that the 18th and 19th centuries, along with the preparatory and succeeding systems, are centuries of doubt."[93] Thus in writing his modern theology, the historical addition to his dogmatics, he declares that "the theme of the present book" is to consider "how theologians have tried to deal with doubt . . . since the Enlightenment."[94] He would not begin his review of doubt-oriented modern theology with any other but the French philosopher René Descartes (1596–1650), the father from whom it is begotten. Indeed, for Thielicke the significance of Descartes cannot be stressed enough. As noted above, when classifying theological methodologies within his systematics, he abandons the standard

---

91. *Temptation*, 2327.
92. Ibid., 2328.
93. *Modern Thought*, 34.
94. Ibid., 45.

labels of "conservative" and "modern" and instead replaces them with the far more accurate descriptions of "Cartesian" and "Non-Cartesian" theology.[95] These terms, used to categorize theological approaches, are derived from Descartes' identity because "the cleavage in intellectual history" is "signified by the name Descartes."[96] As Thielicke asserts about the latter's momentous rank, "Cartesian doubt is an opening chord that calls for quiet, and the concert of the modern age begins."[97]

Descartes' aim is to achieve absolute truth by the exclusive use of human reason independent of any authority. His quest is not to search for an array of novel truths yet undiscovered, but rather to rediscover them with a fail-safe system for finding truth. His intention, instead of rejecting what philosophers before him had taken for granted, is to invent a hack-proof program that would forever firewall truth from the malware of skepticism. In this way, the server of truth would rest secure on an uncrashable network. In short, Descartes' goal is to re-think reality. So he starts over, from the beginning, and by the use of hyperbolic doubt, questions everything traditionally considered as self-evident. Descartes justifies this radical method of doubt:

> Because I wished to give myself entirely to the search after truth, I thought that it was necessary for me to adopt an apparently opposite course and to reject as absolutely false everything concerning which I could imagine the least ground of doubt, in order to see whether afterwards there remained anything in my beliefs which was entirely certain.[98]

Sitting in his fireside chair, Descartes doubts the existence of the external world and his own body. How does he know for certain that his head is not a pumpkin, he questions, for his physical senses are not totally trustworthy, "I have sometimes experienced that these senses were deceptive, and it is wiser not to trust entirely to anything by which we have once been deceived."[99] Maybe he is dreaming, and upon awakening will learn that "all these particulars, for example that we open our eyes, shake our head,

---

95. "Terminological Inadequacy of the Terms Modern and Conservative and Their Replacement with Cartesian and Non-Cartesian" (*Evangelical Faith*, 1:30–37). Some conservatives might question whether Thielicke totally escapes the Cartesian paradigm given his rejection of verbal inspiration *per se* (*God's World*, 81) and the virgin birth (*Evangelical Faith*, 2:407–15).

96. *Evangelical Faith*, 1:34.

97. *Modern Thought*, 57.

98. Descartes, in Copleston, *History Philosophy*, 4:85.

99. Ibid., 4:86.

extend our hands, or even perhaps that we have such hands, are not true."[100] This doubt, however, for the discoverer of geometrical "Cartesian coordinates," would obviously not apply to the propositions of mathematics. For whenever one is awake or asleep, two plus three always equals five, and it is therefore impossible to be deceived in analytic theory. But, "ah," says Descartes to himself, what if "an evil genius, no less powerful than deceitful, has employed his whole energies in deceiving me."[101] Perhaps he is spellbound in an imaginary world and deluded into thinking that two plus three equals five, when in true reality the sum is four. Or in contemporary talk, maybe he is trapped in a computer simulation and brainwashed by its virtual reality, and the only reason he remembers yesterday is because an evil scientist has pre-programmed him with memory.

Despite the universal scope of Descartes' methodological doubt, there is one thing that remains absolutely indubitable, that is, the act of doubting itself. For he cannot doubt that he is now doubting. Though he may doubt the existence of the material world around him, or the reality of mathematical propositions, he cannot doubt his own existence. The reason, because he doubts, for in order to doubt that one is, one must already be. As Descartes asserts, "We cannot doubt our existence without existing while we doubt."[102] So he arrives at the point that had already been proven centuries prior by Augustine, "If I am deceived, I exist."[103] Since doubting is a form of thinking, however, Descartes prefers to formulate the truth in the non-doubtful, now famous phrase, "I think, therefore I am."[104] It is this focal statement that Thielicke calls, "the initial thesis of secularization."[105]

Thielicke's summary of the Cartesian shift is threefold. First, "epistemological interest moves away from objective being to subjectivity."[106] The subjective "I" stands over against objective being and the world and does not integrate itself to it. While before Descartes, the "I" is part of the world and is required to find its place in it, now the "I" is the center of the world and interprets it. Second, "certainty of the self takes precedence over the certainty of God."[107] Descartes' initial statement is not "God is," but "I think, therefore I am." As noted above, the Cartesian shift inverts the ancient

---

100. Ibid.
101. Ibid.
102. Ibid., 4:91n1.
103. Augustine, in Copleston, *History Philosophy*, 4:90.
104. Descartes, in ibid., 4:91.
105. *Modern Thought*, 52.
106. Ibid., 57.
107. Ibid.

principle, "He is, therefore I think,"[108] and sets the world on a drastically different course. Before Descartes the governing thesis is that I must know who God is to know who I am. In the new era, one finds the polar opposite: I must know that I am and who I am to know who and what God is. Third, and to the theme, "doubt undergoes a change of structure."[109]

Prior to Descartes, doubt is an unavoidable necessity, perhaps like a cold or virus that one catches. It was never deliberately given as an antibiotic. In contrast to Descartes, Luther treats doubt by accepting it calmly. For, according to Thielicke, the reformer knows that:

> It can shatter only penultimate certainties and that when I let these go I come upon a solid and impregnable layer which—for Luther at least—cannot be shattered. This layer is the certainty about God which is reached in the first commandment, namely, that he is my God and always in relationship with me. On this basis I ask again about the lost certainties . . . which might for a moment have become doubtful to me. On the solid rock of the first commandment it is clear that God wanted to go this way which I cannot establish rationally. Luther never doubts intentionally; doubt is always something he accepts.[110]

In the Cartesian scheme, conversely, doubt now takes on a heuristic function. No longer a necessary evil, it is a means of knowledge. The fear of the Lord is not the beginning of wisdom (Prov 9:10), doubt is. Knowledge of God does not bring understanding, doubt does. Thus doubt is a sign of humanity come of age. As Thielicke ascertains, "For Descartes and the modern age, doubt . . . is now a virtue, for within the questioning, as a final reality that cannot be questioned, it finds the I and its *cogito*."[111] Basically, the difference between the two is that in Luther doubt has a theocentric focus. In Cartesian doubt, the focus is egocentric. The end result, according to Thielicke, is a "kind of infatuation with doubt, a metaphysical narcissism."[112]

Thielicke's Theological Doubt

With these drastic differences set in juxtaposition, it is difficult to overlook a striking resemblance between Thielicke's *faith-crisis* theology and the

---

108. Ibid., 51.
109. Ibid., 57.
110. Ibid., 56.
111. Ibid., 57.
112. Ibid., 57.

deliberate doubt of Descartes' philosophical program. As one can easily ascertain from the discussion of Luther, doubt for Thielicke is obviously associated with *faith-crisis*. Indeed, they are so closely intertwined that the word *Anfechtung* is even translated as "doubt" at least twice.[113] Doubt is unquestionably related to *faith-crisis*, and it is in this theocentric *faith-crisis* sense, that Thielicke utilizes doubt to reach the certainty of faith. When preaching on the divinity of Jesus, for example, Thielicke challenges his hearers to utilize doubt as a means of discovering the truth:

> As a doubter, I must abandon all Christian traditions and doctrines at the very outset. I must be ready to fall into the void, supported only by one last certainty: if there is a Christ, he will not *let* me fall but will catch me up. The decision depends on him and him alone. And if I should encounter him, as doubting Thomas encountered the risen Lord, and if I must say, "My Lord and my God," then I shall get back all the doctrine that I threw overboard in the wild venture of my doubt.[114]

So convinced of doubt's theological and spiritual place, Thielicke, from the pulpit, dares his hearers: "Only when we drink of doubt to the last dregs will we be able to perceive the real message of our text."[115] Yet in another sermon he challenges: "The doubters are always more blessed than the mere fellow travelers in faith. For they are the only ones who fully learn that their Lord is stronger than any doubt and any hell of despair. So let us take our doubt to Jesus and ask him quite frankly."[116]

Here, Thielicke advances the role of doubt by picking it up from the ground of necessity, as it is found in Luther, and using it deliberately as an apologetic tool, more along the lines of what might be reflected in Descartes' methodological doubt. Indeed, strangely enough, Thielicke acknowledges his indebtedness to the philosopher: "This is the virtue of

---

113. E.g., when discussing what is seen by the Apology of the Augsburg confession, Thielicke lists a "threatened perpetuation of the assaults of doubt [*Anfechtung*] which Luther sought to overcome" (*Ethics*, 1:75; "Mythology," 141; see *Theologie Anfechtung*, 137).

114. *Creed*, 151–52. At the end of the sermon, Thielicke reviews his method with his hearers. "We started with a doubt . . . We have simply thought this doubt through to its end . . . Didn't we suddenly find ourselves on the road to Emmaus, where the risen One drew near to us? Even doubt is an envelope in which messages from God are concealed" (ibid., 159).

115. *World*, 165. For this reason, Thielicke boldly meets Bultmann's challenge to demythologize the New Testament with the conviction that "our faith is steeled in the fires of doubt [*Anfechtung*]" ("Mythology," 141).

116. *Mount*, 65. In agreement with Dostoyevsky, Thielicke "can say of himself that his 'hosanna is achieved through the great purgatory of doubt'" (*Modern Thought*, 7).

the great Descartes, to whose spirit everyone who is intellectually alive and responsible should devote a lock of hair. He knew that one comes to truth only through doubt."[117] Thielicke still insists that his utilization of doubt is categorically distinct from that of modern thought fathered by Descartes. Preaching on "doubt and deicide," Thielicke distinguishes theological doubt from its philosophical imposter by pointing to Christ's question, "My God, my God, why hast thou forsaken me?" (Mark 15:34; KJV). The cry of dereliction *to* God, he explains, "has nothing to do with the modern doubt, which sounds so similar to it, because it too asks the question 'Why' and yet asks it so differently. For in reality it only talks *about* God and cries out *about* God, and in that very act *cries him down*, so that he is no longer heard."[118]

The divergence of a theology of *faith-crisis* from a philosophy of doubt comes into full view on the horizon of open land. Althaus sees the resemblance of doubt in the two programs, but he also foresees the fork in the road that leads the philosophy of doubt down a different path from that which theology takes, the road less traveled:

> The Christian . . . cannot possess the heaven of community with God without repeatedly making the descent into hell which takes place when he doubts and even despairs . . . Theological thinking and speaking does not occur apart from doubt and temptation, and faith's overcoming of temptation; rather it is and remains a thinking within this process, that is, thinking within the framework of *Anfechtung*.[119]

---

117. Continuing he defends Descartes, "And we would be doing him an injustice if we were to assume that he used doubt merely as a dodge, as a heuristic principle, as it were, knowing all the time that in the next moment a brilliant, self-evident proof of God would emerge" (*Nihilism*, 176). Thielicke's opinion of Descartes, however, completely reverses over the decades. He claims that the doubt of Descartes is a "methodological trick" that "takes the very opposite course" of "real, existential doubt" (*Modern Thought*, 77). Moreover, he maintains that Descartes' doubt is indeed a "heuristic construction" and that "from the very first the premise 'God' has been secretly smuggled in, i.e., that the nonexistence of God is an impossible thought for him because God is the normative basis of his structure of thought" (ibid., 77). Essentially, the methodological doubt of Descartes is only an experimental mind-game, "Descartes is not in fact the (total) doubter he makes himself out to be. He is hardly in danger of perishing of doubt, for he is not really at the front but is playing at sand castles. He is on maneuvers, not in battle" (ibid., 74).

118. *Mount*, 96–97.

119. Althaus, *Theology Luther*, 33–34.

Nihilism: Borderline of *Faith-Crisis*

In 1945—after the devastating defeat, occupation, and division of *Deutschland*—the German universities were reopened to forlorn soldiers dressed in the rags of their former uniforms, disheveled refugees from the Eastern states who had lost everything fleeing Soviet control, and those many emaciated figures released from concentration camps. In this context, Thielicke remembers, "It was impossible to deliver a refined, academic lecture. Here one could not be content to give instruction; here there was an intellectual and spiritual hunger that needed to be satisfied; here there were wounds that needed to be bound up."[120] So it was in this situation that the professor, he recalls, "delivered my lectures on nihilism in the largest auditorium in the ancient University of Tübingen, and always I had difficulty getting to my lectern because the young men packed the room to the doors. A loudspeaker carried the lectures to two other lecture rooms."[121]

The rationale for his subject choice and the eagerness with which the students listened is easily explained:

> We may be permitted to begin with the rather banal statement that the word "nihilism" is derived from *nihil*, "nothing," and the even more obvious statement that the word ends with "ism." It is evident that these two facts account for the dubious reputation this word has of being really modern and realistic, so that it is considered to be the representation of the whole spirit of our age.[122]

Nihilism, according to Thielicke, is the *Zeitgeist* of modernity. Unlike other "isms," however,—communism, fascism, capitalism, pluralism, etc.—that try to absolutize a principle or program, nihilism has neither

---

120. *Nihilism*, 11–12.

121. Ibid., 11. The lectures were later published as this book.

122. Ibid., 17. Here Thielicke notes that "the term became popular in its modern signification . . . through Friedrich Nietzsche" (ibid., 179n1). Outside of this book, and excluding references to Nietzsche (see n49; or other "God is dead" theologians such as Jean Paul at n55) who Thielicke obviously equates with nihilism, reference to it is common (*Waiting*, 27–28, 37–38, 66, 79–80, 116, 133, 174, 177; *World Began*, 140; *Meaning*, 14, 27, 133; *Depths*, 42, 88; *God's World*, 19, 152; *Mount*, 137, 170, 214; *Ethics*, 1:251, 253, 257, 261n7, 262, 368; *Evangelical Faith*, 1:87, 249, 256, 396; 3:349, 352; *Believe*, 211; *Diary*, 34; *Human*, 368, 420, 429; *Adventure*, 69, 93; *Modern Thought*, 567). Moreover, these instances do not include the unsearchable references to his favorite synonym for nihilism, "nothingness," or its corollary, "meaninglessness." Rueger states the reason for which Thielicke addresses nihilism: "For Thielicke nihilism is the foundation for the German *Weltanschauung*. It is the force defining the concrete situation of German individuals" ("Individualism in Thielicke," 176).

purpose nor agenda. Instead, "nihilism literally has only one truth to declare, namely, the truth that ultimately Nothingness prevails and the world is meaningless."[123]

Despair

As seen above, Thielicke demonstrates the philosophy by repeatedly returning to Jean Paul's deeply disturbing "Dream of a World Without God." Envisaging himself in the cold graveyard of the galaxy, he overhears Jesus explaining to the children that there is no God. After which Christ, raising "his eyes toward the nothingness and boundless void," cries, "Oh, dead, dumb, nothingness! necessity endless and chill! Oh, mad, unreasoning Chance! when will ye dash this fabric into atoms and me too?"[124] Forlorn in empty space, one becomes the dice of energy and matter in the blind game of chance, for since there is no God, the existence of the universe is totally accidental. It is the unplanned, undesigned, ungoverned, purposeless product of a long causal chain of mindless mechanical forces. Moreover, the completely random origin of the species robs it of any rhyme or reason. A freak mishap of nature, the existence of the human race is ultimately inconsequential, and after its annihilation, will be no more significant than that of an exterminated colony of ants. Everything is meaningless. Surveying the bleak void, Jean Paul draws the only consistent conclusion, "Alas! If every soul be its own creator and father, why shall it not be its own destroying angel, too?"[125] As there is no meaning to life there is no point in living. Thus, one must despairingly take charge of one's own life. Instead of submitting to death, one must accomplish it. Thielicke observes, "What Jean Paul suggests Nietzsche works out in all its logic. The mad self-creator must also master death. As deicide he must also be suicide."[126]

Of course, the black horror of Jean Paul's dream of a galaxy without God was anticipated by the Apostle Paul in his first letter to the Corinthians. In a heuristic exercise, he deals with the resurrection of Christ and the *faith-crisis* question: What would be the fate of humanity if Christ had not risen from the dead? (1 Cor 15:12–32). Pressing the antithesis to its logical conclusion, the apostle reveals that if Christ were not raised then there would be no victory over death, and we would be locked in our finitude. The "death of God" proclaimed in Greek materialistic philosophy would prove

---

123. *Nihilism*, 27.
124. Jean Paul, 198; see *Nihilism*, 130.
125. Ibid.
126. *Evangelical Faith*, 1:238.

true. Since, according to this worldview a person is merely a complex combination of moving atoms, then at death one is annihilated and unavoidably drawn into the yawning abyss of nothingness. This existential nightmare, which the apostle heuristically dreams up, shows that without the resurrection of Christ, Christianity collapses, and all reality reduces to absurdity. The apostle summarizes the desperate case by quoting the atheistic Epicureans: "Let us eat and drink, for tomorrow we die" (1 Cor 15:32).[127] The nihilism ushered by the secular age simply returns us to the nothingness of Greek materialistic philosophy.

Existentialism

The ancient world certainly offered its own solutions to deal with the terror of nihilism. For the twentieth century, however, Thielicke maintains, "One can hardly raise the question of overcoming Nothingness without considering the movement which has come to be called 'existentialism,' a movement which devoted its whole passion to the confrontation with Nothingness and the breaking of its spell."[128] The reason the movement so strongly resonates with Thielicke is because its approach to overcome nihilism is a significantly similar, albeit secularized, version of his own.[129] In order to conquer nihilism the existentialist "must first be confronted with Nothingness. In theological terms, this means that he must face absolute temptation (*Anfechtung*)."[130]

The *Anfechtung*-secularizing existentialists with whom Thielicke primarily engages are Martin Heidegger and Jean-Paul Sartre. The former is known for suggesting that nothingness is confronted when one is removed from all traditional and environmental influences. For those factors which naturally bring healthy stability—family, community, and country—are actually a threat to existence. To the extent that one is supported by familiar custom and culture, the more one is merely a conformist who has achieved no individuality, that is, existence. The props by which one has illegitimately

---

127. Isaiah shows that this was a common proverb of the ancient world (22:13). Here Paul is referring to the Greek philosophers whom he debated in Athens before his arrival in Corinth (Acts 17:16–34). Calvin confirms, "This is a saying of the Epicureans, who reckon man's highest good as consisting in present enjoyment" (*Corinthians*, 2:41).

128. *Nihilism*, 167. Thielicke explains by quoting Jean-Paul Sartre, "Existentialism is nothing else but an effort to draw all the implications of a coherent atheistic position" (ibid., 174).

129. He confirms, "In the final analysis even this type of existentialism is only an echo—though a secularized one—of an idea that appears in Luther's temptation [*Anfechtung*] theology" (*Temptation*, 2329).

130. *Nihilism*, 168.

supported oneself must therefore be removed. One must face doubt and the questioning of all that has hitherto sustained one in order to discover if one is still a "self" apart from these forces or whether one implodes within one's fake self. Only by this dreadful venture can one come to oneself and learn to be one's own person. Otherwise one will simply follow the traditional crowd, ordered around by the "dictatorship of the 'they'" while imagining that one is a self-mover.[131]

Sartre picks up on this individualistic theme and claims, "If God does not exist, there is at least *one* being in whom existence precedes essence, a being who exists before he can be defined by any concept, and this being is man."[132] This means that man shows up on the scene of existence, encounters himself, and only after that can he "become," in other words, define his essence, and then achieve and realize it. Since there is no God, essence is not bestowed upon a person in advance. Rather, the human being creates itself according to its own self-image. As a self-creator, one meets oneself as a *tabula rasa* and resolves by one's own will what shall be written upon it.

In Sartre's play *No Exit*, Garcin—imprisoned within a chamber of hell surprisingly absent of any torture device—finally realizes, "There's no need for red-hot pokers. Hell is—other people."[133] For as others look at me, I am subjected to their opinion of me. I am measured against judgments and standards that are not mine, into which I am consequently assimilated and categorized against my will and within which others objectify me. By staring at me they "fixate" me. They enslave me and take away my freedom. One must therefore practice existential self-defense and retaliate by fixating the other person in order to win back one's freedom. In authentic existence, that is, "freedom," one has no relationship to others. One can only live self-defensively, counterstriking and objectifying the other person who would capture and desecrate one's own existence. Freedom is equivalent to solipsism. Self-being is possessed only in one's solitariness.

In final evaluation of existentialism,[134] and though sympathetic to the cause, Thielicke cannot but disclose its failure in the most vivid of terms:

131. Heidegger, *Being and Time*, 164.
132. Sartre, *Existentialism*, 18, in *Nihilism*, 170.
133. Sartre, *No Exit*, 47; see *Nihilism*, 133.
134. Thielicke provides a simple overview of existentialism in his encyclopedia entry on *Anfechtung*: "In the varied forms of present-day existentialism the idea of temptation [*Anfechtung*] (following Kierkegaard) plays a large role: man finds himself only in so far as he is confronted with the terror of nothingness. For it is only then that he will free himself from the 'functional dependence on the impersonal mass mind' (that dictates values to him and takes over his personal decisions; Heidegger), and from the 'fixation through the others' (who suppress his self so that it cannot assert itself; Sartre). It is only after man has been 'plunged into nothingness' and has been 'freed from all

> We must conclude that here Nothingness is *not* overcome. It is no more than the phosphorescent shine of putrefaction that may look like real light to eyes accustomed to the darkness. Nothingness cannot be overcome by setting one's face against it and taking a negative attitude toward it . . . simply by resisting it by means of self-assertion and possibly the most extreme measure of detachment and "nausea." Anybody who attempts to hypnotize Nothingness will himself be caught in its spell.[135]

Although Thielicke holds the existentialists in the highest regard for their intellectual honesty and courage,[136] he decisively rejects the movement, though, he does not do so as an armchair theologian who provides no constructive alternative. Instead, as already suggested, he offers his own solution to overcoming nihilism:

> We may venture to express it this way: No man will ever come to the truth and thus to a trustworthy bridge over the abyss of Nothingness who has not faced doubt, despair and shipwreck . . . In such cases theology speaks of temptation (*Anfechtung*). Not until a man is in the fiery furnace of utter bewilderment and despair does he see what is really genuine. This is what Luther meant when he said that '*tentatio facit theologum*' (temptation [*Anfechtung*] makes the theologian).[137]

In the reformation of apologetics, the way forward is the way back to Luther's theology of *Anfechtung*. So Thielicke ends his lectures on *Nihilism* with the challenge, "Luther once made this profound and profoundly comforting statement: God creates out of nothing; if you are not yet nothing, God can make nothing of you."[138]

---

conventional value-security' that he can begin to establish his own existence. The only way by which man can come to himself leads along the boundary line of nihilism, that is to say through temptation [*Anfechtung*]" (*Temptation*, 2329). Søren Kierkegaard also treats *Anfechtung* (*Fear and Trembling* and *The Sickness unto Death*, 46, 65–67, 71, 79, 88–89, 91, 127, 267n47).

135. *Nihilism*, 175.

136. That Thielicke harbors great respect for the existentialists is clear: "It would be unfair and Pharisaic to be merely critical. This philosophy has the dignity of being an honest expression of an impossible existence" (ibid., 175).

137. Ibid., 176–77.

138. Ibid., 177. Thielicke utilizes Luther's choice challenge in the parallel ending of *Temptation*, "It is God's nature to make something out of nothing. Therefore: Whoever has not yet reached the point of being nothing, of him God can make nothing" (2329); the conclusion to Thielicke's sermon, "The Primeval Witnesses," about an *ex nihilo* creation, "Luther said, 'God created the world out of nothing. As long as you are not yet nothing God cannot make something out of you'" (*World Began*, 25); and in *Modern*

Conclusion

A theology of *faith-crisis* is that which is needed to advance the current reformation of apologetics. For, to paraphrase Luther, *Anfechtung* "makes the apologist." Not to overlook the task of persuasion, *faith-crisis* functions as the Law, which the apologist proclaims, and which leads one's hearers "along boundary line of nihilism" during Christian conversation.[139] Since God creates out of nothing they must be reduced to nothing. They must be forced to face the *faith-crisis* despair of nothingness at the edge of the abyss "of a complete absurdity which cannot be sustained any longer, which cannot be lived out."[140] To borrow the terminology of one Van Tilian expert, *Anfechtung* is the "antithesis" which the apologist "pushes" toward the logical and negative conclusion of its atheistic or pantheistic position.[141] Chap-

---

Thought, "Thus in the exposition of the seven penitential psalms Luther says that it is God's nature to make something out of nothing so that he can make nothing of us if we are not nothing" (55–56).

139. *Temptation*, 2329. Thielicke recalls one such conversation with the Zen Buddhist master, Hosekei. After the dialogue, he gifted Thielicke a fan on which was painted the word "Nothingness," and a scroll inscribed, "Through great doubt—and thus again through confrontation with Nothingness—to great questions and knowledge" (*Voyage*, 171). Thielicke considers this pantheistic form of nothingness as another variation of nihilism (ibid., 174).

140. *Evangelical Faith*, 1:258. Thielicke offers Nietzsche's insanity as a paradigmatic example. For as his life tragically shows, absurdity is an impossible standard by which to live. "The madness of Nietzsche, although pathologically definable, seems in a kind of pre-established harmony to be the result of his taking this course" (ibid., 1:259). Nietzsche reveals in apocalyptic form that "man cannot escape transcendence, that the act of slaying God is indeed too great for us as the madman testifies, and that the superhumanity which corresponds to the death of God means in the last resort self-destruction" (ibid., 1:259).

141. The phrase, "push the antithesis," is attributed to the late Greg L. Bahnsen who studied under Van Til and was a skillful proponent of the latter's method (Bahnsen, *Van Til's Apologetic*), as told by a recognized student of Bahnsen (Demar, *Pushing the Antithesis: Apologetic Methodology of Bahnsen*, xv). The antithesis is a critical component of Van Til's apologetic. His version originated in Abraham Kuyper (*Sacred Theology*, 152), was developed by Van Til himself (*Apologetics*, 3, 6, 14, 127n3; *Defense*, 8n32, 177, 287n27, 352n27), and popularized by his students. For analysis of its complexity see Frame (*Van Til*, 187–214); Bahnsen (*Van Til's Apologetic* 272–311, 416–18); and Oliphint (*Covenantal Apologetics*, 16, 33, 51, 55).

Karl Barth introduces his *Church Dogmatics* with the concern also to "speak in the *antithesis* of faith to unbelief and therefore apologetically" (1/1:30; italics added). Barth's focus on the antithesis, and his approach in general, however, should be distinguished from Thielicke's *Anfechtung* and method. For the former dismisses any kind of "planned apologetics" as "irresponsible, irrelevant, and therefore ineffective" (ibid.). One reason for his objection is that "in such apologetics faith must clearly take unbelief seriously. Hence it cannot take itself with full seriousness. Secretly or openly, therefore, it ceases

ter 5 shall examine this subversive approach which challenges the hearer's unbelief indirectly. Suffice it now to say that without this vital characteristic, Christian conversation can never rise from the theological ghetto in which it is found and shall merely remain "apologetics" as it was known in Thielicke's day—the old methodologies beholden to philosophical and scientific assumptions—for which he reserves the severest criticism:

> Theology without *Anfechtung* is either (in so far as it carries on a conversation with those outside) *apologetics*, or (in so far as it cultivates dogmatics in the narrower sense) it is confessional morphology; i.e., as an intellectual endeavor it is an esthetic construction and as a foundation for ecclesiastical practice it is repristination. In both cases it loses its relevance—notwithstanding the intellectual and scholarly accomplishments it may achieve and pride itself upon.[142]

---

to be faith" (ibid). Barth's "serious-faith" opposition to traditional apologetics is clearly set in juxtaposition with Thielicke's concern for an apologetic characterized by *faith-crisis*. One should also note that Barth rejects "all independently ventured apologetics" (ibid.). For he is concerned of the risk that "once its task is completed dogmatics will think that its conflict with unbelief has been brought to an end" (ibid.). This criticism, however, should not at all be confused with, nor would it apply to, Thielicke's reformation in which apologetics and theology are one and the same, the task of which never ends as there is no perennial theology.

142. *God's World*, 218; second italics added.

2

A Confession for Apologetics

THIELICKE BEGINS HIS THREE volume dogmatics with the concern to address the citizen of this secular age in his or her concrete historical situation. The urgent reason—which lays the theological foundation for his apologetic—is because "faith by nature always faces *faith-crisis*."[1] And as every theology generates a confession of faith whether formally or not, so too it is with apologetics. From a theology for apologetics is begotten a confession for apologetics, to which Thielicke alludes in the very next sentence. "It exists in the Nevertheless." Resuming this leitmotif in the particularly relevant section, "Theme and Questionability of the Slogan Death of God," Thielicke dogmatizes, "faith can never get beyond the Nevertheless with which it overcomes this *faith-crisis*."[2] According to Thielicke, the "Nevertheless" is that which triumphs over *faith-crisis*. Its significance comes into sharper focus when one realizes that the "Nevertheless" confession of God's existence is the biblical and theological *presupposition* for the task of apologetics—which presuppositional strategy chapter 5 shall feature.[3] We shall now consider Thielicke's conviction that the reformation

---

1. *Evangelical Faith*, 1:25; translation mine, cf. *Evangelische Glaube*, 1:6.

2. *Evangelical Faith*, 1:231; translation mine, cf. *Evangelische Glaube*, 1:324. The theme continues to resurface in this volume through the appendix, where Thielicke evaluates modernity's dream of utopia on earth and completely rejects the secularistic vision since it "abandons the category of the Nevertheless" (*Evangelical Faith*, 1:391). He ends, "How can there be anything of faith or of the defiance of the Nevertheless in a man who imagines that the resurrection and eternal life have to compete with earthly dreams?" (ibid., 1:402).

3. Thielicke shows that the awareness of competing presuppositions or worldviews is vital to apologetics. When dialoging with unbelievers, he believes that "the reality of God as the one who addresses them is always presupposed" (*Modern Thought*, 456). For anyone to view reality "with no presuppositions at all is impossible" (*Evangelical Faith*, 2:278–79). Therefore Thielicke forbids Christian persuasion, or "missionary work without paying any attention to their presuppositions" (ibid., 3:375), on which the apologist "turns the tables," that is, "attacks" (*Between*, 26; *God's World*, 217).

of apologetics is impossible without "a Nevertheless which is the basis of the presuppositions of life and thought."[4]

Psalm 73

The "Nevertheless" to which Thielicke refers is taken from the *faith-crisis* confession of the believer in Thielicke's favorite Psalm, the 73rd: "Nevertheless I am continually with thee" (Ps 73:23; KJV).[5] The sacred poem was quickly considered in the survey of Thielicke's works while searching for a definition of *Anfechtung* that would most adequately convey his meaning of the term. As discovered, the theologian considers Psalm 73 to be the paradigmatic example of *faith-crisis* belonging to a unique class of "unchanging primal models of *Anfechtung* (that is why we can understand directly *Anfechtungen* such as those of Psalm 73)."[6] Given its dominant role in Thielicke's theology, a more thorough consideration would prove valuable at this juncture. It would also seem beneficial to consider the Psalm in a somewhat colloquial manner as per Thielicke's sermons, although to suggest that this could serve as a model of his preaching style would be an insult to his pulpit.[7]

> [1] A Psalm of Asaph. Truly God is good to Israel, to those who are pure in heart. [2] But as for me, my feet had almost stumbled, my steps had nearly slipped. [3] For I was envious of the arrogant

---

4. *Evangelical Faith*, 3:23. Van Til states similarly, "For me the *presupposition* of the possibility of theoretical *thought* and *experience* is the truth of Christ's words . . . " (*Jerusalem and Athens,* 97; italics added). Oliphint follows Van Til closely, "A transcendental [presuppositional] approach looks for the (so-called) *preconditions* for knowledge and life" (*Covenantal Apologetics*, 46).

5. In addition to textual references to Ps 73 (see ch. 1n75), there are specific references to the term *Nevertheless* (*World Began*, 246, 258; *Meaning*, 15; *Depths*, 89; *Freedom*, 199; *God's World*, 138, 139, 141, 144; *Mount*, 140; *Conversations*, 4, 96, 189; *Ethics* 1:xvii; 2:96, 190, 322; *Creed;* 8, 9, 19, 59, 203, 209; *Evangelical Faith*, 1:25, 230–31, 291, 356, 391, 402; 2:12, 33, 37, 82, 186, 188, 192–93, 195, 197, 219, 238; 3:23, 29, 76, 152, 168, 172, 181n11, 353, 362, 418, 433; *How Modern?* 50, 69; *Believe*, 165, 177, 191, 213, 216; *Letters*, 33–34; *Living Death*, 187; *Human*, 323, 441, 462, 469; *Adventure*, 80; *Modern Thought*, 37, 38, 380, 511, 563).

6. *Evangelical Faith*, 1:25; translation mine, cf. *Evangelische Glaube*, 1:6. Van Til recognizes the significance of the psalm: "Asaph's lament in Psalm 73 is eloquent proof that the saints of God have, throughout the ages, but especially in ancient times, struggled with the problem of the 'unevenness' of the ways of God with man" (*Theology*, 141).

7. Doberstein explains that Thielicke's homiletical philosophy is to speak the everyday language of the common person and "translate his message into contemporary, colloquial terms" ("Translator's Introduction," *Waiting*, 7).

when I saw the prosperity of the wicked. ⁴ For they have no pangs until death; their bodies are fat and sleek. ⁵ They are not in trouble as others are; they are not stricken like the rest of mankind. ⁶ Therefore pride is their necklace; violence covers them as a garment. ⁷ Their eyes swell out through fatness; their hearts overflow with follies. ⁸ They scoff and speak with malice; loftily they threaten oppression. ⁹ They set their mouths against the heavens, and their tongue struts through the earth. ¹⁰ Therefore his people turn back to them, and find no fault in them. ¹¹ And they say, "How can God know? Is there knowledge in the Most High?"¹² Behold, these are the wicked; always at ease, they increase in riches. ¹³ All in vain have I kept my heart clean and washed my hands in innocence. ¹⁴ For all the day long I have been stricken and rebuked every morning. ¹⁵ If I had said, "I will speak thus," I would have betrayed the generation of your children. ¹⁶ But when I thought how to understand this, it seemed to me a wearisome task, ¹⁷ until I went into the sanctuary of God; then I discerned their end. ¹⁸ Truly you set them in slippery places; you make them fall to ruin. ¹⁹ How they are destroyed in a moment, swept away utterly by terrors! ²⁰ Like a dream when one awakes, O Lord, when you rouse yourself, you despise them as phantoms. ²¹ When my soul was embittered, when I was pricked in heart, ²² I was brutish and ignorant; I was like a beast toward you. ²³ Nevertheless, I am continually with you; you hold my right hand. ²⁴ You guide me with your counsel, and afterward you will receive me to glory. ²⁵ Whom have I in heaven but you? And there is nothing on earth that I desire besides you. ²⁶ My flesh and my heart may fail, but God is the strength of my heart and my portion forever. ²⁷ For behold, those who are far from you shall perish; you put an end to everyone who is unfaithful to you. ²⁸ But for me it is good to be near God; I have made the Lord GOD my refuge, that I may tell of all your works

The first verse of the Psalm reveals its author as Asaph. This author of eleven more of the Psalter's poems is a man intimately acquainted with the temple system in Jerusalem and one for whom belief in the God of Israel seems to be genetically encoded into the very fabric of his being. He begins the psalm with a general confession of God's goodness to the nation of Israel, and especially to "those who are pure in heart" (v. 1). These are the true Israelites whose clean lifestyles reflect the faith in Yahweh possessed by the national forefather, Abraham. Immediately after this affirmation of Yahweh's goodness, however, the poet surprisingly calls it into question. For he informs of a very dark time in his life when the gloomy clouds of doubt overshadowed any rational certainty of God whatsoever. This was during a *faith-crisis* that he amazingly survived, summarized by the heading of Franz Delitzsch's exposition, "Temptation to Apostasy Overcome."[8] The psalm is Asaph's own story, his autobiography of *Anfechtung*.

Faith-Crisis

The author candidly admits, "But as for me, my feet had almost stumbled, my steps had nearly slipped" (v. 2). Within the Old Testament, the life of faith is often portrayed as a walk along a path, most famously expressed in the 23rd Psalm, "He leads me in the paths of righteousness" (Ps 23:3). And it is from this narrow road of righteousness that the faithful Asaph almost falls headlong into the nearby ditch of disastrous unbelief. The reason, he explains, "For I was envious of the arrogant when I saw the prosperity of the wicked" (v. 3). When the psalmist looks at those who live in open defiance of God, it is like viewing yet another episode of the "Lifestyles of the Rich and Famous." The revolting spectacle, however, is all the more difficult to face for the devout, like Asaph, who personally suffer relentless hardship (vv. 5, 14) and even endure national catastrophe (Ps 74). Moreover, the troubling phenomenon completely contradicts his basic presuppositions of reality. For according to his ancient worldview—as the very beginning of the Psalter (Ps 1) testifies—there is an unseen metaphysical law that visibly governs the relation between guilt and punishment, on the one hand, and righteousness and reward on the other.

So to prove his case about the inversion of justice, the psalmist displays the evidence in the following verses (vv. 4–12). He points first to the fact that "they have no pangs until death" (v. 4). The rebellious are not only wealthy, but healthy. Common medical conditions are totally foreign to them. They do not squint with near-sightedness nor suffer from a hemorrhage as those among Asaph's social network. Indeed, they are like the cover models of glamour magazines; "their bodies are fat" (v. 4); and further emphasizing his point is that even their "eyes swell out through fatness" (v. 7). Granted, in the reader's modern, botoxed, photo-shopped culture, the picture of obesity does not do much to sell the psalmist's argument. In the ancient world, however, heaviness is a head-turning image of envy. For it is an unmistakable status symbol as only the extremely rich can afford the

---

8. For the purposes of this discussion we shall consult the exposition of Delitzsch, professor of exegesis at Leipzig, who in collaboration with C. F. Keil produced commentaries on the Old Testament that became the standard for 19th century Lutheran scholarship, with which Thielicke would have surely been acquainted (Keil and Delitzsch, *Commentary*, 5:485).

luxury of overeating. Strengthening the psalmist's point is the fact that the incredible income which subsidizes such extravagant consumption is often due to the exploitation of the poor,[9] who remain lean and are sometimes visibly malnourished. Like Hollywood movie stars, the God-mockers are always sporting the latest fashion; for jewelry, "pride is their necklace," and for designer clothing, "violence covers them as a garment" (v. 6). The sight of the rebellious alone is repulsive.

For their creed, they scorn any idea of God and openly "set their mouths against the heavens" (v. 9). Like rock stars in the constant spotlight, their anti-theistic propaganda is uncritically covered by the media and mindlessly believed by national fans so that God's "people turn back to them, and find no fault in them" (v. 10). Indeed, the catchy commercial for their religion-free cause is "How can God know?" (v. 11). The ancient anti-theists fervently deny the omniscience of God and thereby, long before Nietzsche, declare that "God is dead."

As a result, the blatant contradiction of reality drives Asaph to the edge of unbelief, "All in vain have I kept my heart clean" (v. 13). Here in juxtaposition from the confession of the first verse—God's goodness bestowed upon those with a pure heart—the poet laments that his clean-hearted life of faith has been all for nothing. His life spent scandal-free, constantly washing his "hands in innocence" (v. 13) because of his belief in God, is totally meaningless. Delitzsch asserts that "doubt is become the transition to apostasy."[10] The only reason that Asaph does not give vent to his dangerous doubt is because "I would have betrayed the generation of your children" (v. 15). Although flirting with the philosophers, the psalmist does not want his unbelief to become a stumbling-block that would destroy the faith of his friends. So he decides to remain a closet apostate until he can think it all through. But there is only one problem with this plan, specifically, "When I thought how to understand this, it seemed to me a wearisome task" (v. 16). Delitzsch explains, "Thinking alone will give neither the right light nor true happiness."[11] It is impossible for the poet to sort out the contradiction rationally. Neither human reason, philosophical speculation, nor epistemological theory can resolve the riddle. The door is shut on his secret skepticism, and there is no way to come out.

---

9. For such an example in antiquity, see the obese oppressor of Israel; Eglon, the king of Moab (Judg 3:17).

10. Keil and Delitzsch, *Commentary*, 490.

11. Ibid., 491.

Triumph

Yet the unexpected happens. For whatever unlikely reason—cultural expectation, social pressure, or the desperate search for existential authentication—the poet surprisingly attends public worship. Delitzsch comments, "He went into God's dread sanctuary" (v. 17).[12] The worship atmosphere alone evokes a sense of reverence and awe for the transcendent Creator who dwells in remote majesty, before whom the stars are like dust at his feet. Then here in this sacred space the unpredictable occurs; the skeptic is given a glorious glimpse of eternity, "Then I discerned their end" (v. 17). He sees his own eternal destiny, which is especially highlighted in contrast to that of the anti-theists' destruction (vv. 18–20). With this newfound perspective of the invisible spiritual realm, his confusion is cleared away. It is also important to note that the certainty of God's existence is not the result of philosophical proof or even prior theological reflection; rather, it comes from an encounter with the God who discloses himself.

Even so, "the poet, from the standpoint of the explanation he has received, speaks of a possible return of his temptation, and condemns it beforehand."[13] The psalmist is painfully aware of his faltering faith and is convinced if he were ever again thrown into *faith-crisis,* he would be "brutish and ignorant . . . like a beast toward you" (v. 22). As a brute beast that is unable to reason its way to God, he would be found out of communion with the Creator.[14]

Finally, it is this possibility of recurring *faith-crisis* that brings us to the focus of this discussion: Asaph's triumphant confession of faith, "Nevertheless I am continually with thee" (v. 23; KJV). Delitzsch explains, "Confidently does he yield up himself to the divine guidance, though he may not see through the mystery of the plan of this guidance . . . The future is dark to him, but lighted up by the one hope that the end of his earthly existence will be a glorious solution of the riddle."[15] In other words, the term "Nevertheless" is an expression of the psalmist's defiance to "the contradiction between reality and God,"[16] a confession that he will worship in the dark until the dawn breaks.

---

12. Ibid.

13. Ibid., 492.

14. Ibid. Delitzsch adds, "The meaning of the poet is, that he would not be a man in relation to God . . . if he should again give way to the same doubts, but would be like the most stupid animal, which stands before God incapable of such knowledge as He willingly imparts to earnestly inquiring man" (ibid., 492).

15. Ibid., 492–93.

16. *Evangelical Faith,* 1:229.

With this survey of Psalm 73 in view, now we can stand fast on the theological foundation of Thielicke's apologetic and understand this confession of "Nevertheless" to which he indefatigably returns. For as in yet another instance, when preaching on "What Does It Mean to Believe?" Thielicke alludes:

> Was it a purely natural thing for the psalmist to say, "Nevertheless I am continually with thee"? After all, what he was saying was this: Everything contradicts the faith that there is such a thing as justice, that a higher power rules this world, and that there is anyone who concerns himself about me. Nevertheless, I hold fast to thee, I push on blindly through the fog and know that thou art waiting for me on the other side.[17]

"Nevertheless" Cry of Dereliction

As a theologian of the cross and not of glory, the culminating example of the "Nevertheless" to which Thielicke finally turns is the Golgotha event. "The saying: 'Nevertheless I am continually with thee' (Psalm 73:23) which the devout say to the hidden God . . . recurs in a deeper and more radical form in the NT. The crucified Jesus utters this Nevertheless in his cry of dereliction on the cross."[18] The psalmist's confession of "Nevertheless" foreshadows Christ's "Nevertheless" cry—"My God, my God, why hast thou forsaken me?" (Mark 15:34)—which reveals an existential certainty of God's existence over against the reality which contradicts it. Thielicke explains in arguably the most profound passage of his entire dogmatics:

> Faith breaks through the encircling reality which is bearing witness against God. Appeal is made to him who is not seen (Hebrews 11:1). The complaint of Jesus, his cry of dereliction, is not a shriek in the void. It does not proclaim the death of God. This confession of God's remoteness is an assurance of his nearness.
>
> Jesus is not speaking *about* God and his absence. He addresses him as Thou. His confession of dereliction is thus a prayer to him who has forsaken him. In this confession he also adopts the formulated prayer of the OT community (Psalm 22:1). He uses the Word of God to cry to the remote and absent God . . . An impossible prayer is prayed. A prayer is ventured which, if God's absence is not ultimate, can only be a questioning of reality. In the praying of this prayer, and in the implied

17. *Creed*, 8–9.
18. *Evangelical Faith*, 3:172.

breakthrough of faith, the absence of God becomes a vanishing dream and the death of God becomes a vanquished illusion.[19]

With the cross in view, Thielicke begins the last volume of his dogmatics with the *Anfechtung* antithesis against which the apologist ventures a confession: "Faith can only go *against* appearances, *against* the evidence, in the power of a Nevertheless."[20]

Not "Therefore"

Theologizing about the "Nevertheless," Thielicke brings further clarity to the meaning of the psalmist's confession by a precise syntactic apophasis:

> The contradiction between reality and God is never overcome by perception. If it were, Psalm 73:23ff. would have to run: "Because thou hast thought thus, I see that the wicked may triumph and I must suffer. Therefore I am continually with thee." We do not find this solution, however, in . . . Psalm 73.[21]

In the next volume of his systematics he continues, "Faith is not an insight into the nexus of meaning which enables us to speak in terms of a Because and which thus achieves continuity with our causal thinking. Instead, it finds itself referred to a Nevertheless. 'Nevertheless I am continually with thee . . . ' (Psalm 73:23)."[22] For Thielicke, the absence of a causative "Therefore" and the placement instead of a countercausative "Nevertheless" is not a matter of semantics, but of theology proper. He thus adds:

> The impossibility of making world occurrence intelligible by bringing it under a formula and establishing the statement: 'Because . . . therefore this is so and this happens'—this impossibility is accompanied by the confession of the righteous: 'Nevertheless I am continually with thee' (Psalm 73:23).[23]

What fact and reason show do not lead the psalmist to confess, "Because . . . Therefore." Instead, in defiance against the empirical and rational, he protests, "Nevertheless." Resuming this thought in the final volume of his systematics he asserts:

---

19. Ibid., 1:230.
20. Ibid., 3:23.
21. Ibid., 1:229.
22. Ibid., 2:33.
23. Ibid., 2:82.

> Even believers cannot understand the individual steps by which God's thoughts are realized in history. They find comfort in facing puzzling things (e.g., the good fortune of the wicked who swell with fatness and are praised by the mob [Ps. 73:7, 10] while the righteous suffer . . .)—in facing these things in all their stringency and replying in a relieved "Therefore"—but no, even for believers the only possibility is to say: "Nevertheless I am continually with thee" (Psalm 73:23).[24]

Yet Thielicke will not drop the matter and continues in his textbook on modern theology. Commenting on Asaph's quarrel with God about his government of the world, Thielicke writes, "The Psalmist [and Job] . . . find it unjust until they get through to God with a Nevertheless, not an understanding or conjectural Therefore."[25]

Thielicke continually emphasizes the crucial point from the pulpit. During the Second World War, Thielicke encourages the defeated:

> The author of Psalm 73, who does not get at these dark passages by seeking and finally discovering *reasons* behind the mysterious leadings of God, so that he can then say, "Because of such and such, God did this or that." Rather he confesses and declares (and does so in the face of impenetrable *darkness*): "*Nevertheless*, I am continually with thee."[26]

When preaching on "Overcoming Anxiety" and despair caused by the looming threat of "whether the atom bomb will lay in dust and ashes the summer landscape," Thielicke expounds:

> How does the psalmist arrive at this peace in the midst of an unpredictable world? Does he arrive at it, say, by a process of reflection in which he discovers the meaning and suddenly the light dawns on him? Does he reflect and then say, it was "because" God wanted to mature me through suffering; "because" he wanted to test my faith in the midst of this crazy, unpredictable world; he robbed me of my position, my living, my home, my dearest "because . . ."? No; we shall look in vain in the whole psalm for this kind of argument. It is the feverish thinking of the worldly wise, who think they can fathom the meaning of life

---

24. Ibid., 3:152. Anticipating the positive side of his apologetic approach addressed in ch. 6, we should add his assertion that the "relation of trust does not arise out of a causative reasoning of a Therefore. It is a *venture* of a Nevertheless that 'I am continually with thee' (Psalm 73:23)" (ibid., 3:362; italics added).

25. *Modern Thought*, 37.

26. *God's World*, 138; see *Depths*, 89; *Human*, 323.

that grasps for this kind of argument. The psalmist scorns it. He simply says: *"Nevertheless I am continually with thee."*[27]

Sermonizing on "The Mystery of Death," he counters "our doubts and objections":

> Never can we say: "*Because* certain conditions are such and such, certain things happen to me." We'll never get by with that answer. It sticks in our throat, doesn't it, when we think of the millions who died in the last war, the subterranean terror in the cellars and bomb shelters, the stricken women and children? The fact is that we do *not* know why this had to be; but now we can say: [Nevertheless] "I will abide with Thee."[28]

The confession, or presupposition, of "Nevertheless" is categorically distinct from and can never be confused with a causative and postsuppositional "Therefore."[29] Rather, "Nevertheless" is a repudiation of "Therefore."[30]

---

27. *Mount*, 139–40. Thielicke continues to caveat, "I beg you to note that faith does not say, 'Nevertheless I will remain standing; 'what does not get me down makes me stronger'" (ibid., 142).

28. *World*, 177, 183.

29. Given this vehement opposition to "Therefore" as a confession for apologetics instead of "Nevertheless," one must conclude that there is a typographical error in the German text—transmitted into the English translation—about the *faith-crisis* confession of John the Baptist since it stands in blatant contradiction to the above: "He evokes this confession in John, forcing him to say: *Therefore* he is the one that should come" (*Evangelical Faith*, 2:335; italics added). That John questions the identity of Christ while in *faith-crisis* is clear, as Thielicke explains two pages prior: "This comes to expression in that he asks in *Anfechtung*" (*Evangelical Faith*, 2:333; translation mine, cf. *Evangelische Glaube*, 2:409). Accordingly, the faithful confession of the Baptizer could never have been a postsuppositional "Therefore" but only a defiant "Nevertheless."

30. Oliphint approaches the "Nevertheless" in his endeavor to translate Van Til into more biblical and theological categories. In explaining the apostolic mandate for apologetics (1 Pet 3:15), he points to Peter's first century readers, suffering believers scattered throughout the Roman Empire, who are persecuted by those hostile to the faith (1:6; 3:13–17; 4:12–19; 5:9–10). In this context, Oliphint focuses on Peter's preparatory command to "sanctify Christ as Lord in your hearts" (NASB) in order to do apologetics. The Lordship of Christ, as a conviction of one's heart, means that "we are to think about and live in the world according to what it really is, not according to how it might at times *appear* to us" (*Covenantal Apologetics*, 35). Peter issues the command because he "recognizes that one of their paramount temptations is to interpret their circumstances in such a way that would not acknowledge Christ as Lord" (ibid.). So Oliphint concludes that "instead of looking at the overwhelming suffering around them and declaring that there is no God, they are rather to declare, 'Jesus is Lord'" (ibid., 34)—a New Testament formula of "Nevertheless."

Faith "Against"

Theologizing about modern theology's theme of doubt and appropriation, Thielicke employs the "Nevertheless" illustratively to teach on the nature of faith, "As it traverses this doubt, faith achieves self-clarification. It is not just faith *in* but always, to the end of the aeon, faith *against*—the faith of a Nevertheless."[31] This "in" and "against" assertion is not superfluous theological gymnastics, but a core exercise that he routinely performs from the very beginning of his systematics, "It is faith against something as well as faith in something."[32] Exactly what it is that faith is "in" and "against" is explained later in the same volume, "Faith is not just faith in God. It is also faith against reality."[33] This "reality" against which faith flings itself is a false perception of reality that seemingly contradicts God's sovereign rule and hence his existence. "Thus," explains Thielicke, "the contradiction between reality and God which brings us under the *faith-crisis* of God's supposed absence arises, in the end, from the fact that we have made an idolatrous image of this reality and this image has to be shattered."[34] In other words, the "Nevertheless" is a confession of the absolute antithesis between belief and unbelief—the *Anfechtung* antithesis against which the apologist believes and pushes in Christian persuasion.[35]

In the second volume of his dogmatics Thielicke brushes some color onto the pagan portrait of reality and highlights the antithesis against which the "Nevertheless" is directed:

31. *Modern Thought*, 38.

32. *Evangelical Faith*, 1:25; see 228, 231; 2:51, 59–60, 74, 238; 3:23, 29; *Theologie Anfechtung*, iv; *Human*, 469; *Modern Thought*, 5, 18, 38.

33. *Evangelical Faith*, 1:228. Thielicke elaborates from the pulpit, "Believing is by no means merely a question of *what* I believe in, but always also the question of *against what* I believe. For faith must always struggle against appearances. We do not see what we believe, at any rate not until the moment comes when faith is permitted to see what it has believed, and unbelief is *compelled* to see what it has *not* believed" (*World Began*, 10).

34. *Evangelical Faith*, 1:229; translation mine, cf. *Evangelische Glaube*, 1:320. Oliphint translates Van Til's antithesis in terms similar to Thielicke's "idolatrous image of this reality." He asserts that "the views of any who remain in unbelief are, in *reality*, *illusions*. They do not and cannot make sense of the world as it really is" (*Covenantal Apologetics*, 51–52; italics added; see 150, 191, 229).

35. Thielicke stresses the antithesis by showing that "in" and "against" is reflected in the historic confessions of the Reformation, as well as the Barmen Declaration of 1934 directed against the "German Christian," or Nazi, accommodation. The clause "We confess and teach" followed by the "We reject" is a grammatical formulation of the antithesis between faith "in" and "against" (*Modern Thought*, 5–7). Van Til speaks similarly of an *"absolute ethical antithesis"* in order to emphasize the noetic effect of sin (*Theology*, 64).

> Psalm 73 present us with a rationally insoluble problem, namely, that of reconciling the divine overruling of history with the complete absence of any such relation, and hence of bringing it out of its obscurity (Psalm 73:12, 16). The Lord of history is not in fact manifest in his works. On the contrary, he is hidden in these works, so that faith in him can consist only in the protest of a Nevertheless against what the *senses see* and what *reason recognizes* to be the law operative in events of this kind (Psalm 73:23ff.).[36]

The hiddenness of God draws one's focus to two aspects of the idolatrous image of reality against which the "Nevertheless" rails. The "Nevertheless" is a protest against what the "senses see" and what "reason recognizes"—which counterdemonstrationism chapter 4 shall treat.

"Higher Thoughts"

Viewing the *Anfechtung* antithesis from yet another angle, Thielicke sees it arising from the collision between human thoughts and the "higher thoughts" of God:

> The "higher thoughts" which may make such odd thing as the suffering of the good and the prosperity of the wicked intelligible in the self-consciousness of God are certainly not "our thoughts" . . . The *faith-crisis* arises, then, because our thoughts are not content to be trusting and waiting thoughts but grant themselves normative rank.[37]

The "higher thoughts" to which Thielicke refers throughout his corpus are those revealed through the prophet, "For as the heavens are higher than the earth, so are my ways higher than your ways and my thoughts than your thoughts" (Isa 55:9).[38] The broader context of the passage speaks of

---

36. *Evangelical Faith*, 2:12; italics added. Thielicke also applies the "Nevertheless" nature of faith "in" and "against" to the question of whether Christ is the hidden Pantocrator: "There is no syllogism by which we may say, 'Therefore he is the Christ of God.' He discloses himself only to a trust which withstands the hiddenness, the concealment of the cross, and the counterargument of appearances. 'Nevertheless I am continually with thee,' even though everything speaks against it (Psalm 73:23). It is of a piece with this that faith can be understood only in terms of two dimensions, namely as faith 'in,' but also as faith 'against'" (*Human*, 469).

37. *Evangelical Faith*, 2:52; the last sentence is the translation mine, cf. *Evangelische Glaube*, 2:62; see *Between*, 7; *World Began*, 193).

38. Thielicke refers to "higher thoughts" repeatedly (*Waiting*, 143, 192; *Between*, 7; *World Began*, 18, 51, 111, 193, 197, 222, 226; *Nihilism*, 112; *Meaning*, 28, 126, 158, 164,

a promised restoration for the exiles after their Babylonian captivity. The immediate verse shows the certainty of its fulfillment is that God's totally other thoughts for his people's welfare far transcend the finite limits of human reason. For his thoughts are not at all ineffectual wishes or helpless hopes. Rather, his omniscient thoughts correlate to his sovereign authorship of the future which assures that he is the absolute Lord of history. Thielicke writes, "If God gives this kind of revelation, it implies much more than mere prediction of the course of things . . . God does not merely declare the future; He brings it to pass."[39] History in this sense is "his-story" which carries with it an assurance that God will make the future his future. So the direction of history steered by these "higher thoughts" can in no way to be compared to the contested outcome of ancient dualism or to an unknown future espoused by contemporary open theism. God's "higher thoughts" are his eternal plan by which he governs the galaxies and incontestably rules the world.

One must stress, however, that these "higher thoughts" are not the predictable plan of a removed, deistic God who does not interfere in human affairs but works strictly according to the laws of planetary motion and thermodynamics. "Tell me how lofty God is for you," Thielicke challenges, "and I'll tell you how little he means to you."[40] The theological axiom teaches that the "lofty God" of deism "has been lofted right out of my private life."[41] Instead the God whose timeless "higher thoughts" are beyond human imagination has very personal plans for private individuals: "Before the foundation of the world, there begins the history of a great love and a great search. Here, there begin to take shape those higher thoughts that God is thinking even about my life."[42]

Trust in these "higher thoughts" should thus embolden faith. From the pulpit, Thielicke once again returns to Jean Paul's "Dream of a World

---

170, 175; *Silence*, 30; *Freedom*, 198, 216; *God's World*, 138, 139, 210; *Mount*, 126–27; *Conversations*, 41, 84, 108; *Trouble*, 8, 54; *ThE* 1:661–62, 665; 2:237; *Creed*, 6, 16, 22, 41, 42, 124, 195, 213; *Evangelical Faith*, 1:229; 2:52, 56, 82, 84, 441; 3:151, 164, 432; *How Modern?* 11, 50, 66; *Believe*, 9, 49, 82, 88, 100, 120, 138, 173; *Human*, 324, 337–38; *Notes*, 120).

Van Til also believes that "higher thoughts" play a significant role in apologetics. Describing man's autonomy referred to above, Van Til states, "He would not think God's thoughts after him; he would instead think only his original thoughts" (*Apologetics*, 80). He therefore maintains that the apologist must learn to think analogically, i.e., "to think God's thoughts after him" (*Apologetics*, 77n19, 78, 131, 140).

39. *Human*, 324.
40. *Creed*, 33.
41. Ibid., 33.
42. *World Began*, 18.

Without God" to illustrate that the "man who knows and trusts that there is One who thinks higher thoughts about his life develops a new attitude toward and relationship to the future."[43] Indeed, he need not know or fear what the future will bring because he knows the One who holds the future in his hand. Moreover, the faith that his will for one is good and that he considers everything that is to happen before he sends it provides far more elemental and decisive certainty than the uncertainty about that which chance has in store. For those caught in the blind dice game of meaningless chance—the accidental outcome of the interaction between random energy and matter—there is only pointless resistance or the despair of *amor fati*. The latter might superficially resemble a kind of reconciliation to fate; however, in reality it is only a heartless resignation to that with which there is no basis of rational discussion or negotiation. Either case "there are no more 'higher thoughts' that rule over us, and there is no God to 'think' anything about it or to watch lovingly over our life."[44] On the other hand, Thielicke assures, "I do not capitulate to mindless fate and meaningless chance. I bow before the higher thoughts of God who knows better than I myself what I need and what will work to my good."[45] Yet more, he can not only face the future calmly, but become "an adventurer of a higher order" eagerly and expectantly looking "for the surprises God has in store for me."[46] He can readily await to see how God "will deal with the great motif which he has given to my life, that motif which affirms that everything works for good if only I love him and remain confident that he will sustain and uphold me."[47]

This motif, Thielicke maintains, mysteriously includes even the dark providences of life. For the faithful who find encouragement by the fact of "higher thoughts" confess:

> "Nevertheless I am continually with thee" (Ps. 73:23)—*even though* we see nothing but the blindly raging elements, *even though* the power of darkness seems to have the last word . . . it is only in the midst of menacing forces that we can confess and declare who or what God is for us. Here is where it becomes apparent whether we truly believe that even the darkness is only a part of his "higher thoughts."[48]

---

43. *Creed*, 6.
44. *Believe*, 173.
45. *Conversations*, 84.
46. *Creed*, 6. He again stresses, "That, in his name, we may be adventurers on a new level" (ibid., 244).
47. Ibid., 6.
48. *How Modern?* 50.

The audacious claim that included in these "higher thoughts" is the dark sight "of a brutally murdered child" or that "four small children are robbed of their mother through the act of a drunken driver" does not cause Thielicke to blush in the face of the protest:[49] "How can God permit this?" For the riddle that is insoluble to our thoughts is resolved in the hidden thoughts of God. Moreover, as one himself who asked the question for years while often chained to a wheelchair,[50] Thielicke confirms, it is exactly at this very point that "the urgent question arises whether I can simply trust that God has a purpose in mind for me, that he is realizing his higher thoughts in the very thing which in *my* thoughts must necessarily be meaningless."[51] The desperately sought answer for meaning—which requires "trust," that is, faith—is ontic rather than noetic. That is why "higher thoughts" cannot be taken for a cosmic formula or Theory of Everything (TOE) type answer which constructs a therapeutic bridge over the dreaded abyss of nothingness for the intellectually weak or frightened. The "higher thoughts" must be believed in order to be understood. "Only in the sanctuary,"[52] in the vestibule of faith, does the psalmist come to apprehend them (Ps 73:17–20; see 36:9).

Overcoming *Faith-Crisis*

As the "Nevertheless" is a repudiation of the false appearance of reality, *faith-crisis* is overcome neither by sense experience nor human reason. To illustrate how "the Christian overcomes the onslaughts upon his faith,"[53] Thielicke offers a favorite hymn with which some of his German audience would have been familiar, that of Paul Gerhardt's "Commit thy way, confiding."[54] This hymn does not at all reflect an attitude of the "victorious Christian life" but instead expresses all the fiery furnaces of hellish *faith-crisis*. Referring to the demonic forces that cloud any higher thoughts of the hidden God, the hymn climaxes in the words: "Blessed be thou, thou child of faithfulness!" Using this crescendo as a rhetorical device, Thielicke reminds his audience that those who overcome *faith-crisis* are not those about whom the hymn says: "Blessed be thou, thou thinker, thou philosopher who with thine ingenious mind has found the cosmic formula that resolves the enig-

---

49. *Creed*, 124; *Meaning*, 164.

50. *World Began*, 50. While a young student, Thielicke contracted a crippling tetany which was eventually cured by experimental medication; see ch. 6.

51. Ibid., 51.

52. *Evangelical Faith*, 2:84.

53. *God's World*, 140.

54. Ibid., 139–40.

matic and tormenting mysteries of the world."⁵⁵ Nor, expanding Thielicke's rhetoric, could it be said about those who conquer *faith-crisis*: "Blessed be thou, thou researcher, thou scientist, who with thine empirical evidence has discovered the origin of the universe and Theory of Everything." Instead *faith-crisis* in only overcome by the grace of God.

Grace

As Thielicke insists from the pulpit, *faith-crisis* is that from which one must be saved by a miracle of grace:

> Thus the Nevertheless is a part of faith, just as the cup of suffering is part of Gethsemane and as Golgotha is part of the miracle of the Resurrection. Sometimes the fog grows so thick as I look ahead that I have no idea how I shall ever get through. But then I am given the *grace* to say Nevertheless, for suddenly He who was a man like you and me and who took upon himself the burden of this same misery is there beside me. Then suddenly, with him at my side, the barrier is broken and I am in the clear; I have experienced the *miracle* of getting through.⁵⁶

The believer survives *faith-crisis* only by an act of grace, that is, the miraculous intervention of Christ.

Indeed, the grace of God required for conversion is just as vital after regeneration to preserve faith from the onslaught of *faith-crisis*. This intervening miracle, Thielicke stresses from the beginning of his theological work, is due to the nature of faith: "For he thinks the faith must be so understood, that he faces it not as a constant, which he ever possesses, rather that the Lord over him creates the event of faith anew daily and rescues him from the spell of *Anfechtung*."⁵⁷ Faith is not a possession kept in the failsafe vault of self-confidence which can provide peace of mind for the cultural Christian who perhaps attends Christmas and Easter services. Rather the life of faith is a journey, a pilgrimage on a road from "faith" to "sight." Thielicke elaborates:

> Faith is never something "finished," which one "has" once and for all and could smugly boast of possessing. No, faith is always traveling a definite way, a particular road. We can characterize the starting point and the terminus of that road by saying that

---

55. Ibid., 140.
56. *Creed*, 9; italics added.
57. *Theologie Anfechtung*, iv; translation mine.

> it is a way that leads from the trial of doubt and despair to the praise of God. It is the faith of the church militant which, like that of the writer of Psalm 73, is always in danger of foundering on the dreadful incongruities of this world, the underserved fortune of the wicked and the equally underserved misfortune of the good. It is the faith of that company of people who . . . want to curse the day of their birth, because the meaninglessness of life—especially in time of catastrophe—overwhelms them and forces them to fight their way through to the "Nevertheless" of faith.[58]

It must be stressed, however, that this reaching or fighting for faith's "Nevertheless" should not be viewed as a human effort. Rather, Thielicke confirms, "We believe because 'the power of his might worked in us' (Ephesians 1:19)."[59] It is God who is at work in us to desire him, and more of him, and thereby draw us unto himself (Phil 2:13). So, following Luther's thought, if one is to see faith as a work, then one must view it as "God's work and not man's."[60] The grace of God alone is that which sustains faith and empowers it daily with new might—bringing faith to its "Nevertheless"—in order to overcome *faith-crisis*. Thielicke remembers:

> That precisely in the darkest hours of our lives, when no human being could help us and the deepest agony of being forsaken ate at our hearts, precisely then we felt the miracle of this Nevertheless and God sent his stars to rise over us. That is why it is precisely these most difficult hours that we don't want to do without, not because they are so difficult, but because it is at such times that we experience that faith which can break through steel and stone.[61]

Predestination

The miracle of the "Nevertheless" experience leads one, in retrospect, to perceive a deep and profound mystery regarding the overcoming of *faith-crisis*, and moreover one's conversion:

---

58. *God's World*, 140–41.
59. *Evangelical Faith*, 3:13.
60. Ibid., 3:19.
61. *Creed*, 59. In Thielicke's view, "He who simply cultivates and preserves the sheltered garden of his childhood faith and the ideals of Western Christian civilization, always fending off the destructive onslaughts of doubt, can never really experience the miracle of grace" (*Nihilism*, 176).

> There, because a man knows that he has been found by this strange and underserved love, because he sees the grace of God winning the victory in that battle without any contribution on his part—"if God is for us, who is against us?"—he realizes in wonder and adoration *that the reason why he became a Christian and countless others have not does not lie in himself, but that it was all a miracle that simply fell to his lot.*[62]

What distinguishes the believer from those outside the faith is that he or she was predestined by God for salvation while others were passed over and left in their unbelief.

At this point in Thielicke's *Anfechtung* theology, the age-old subject found in almost every philosophical system—usually couched in terms of fate or freewill—emerges.[63] Whereas the question usually arises on an abstract level in the speculative discussion of a classroom, Thielicke applies it to concrete existence in the real world. Moreover, he emphasizes the time when the subject becomes relevant, for it is only after *Anfechtung* that predestination suddenly "comes into the picture":

> It appears in that moment when I have struggled with the devil and my own flesh, when I have passed through the mortal conflict, engaged to the quick in the battle of God and Satan for my soul, and suddenly find myself on the side of the victorious Christ, without really knowing, and certainly not being able to explain, how I got there. Instead of questions, I have on my lips only gratitude that I have been drawn over to that side by a power which is greater than I.[64]

Faith-crisis is that which provides the necessary perspective for any consideration of predestination. After *Anfechtung*, after the smoke of battle vanishes, the believer does not ask the typical *Why?* question inquisitively and speculatively seeking to solve the secret meaning in God's higher plan with a rational answer: Rather the subject of predestination emerges as praise to God after the life-or-death struggle has been won, not by one, but by *Christus Victor* for one. Luther confirms, "In the absence of suffering and the Cross and the perils of death, one cannot deal with

---

62. *God's World*, 204.

63. Neither does modern atheism escape the labyrinth, but instead espouses a very rigid doctrine of fate. For the human being can only behave according to one's pre-programmed genetic code. As Richard Dawkins delights in repeating, "DNA neither knows nor cares. DNA just is. And we dance to its music" (*River Out of Eden*, 133). He concedes that freewill exists only to the extent as allowed by slavery to one's DNA code.

64. *God's World*, 204–5.

predestination without harm and without secret anger against God."[65] In other words, the uncommitted intellectual is in no position to deal with it apart from epistemic shipwreck washing him or her ashore a dark labyrinth of unfathomable mystery.

Yet for those struggling searchers laden with guilt and doubt, predestination is a truth of magnificent comfort. Here believers learn that there is nothing more secure than their eternal destiny. For despite their sin, misery and unbelief, God still chose to save them. In his eternal plan, he foresaw their epistemological, that is, ethical rebellion, and determined to elect them anyway. He said "Nevertheless" to them and to the forces of hell about them.[66] They further realize that God's choice is completely unconditional and therefore not influenced by their Faustian strivings or their accomplishments or their character.[67] Rather they are simply "predestined according to the purpose of him who works all things according to the counsel of his will" (Eph 1:11). In other words, it is God's sovereign prerogative to do as he pleases. "I will have mercy on whom I have mercy, and I will have compassion on whom I have compassion" (Rom 9:15). The assurance of their salvation, therefore, does not depend upon their own effort, but as Thielicke explains is

> rather an assurance given to me through a miracle, a miracle that lies completely outside the realm of my self, solely in the unfathomable, self-authenticating love of God, then the concept of predestination becomes the ultimate expression of praise and gratitude. Then it is the adoration of a man who is at the end of all his potentialities, who is conscious only of the disaster to which his guilt has doomed him and now is snatched away from

---

65. *LW* 35:378, quoted in *God's World*, 205. Van Til charges Lutherans with an Arminian theology that lends to traditional apologetics (*Jerusalem and Athens*, 9–10, 91). But this criticism would not apply to Thielicke, a neo-Lutheran. Later Van Til sharpens his aim on those, in his opinion, that are Lutheran in name only like the fictional Mr. Martin Marty, whom Luther scolds for abandoning his teaching on the *Bondage of the Will* (Response to John Warwick Montgomery, "Once upon an A Priori," in *Jerusalem and Athens*, 400–403). Montgomery's criticism of Van Til is a result of his misunderstanding of the latter, as are his charges against Thielicke ("Thielicke on Trial," 57).

Thielicke's reception among American Lutherans largely divides into polar camps. Opposite of Montgomery's one-sided criticism is unrestrained enthusiasm for Thielicke (Fry, "Helmut Thielicke," http://biblecentre.net/theology/books/het/het200.html/).

66. Thielicke also refers to the "Nevertheless" or "Yes" that God says to the believer (*Evangelical Faith*, 2:186, 188, 192–93, 195, 197, 219; see Barth, *CD* 2/2:28–29).

67. *God's World*, 211.

all this by the strange initiative of God and led by the Father's hand into the cheerful light of home.[68]

Role of Apologetics

As in any discussion of fate or freewill, the classical question of human responsibility is also applied to the doctrine of predestination. Yet moving beyond the mind-game question—as in the case of Judas' necessary role in redemptive history—the inquiry rightfully arises, "If God has predestined those whom he will save, then why bother with apologetics?" More specifically, how does the subject of predestination affect the role of apologetics to Thielicke which so clearly holds? As Thielicke's apologetic incorporates a characteristic influenced by Pascal's *Wager* (see chapter 6), the theologian allows the mathematician to answer: "I would not seek thee, O God, if thou hadst not already found me."[69] Those whom God has already found in his eternal plan shall seek him, and he uses Christian conversation to help stimulate their search. So in this context Thielicke is fond of repeating that which was revealed through the prophet, "You will seek me and find me, when you seek me with all your heart" (Jer 29:13).[70]

Apologetic Conversation

The role of apologetics finally brings into focus a vital outcome of the "Nevertheless": *faith-crisis* conversation with unbelievers, which is approached through such a conversation within oneself. This emerges in a discussion on the idolatrous image of reality which contradicts God's existence. Thielicke informs, "The Nevertheless which faith continually opposes to these obfuscations may be seen also in theological reflection. This, too, is always an inner dialog between the spiritual man and the natural man."[71]

This inner dialogue is integral to Thielicke's apologetic methodology. Indeed, it is only after this inner conversation has taken place that one is prepared to converse with unbelievers:

> Consequently the dialogue with those outside can be carried on only if it has first taken place within myself as a monologue, that

---

68. Ibid., 205–6.
69. Pascal, in Thielicke (*World Began*, 86, 209; *Nihilism*, 104, 178; see *Believe*, 21). Thielicke also attributes the formula to Augustine (*Believe*, 86).
70. *God's World*, 130; *Creed*, 67; *Believe*, 19, 165; *Evangelical Faith*, 2:93.
71. *Evangelical Faith*, 1:231.

is to say, as a dialogue of the spiritual man within me with the natural man within me. And to that extent this dialogue is carried on, not in certainty and security, but in *Anfechtung*, in faith assailed and tempted by doubt and despair.[72]

It is precisely at this *faith-crisis* dialogical juncture, according to the theologian, that traditional apologetics fails so miserably. For it only "speaks from a position of certainty and from its secure position addresses others who have gone astray. The apologist is sure that he possesses the truth and is confident that error is abroad somewhere fairly far from his gates."[73] Contrary to this approach, however, the *Anfechtung* apologist never speaks from an unassailable citadel of certainty and from its secure position confidently corrects secularists regarding their mistakes. Instead, he addresses skeptics only after he has first addressed his own doubt. A conversation within himself must initially be conducted; a dialogue between the natural and spiritual sides of his personality. Only by relentlessly wrestling through this doubt-laden dialogue in his own person is he able to dialogue with skeptics about their doubts.[74]

---

72. *God's World*, 218; see Thielicke's early statement that apologetic conversation should not take the character of an argument with the outside, but with the character of "the inward *faith-crisis*. It conducts itself like a conversation between the spiritual man and the natural man in ourselves" (*Fragen*, 10; translation mine; see Speier, *Initiator*, 14).

73. *God's World*, 217–18. Van Til actually employs "the figure of a fortress or citadel" (*Apologetics*, 22–23) to describe the apologist's position of certainty, i.e., a rational certainty achieved without *Anfechtung*. This is the most significant distinction between the two presuppositional approaches. Van Til asserts, "Thus there is absolutely certain proof for the existence of God and the truth of Christian theism" (*Apologetics*, 133–34). He teaches that "we as Christians alone have a position that is philosophically defensible" and is "certain . . . that Christianity is objectively valid and that it is the only rational position for man to hold" (*Common Grace*, 8, 82, in Bahnsen, *Van Til's Apologetic*, 74). In following, Oliphint maintains that this "certainty should inform part of our apologetic approach" (*Covenantal Apologetics*, 217n25). Van Til's notion of certainty seems to leave no room for doubt, at least as his use of the term "certainty" is defined by Bahnsen: "The claim that a basis for doubt is inconceivable is justified whenever a denial of the claim would violate the conditions or presuppositions of rational inquiry" (*Van Til's Apologetic*, 78–79n98). In this context, it should be noted that Thielicke's allergy to certainty does not imply that his apologetic operates on "probability," for that would contradict the existential "*certainty* of the reality of God" (*Modern Thought*, 451; italics added) confessed in the "Nevertheless," which is a "*certainty* about God . . . which I cannot establish *rationally*" (ibid., 56; italics added). So Thielicke's reaction to *rational* certainty is triggered by what he perceives as an apologetic high-handedness which is based in philosophical rationalism—for which reason he categorically rejects traditional apologetics. Would this distinction hint to a more radical and thorough break from traditional approaches than Van Til's project?

74. Thielicke's dialogical approach seems to correspond with the apologetic culture

Goal of Solidarity

Thielicke argues that the inner conversation of the apologist effects the persuasiveness of his or her outer conversation with unbelievers. He confirms that there are many methods by "which the believer bears witness to the logos of his hope and develops it as logos (1 Peter 3:15f.), trying to make it clear to every man."[75] Yet the criteria of responsible God-talk are such that "he who speaks about God as indicated will find himself in *solidarity* with all thinking people as he renders *to himself* and others the *logos* of his talk."[76] Solidarity allows the apologist to identity with and connect to his hearer. Solidarity vouches for his sincerity and, Thielicke maintains, is a "very pastoral 'method' which, after all, requires that communication be established in order to become effective."[77]

The goal of solidarity reflects Thielicke's rigid conviction that one's hearer cannot be objectified. Personal understanding of another individual is categorically distinct from a scientific explanation of that person as the product of biological and environmental factors. In other words, insight into the life of someone else requires a particular existential precondition, specifically, that one duplicate in one's own self the same form of existence that frames the life of the other person. Only in this way can one empathize with his or her loneliness, anxiety, or fullness of being. Yet here again traditional apologetics fails, in Thielicke's judgment, especially the theistic proofs. For no regard is given to the individuality of the hearer. The approach objectifies the unbeliever by assuming that the same memorizable proofs are universally valid, irrespective of the person. The standardized approach does not need to vary from any particular hearer to another. All that anyone needs is just to hear of more causality, design, or superiority of being. In contrast, Thielicke seeks to win his audience by establishing

---

in Germany after the Second World War: "In the last years the concept of 'apologetics' was frequently replaced with the concept of 'dialogue'" (Speier, *Initiator*, 222n3; translation mine).

75. *Evangelical Faith*, 2:96.

76. Ibid.; italics added. In Oliphint's translation of Van Til from philosophical to theological categories, he finds these three aspects of Thielicke's inner-outer dialogue in Aristotle's "Rhetorica" where the philosopher lays out the "*trivium* of persuasion" (*Covenantal Apologetics*, 139). Aristotle's categories are the personal character of the speaker (*ethos*), the audience's frame of mind (*pathos*), and the speech itself (*logos*).

77. *God's World*, 218. Thielicke emphasizes solidarity throughout his dogmatic work (*Evangelical Faith*, 1:71, 78, 82, 204–5, 213, 215, 223, 226, 228, 383, 399; 2:59, 96, 133,135; 3:353–54; *Modern Thought*, 8, 20, 120).

solidarity with his conversation partner,[78] and the way to find solidarity in dialogue is first and continually to speak to oneself in monologue.

Ground for Solidarity

Thielicke's goal of achieving solidarity with his audience is motivated by two theological reasons. First, he has in mind the "fact itself, namely *justification.*"[79] For the apologist does not speak as a stranger to *faith-crisis*. One understands doubt and despair. Thielicke assures that all the apostasy in the outside world "is actually what I am, a condition from which I have been removed only by an act of grace over which I have no control."[80] Conversion does not borrow from human effort. The impossibility is due to the original condition of human nature found in its state of spiritual death and bondage. A person must be removed from a state of unbelief by a power that is outside of him or her. One is placed in a condition of belief in God only by the regeneration of one's being. A person is brought from death to life through an act of new birth by the mysterious operation of the Holy Spirit who then bestows faith. Faith itself is a gift (Eph 2:8). The very faith that is required for a person's justification is given by God. Looking at this objective reflection of oneself, one can only say, "It is no longer I who live, but Christ who lives in me" (Gal 2:20).

For apologetic method, this means that the believer is not to stand triumphantly on Christian ground, demonstrating the truth of one's message as the realization of one's own intellectual effort. Rather one is to seek solidarity with the unbeliever—that is, to love one's secular neighbor—by presenting their conversation as a continuation of the conversation within oneself. To this end, Thielicke would "take down my theological barricade, apparently go over to the enemy, and take a stand on the ground" of his dialogue partner for the sake of argument[81]—which approach chapter 5 continues to address.

---

78. Oliphint underscores Thielicke's stress on solidarity, which the former believes is essentially missing from traditional methods. Using Aristotle's category "of *pathos*," he explains, "we are interested in a proper and personal understanding of those to whom we speak" (*Covenantal Apologetics*, 146; see 193, 196–98, 228, 235).

79. *God's World*, 218.

80. Ibid.

81. *Modern Thought*, 452. Thielicke sees that Friedrich Schleiermacher also uses this method, whom he describes as "the first great modern apologist" (ibid., 162)—yet not without qualification (ibid., 203). In the "confession of solidarity, Schleiermacher seeks to win a hearing, not by addressing the cultured authoritatively from outside, but by assuring them that he is one of them and will *argue on their own ground*" (ibid.,

There is a second theological reason to show solidarity by standing on the unbeliever's own ground for argument's sake. God is disclosed, not mythologically, but incarnationally, that is, in solidarity with humanity on its "ground." Thielicke writes:

> God's self-disclosure takes place in such a way that God has a history with us. This means that he enters our history, dwells among us, has the Word made flesh . . . this means that God gives up his transcendence, sets himself against the horizon of our history, and in *solidarity* with our historical existence "is tempted like as we are" (Hebrews 4:15f). Making himself present, God comes into our world and experience.[82]

The incarnation reveals ultimate solidarity. So as a follower of Christ, the apologist is bound to seek solidarity with one's secular neighbor in order to follow the example of the incarnation. For the eternal Logos relinquished his traumatizing majesty to become human, and moreover remained incognito as a despised and rejected outcast. Accordingly—in contrast to ancient docetism which denied the physical body of Christ and instead conceived of him as a "shadowy or unreal heavenly being lacking any *solidarity* of existence with other men,"[83] incapable of temptation or suffering—genuine solidarity cannot be achieved by a docetic "seeming" or "appearing" to identify with the unbeliever via an apologetic of glory, incapable of sharing *faith-crisis* existence with them.

Indeed, a theology of the cross shows that the solidarity which Christ shares with humanity does not end in the manger, with a bare incarnation, but at Golgotha since "the crib and the cross are hewn out of the same wood."[84] Here, however, Thielicke's focus is not on Christ's physical suffering, but rather his spiritual torment as he descends into hell. Though Thielicke wholeheartedly subscribes to Luther's view of Christ's descent as the first stage of his exaltation—a victorious journey to the netherworld to declare its doom and triumph over the demonic hosts—the former does not see it as incompatible with, but rather complementary to, Calvin's view of it as the last stage of Christ's humiliation:

190–91; italics added; see Rueger, "Individualism in Thielicke," 38). Van Til uses a similar approach and insists that "the Christian apologist must place himself upon the position of his opponent, assuming the correctness of his method merely for argument's sake (*Apologetics*, 129, see 7).

82. *Evangelical Faith*, 1:78; italics added.

83. Ibid., 1:383; italics added.

84. *Evangelical Faith*, 3:xvi; *Creed*, 97.

> Some, especially Calvinists, intended to say in this way that Jesus even took upon himself the extreme humiliation of stooping to *solidarity* with the lost and becoming *their* brother, too. Didn't he cry out from the cross, "My God, my God, why hast thou forsaken me?" Here in the last hour of his life, hadn't he already taken upon himself the uttermost darkness of the godforsaken? Didn't he expose himself to the despair of nothingness so that even on the bottommost level of soul torment he could be *with* us to hold us by the hand?[85]

Consequently, in the display of solidarity—by which one stands on the unbeliever's ground for argument's sake—the apologist "descends into hell" with the nonbeliever as they are together exposed to the despair of nihilism[86]—the borderline of *Anfechtung*.

The persuasiveness of this dialogical, solidarity-oriented, apologetic method is that which Thielicke reminisces about in his autobiography:

> In this way my theological work acquired from the outset a motif which freed it from becoming esoteric and dogmatic, and gave it the character of a *dialogue*. When in some of my later works I conducted an impassioned conversation with the present age . . . I never thought of myself as an apologist defending the Christian faith from a secure position and anxious

---

85. *Creed*, 130; first italics added. The Calvinists to whom Thielicke here refers are the authors of the Heidelberg Catechism with their answer to the question, following Calvin, about why Christ descended into hell: "That in my greatest temptations I may be assured that Christ my Lord, by His inexpressible anguish, pains and terrors, which He suffered in His soul on the cross and before, has redeemed me from the anguish and torment of hell" ("Question 44," *Heidelberg Catechism*, in Schaff, *Creeds of Christendom*, 3:321). This confession, Thielicke maintains, locates the "saving significance of this final suffering in *solidarity*" (*Evangelical Faith*, 2:420; italics added). In this interpretation—though theologically profound—Calvin reacts to an urban legend propagated among the reformers which taught that Christ's descent into hell was simply His burial in the grave. The revisionist history had considerable influence on the Reformation (Hamm, "*Descendit*: Delete or Declare? A Defense against the Neo-Deletionists," 93–116).

86. Thielicke does not actually label this step as a "descent into hell." Rather, we apply it as the natural product of his logic. Althaus foretells it: "The Christian . . . cannot possess the heaven of community with God without repeatedly making the *descent into hell* which takes place when he doubts and even despairs . . . within the framework of *Anfechtung*" (*Theology Luther*, 33–34; italics added). Van Til refers to this *descent* in the language of quicksand. He states that the apologist must argue on his opponents ground to "show him that on his view of man and the cosmos he and the whole culture is based upon, will sink into quicksand," which sinks of its own weight (*Jerusalem and Athens*, 91). Oliphint translates as the "Quicksand Quotient" (*Covenantal Apologetics*, 76, 85, 115, 165, 221, 224, 228). In applying it, the apologist shows that "the 'ground' chosen by the position is insufficient to support its own principles" (ibid., 77).

to prove to the secular human being his errors. Rather, I always regarded the lack of truth and the wretched ideological surrogates I observed in the "outside world" as something present in *me* from which I had been saved through no merit of my own. To me, the neopaganism of the Third Reich was merely a gigantic projection and objectification of what *my* "blood" and *my* "soul" were also continually bringing forth. For this reason, I was only able to overcome this by withstanding the temptation [*Anfechtung*] into which this neopaganism thrust me. It possessed a bridgehead in me. I was myself susceptible to it. I was not at all sure of myself and knew only too well that I could not regard myself as Christ's representative and the Antichrist as something outside of me. Rather, I myself was the "battleground," and I was well aware that wild wolves were howling in *my* subconscious too. I regarded it as a confirmation of this position when neopagans told me that I had understood them and sometimes asked me if I was one of them. Consequently, I conceived of theology . . . as a conversation between the spiritual and natural sides of my personality. And only after I had thrashed out this dialogue in my own person, could what I had to say to the outside world gain credibility.[87]

Conclusion

Thielicke closes his memoir of modern theology with an *Ecclesiastine* epilogue to the narrative of apologetics, memorializing its biography as an unending theology of *faith-crisis* that can only be overcome by—not unpredictably—a confession of "Nevertheless":

> Is there, then, nothing new under the sun, even in theology? Has everything already been? Yes, it has already been, and it always will be again as long as this aeon lasts and there is in it both faith and thinking about faith. Yet it will always be again in a new way, and faith will always be a venture. As before, it will involve not a Because but a Nevertheless. It will constantly learn to utter this Nevertheless in face of the reality of the human and therefore in spite of appearances to the contrary.[88]

87. *Notes*, 79. Does an apologetic of *rational* certainty foster this kind of solidarity with unbelievers? Perhaps the attitude can lead unhappily to rather condescending and polarizing conversation, as in Oliphint's fictional encounter with Daniel Dennett, "Unless you've had your naturalistic head in the ground, you will recognize that . . . " (*Covenantal Apologetics*, 213).

88. *Modern Thought*, 563. Thielicke concludes his catalogue of defective theology

3

The Rejection of Traditional Apologetics

EARLY IN HIS THEOLOGICAL career Thielicke provides a working, although sarcastic, definition of traditional apologetics: "Apologetics claims to be the science of defending the faith, and even of defending against *faith-crisis*."[1] That would seem fair enough. Yet his criticism of the subject—as suggested by the polemically entitled heading, "The Shadow Art of Apologetics"— only becomes more severe. Essentially, "apologetics is like trying to chase away shadows with a shadow."[2] From this beginning through the last of his theological works, the descriptors he uses with the term "apologetics" are only such disparaging labels as "evasion," "propaganda," "mask," "futile," "patchwork," and "nonsense," to name but a few.[3] Indeed, Thielicke even seems fearful of the word itself. Describing the real apologetic mission of a

---

with Barth: "For a while dialectical theology seemed to be opening up a new panorama from which the dualism of assault and appropriation had retreated and only the 'vertically from above' held the stage. But this was only an interim in the history of theology—not a cessation of breathing but a catching of breath" (ibid., 562–63). In Thielicke's view, the crisis of Barth's unrealistic theology is that it cannot be characterized by the "Nevertheless." Thielicke also ends other works with a similar call, "We are the people who must learn from an ancient Book to say, 'Nevertheless I am continually with thee'" (*Conversations*, 189; see *Evangelical Faith*, 1:402).

1. *Between*, 26; translation mine, cf. *Zwischen*, 52. Thielicke's analysis is confirmed by the Ligonier theologians who claim—without a hint of irony—that apologetics liberates "the Christian plagued by the darts of doubt" (Sproul et al., *Classical Apologetics*, 22). Thielicke believes instead that apologetics challenges the *believer's* unbelief (Mark 9:24) by using doubt as a heuristic tool to push the *Anfechtung* antithesis of faith in order to reach its "Nevertheless." Indeed, to paraphrase Luther, "*Anfechtung* makes the apologist."

2. *Between*, 26; see Speier, *Initiator*, 163–64. Kierkegaard uses a similar metaphor in his complaint about apologetics, "The battle against objections has been *shadowboxing*, because it has been intellectual combat with doubt instead of being ethical combat against mutiny" (Hong and Hong, *Journals and Papers*, 1:359; italics added).

3. *Modern Thought*, 6, 202, 247, 333, 450, 452. His dim view of the subject is also magnified by the title of the section, "Critical Appraisal: The End and New Beginning of Apologetics" (ibid., 449–57); see also the revolutionary section, "The Pastoral Conversations of Jesus: The Reversal of Apologetics"; translation mine, *Fragen*, 5–7).

theologian, he cautiously adds the disclaimer, "Here, if we are not afraid of an overloaded term, is the *apologetic* task of theology."[4]

Those bold enough to wade through Thielicke's corpus in search of a manual on apologetics might initially rejoice at *Man in God's World*, only to find surprisingly tucked into the "Postscript for Theological Readers" a blistering criticism of traditional apologetics.[5] Yet to perceive Thielicke's disgust with apologetics and therefore to conclude that he is not interested in the subject is to misunderstand him totally. For here he daringly admits that the mission of his lifelong career as a theologian, as seen in our introduction, is to help usher the reformation of apologetics:

> Perhaps this may even be the particular goal that hovers before the author and his work—that it must take over the task of previous apologetics in a *new way* and perhaps contribute in a small way to transplanting the task of Christian discussion to a different and *theologically genuine level.*[6]

In order to draw attention to this urgent apologetic venture, Thielicke contrasts his own apologetic approach with the problematic features of traditional methods: "There are however, three characteristics of conventional apologetics which I have diligently, and I hope with some consistency, sought to avoid."[7] The first problem, as laid out in chapters 1 and 2, is that traditional apologetics speaks from a citadel of certainty instead of *faith-crisis*. Thielicke, however, shows that "all theology which pursues the genuine goal of ungenuine apologetics has a character of a 'theology of *Anfechtung*.'"[8] A second concern is that traditional "apologetics leaves no room for genuine offense because it seeks to *demonstrate* the Christian faith . . . and therefore confuses faith with sight and sets itself, not *under* the Word, but rather above it."[9] The third faulty "characteristic of apologetics is that it proposes to give Christian answers to human questions."[10] This is the exact reverse of what he sees as the offensive task of Christian conversation which rightly "attacks the world with *its* questions and forces it to face them."[11] This counterquestion approach aims to strike one's hearers in the *imago Dei* at the

---

4. *Modern Thought*, 9.
5. *God's World*, 213–18.
6. Ibid., 217; italics added.
7. *God's World*, 216.
8. Ibid., 218.
9. Ibid., 216.
10. Ibid., 217.
11. Ibid.

center of their being which they try to suppress (Rom 1:18, 25).[12] These last two distinctives, the counterdemonstrationism of Thielicke's cross-centered strategy, and his table-turning method, are the subjects of chapters 4 and 5, respectively. Now we shall consider his evaluation and rejection of traditional apologetic methods because of their enslavement to sublevel—that is, natural—theology.[13]

Logos Apologists

Thielicke begins his review of previous apologetic methodologies with the early defenders of Christianity after the apostolic era, the "Apologists" or Logos theologians. For these apologists are the archetypal representatives of the three distinctives of traditional apologetics which Thielicke categorically rejects. Among these Church fathers he continually mentions Justin Martyr (110–165) and his pupil, Tatian (110–172), attending to the former in particular.[14] For Justin, by universal consent, was the greatest apologist of the second century. Seeking that knowledge which would satisfy the cravings of his soul, he had wandered through the philosophical schools of the Stoics, Aristotelians, Pythagoreans, and Platonists. After converting to Christianity, Justin continued to wear his philosopher's robe to signify that he had found the one true philosophy. Yet Justin's fashion is what would anticipate his apologetic façade in Thielicke's assessment. For in Justin, "Christ is placarded as the fulfillment of Greek philosophy" and "becomes the Son of the God of the philosophers."[15] In the Apologists, Christianity is simply a higher philosophy, for Christ is what human reason can theorize instead of the One who must be revealed (Matt 16:17).

---

12. *Between*, 26; *Ethics*, 1:169; *Modern Thought*, 452.

13. Speier confirms that "Thielicke's apologetic is a definite ecclesiastical and theological reaction to the history of apologetics" (*Initiator*, 240; translation mine). However, he limits his analysis to Thielicke's rejection of the deistic apologetics of the 18th and 19th centuries (ibid., 223–28).

Van Til provides a litany of complaints against traditional apologetics which parses Thielicke's threefold criticism. "The traditional method," Van Til argues, "compromises the biblical doctrine of God . . . the biblical doctrine of the counsel of God . . . the *clarity* of God's revelation to man . . . the *necessity* of supernatural revelation in relation to natural revelation . . . the *sufficiency* of redemptive supernatural revelation in Scripture . . . the *authority* of Scripture . . . the biblical doctrine of man's creation in the image of God . . . the biblical doctrine of the covenant . . . the biblical doctrine of sin" (*Defense*, 340–41).

14. *Evangelical Faith*, 1:79, 126, 148; 2:8, 85; 3:22, 339, 369; *Modern Thought*, 11, 46.

15. *Evangelical Faith*, 1:126; 2:85.

Logos Principle

What concerns Thielicke about Justin's apologetic is evident in the passage entitled "Christ Compared with Socrates":

> But these things our Christ did through His own power. For no one trusted in Socrates so as to die for this doctrine, but in Christ, *who was partially known even by Socrates* (for He was and is the Word who is in every man, and who foretold the things that were to come to pass both through the prophets and in His own person when He was made of like passions, and taught these things), not only philosophers and scholars believed, but also artisans and people entirely uneducated, despising both glory, and fear, and death; since He is a power of the ineffable Father, and not the mere instrument of human reason.[16]

In order to demonstrate Christianity to readers molded by Greek tradition—a characteristic of traditional apologetics which Thielicke loathes—Justin employs the idea of the Logos. According to the Stoic worldview, the Logos was that reality which solved the perennial problem of the one and the many; the unity that provided stability over against the diversity and held all things together in coherence. Specifically, the Logos was the cosmic force, or *Reason*, permeating the universe and governing its constant change. So this philosophical concept is that to which Justin appeals to show Christianity's attractiveness and credibility. "The apologetic aim," Thielicke contends, "was that those influenced by Greek thought should not find in Christ something absolutely new and hence scandalous and offensive (1 Cor 1:23), but a confirmation of their own thinking."[17] So Justin claims that because of the Logos even Socrates (470–399 BC), who lived before Christ, was "a Christian." For Christ was "known" by Socrates—and other philosophers before him, among whom Heraclitus (525–475 BC) who coined the term *Logos* would naturally be included—as the seed of the Logos resides within every person and thereby reveals fragments of truth to them. In part, Christ is what the philosophers had already speculated.

Similarly, Tatian, serves the Logos concept to demonstrate the Gospel message to his hearers. Explaining the creation of the world through the pre-existent Christ, he writes, "By Logos-power, the Logos Himself also, who was in Him, subsists . . . and came into being by participation."[18] According to

---

16. Justin Martyr, *ANF* 1:191–92; italics added.
17. *Modern Thought*, 11–12.
18. Tatian, *ANF* 2:67.

Tatian, the Logos Himself was brought into being by Logos-power. In other words, Christ is a mere illustration of the Logos principle.

Warrant for the Apologists' approach can certainly be found in the prologue to the Gospel of John, which utilizes "Logos" to introduce the message of Christ (John 1:1). Though superficially the two methods would appear the same, closer inspection shows that they differ drastically, for, in Thielicke's view, the apostle does not leave the philosophical term in its old sense. The old wineskin containing its former content cannot hold the new wine of the identity of the Nazarene; therefore, John "baptizes" the term so that it acquires a new meaning.[19] The old passes away, and the term becomes a new creation. So in the Gospel of John, "Christ is not defined by what the philosophers meant when they used the term."[20] The case is the exact opposite. Thielicke asserts that "Who (not what) the Logos is, is defined by Christ, or, more precisely, by the Logos incarnate," that is, the God-Man.[21] Thielicke argues:

> The reverse process took place in the early Apologists (Justin Martyr or Tatian). Here the 'Logos' of Greek philosophy is taken over unaltered and Christ is defined by the concept. He is thus the fulfillment of secular wisdom rather than its contradiction (1 Corinthians 1:18ff.; 2:14). The Logos concept is the bridge on which the philosopher meets the Christian message, not finding in it something different that transcends wisdom, but rather recognizing himself in it.[22]

The tragic result of the apologetic accommodation, is that Christ is simply the fulfillment of Greek philosophy. "Christ is defined by the 'logos,'" Thielicke concludes, "and becomes universal Reason in the Stoic sense."[23] What John had demythologized "is thus remythologized."[24] The scandal of the cross is

---

19. *Evangelical Faith*, 1:79. This tactic, to "baptize" or redefine the language of philosophical systems in order to connect to his audience, is a favorite of Thielicke's (ibid., 1:80, 100, 104, 125, 202; 2:27, 98, 356; *Trouble*, 35). Van Til also advocates using "the language of the philosophers" and rightly warns that we must "be on our guard to put Christian content into this language that we borrow" (*Defense*, 46; see 60n23, 242). Oliphint translates Van Til's practice into the terms of "co-opted," "adopted," and "surgically removes . . . and transplants" (*Covenantal Apologetics*, 53, 148, 149).

20. *Evangelical Faith*, 1:79.

21. Ibid., 2:85.

22. Ibid., 1:79. The Westminster apologists also remain wary of Justin's use of the Logos, "In what way, we could ask, did Socrates know Christ . . . did he [Justin] fall prey to Greek speculation? (Edgar and Oliphint, eds., *Christian Apologetics*, 1:41).

23. *Evangelical Faith*, 1:126.

24. Ibid., 1:126.

removed and its folly rationalized (1 Cor 1:23); hence, the apologetic aim is self-defeating, for it confirms the philosopher's own presupposed autonomy rather than challenges one in one's unbelief.

False Analogy

According to Thielicke, the flawed approach of the Apologists lies on the false "doctrine of the analogy of being" which "forms the theological background of the intended synthesis."[25] Moreover, the position is a precarious one as Thielicke understands "the problem of the analogy of being not as a worldview nor an epistemological problem, but as a *faith-crisis*."[26] In other words, the analogy itself tempts faith to unbelief and *against* which one must believe! Exactly what is this illegitimate theological concept that exposes faith to shipwreck? The analogy of being is a method of predication that specifically addresses the question of "God talk."[27] How can the finite apologist speak of the One who is infinite and incomprehensible? Thus: the analogy of being. A recent contribution explains that it

> is based on the assumption that a likeness or analogy exists between the infinite being of God and the finite beings of his creature. This likeness, or similarity-resemblance, lies at the basis of all arguments for the existence of God and serves as the power and capacity of language to speak of God in terms of his being and perfections.[28]

At first glance the concept would not seem too suspicious, especially in light of the fact that the Scripture is full of such analogies. Indeed, Thielicke's favorite parable of the Prodigal Son, contains the analogy of God as father (Luke 15:11–32). As he clearly states, "Analogies exist. Otherwise there could be no God talk at all."[29] In contrast, however, the analogy of being, as Thielicke sees it, is ultimately rooted in Aristotelian metaphysics which contradicts, and even supplants, the biblical mode of revelation. He therefore insists that "the God-world relation . . . does not consist in an ontically given and hence demonstrable analogy between the two realities."[30] It can-

---

25. *Modern Thought*, 46.
26. *Theologie Anfechtung*, iii; translation mine.
27. *Evangelical Faith*, 1:376.
28. Spencer, *Analogy of Faith*, 16.
29. *Evangelical Faith*, 1:376.
30. Ibid., 1:369. Thielicke also stresses that analogies, like the parables, can actually obscure truth, which raises the critical doctrine of the Holy Spirit and the miracle of a new creation. Analogy cannot replace the inward illumination of the Spirit and can be

not be proven with a system that claims to coordinate both transcendence and immanence onto one schema and yet relate them as two different strata of reality. Whenever metaphysical leaps like this are made they either equate God and the world monistically (pantheism) or separate God from the world dualistically (deism). "Either way," Thielicke assures, "the world is no longer worldly and God is no longer divine."[31] The two realities, divinity and humanity, God and the world, are brought together in the "exemplary union" of the incarnation.[32] Herein lies the problem with the analogy of being—classically illustrated by the Logos apologetic—that tries to map an ontological grid which includes both God and the world as dimensions of the one and same reality. It eliminates the need of the hypostatical union of the God-Man. Indeed, when the Apostle John discusses the Logos, he means Christ is "the climax of the mighty acts of God in which God establishes his relation to the world."[33] The Apologists, however, mean that Christ is:

> An illustration, confirmation, and final culmination of the logos principle which embraces both God and the world. The salvation event is thus drawn into a given schema which can be perceived apart from faith. The procedure is *apologetic* in the sense that both pagans and Christians can thus contend for a common principle which claims them both.[34]

In Thielicke's evaluation of the Apologists' methodology, the unique identity and sovereign agency of the person of Christ is compromised. Furthermore, this scornful description of "apologetic" procedure reveals that the approach fails because it leaves the unbelief of the pagan unchallenged—the last characteristic of traditional apologetics which Thielicke so loathes. Instead of a counterquestion approach which "attacks the world with *its* questions and forces it to face them,"[35] it seeks to establish the Christian message on "common ground" apart from faith, thereby eliminating

---

appreciated only when the light is kindled in which one sees light (Ps 36:9; *Evangelical Faith*, 1:367). So Thielicke's problem with analogy is when it ignores the impassable barrier between nature and grace. His angst is not over analogy itself, but the particular type. He summarizes, "Rightly, then, an analogy of being which can be demonstrated as a truth of reason has been rejected in favor of an analogy of faith, which is disclosed only in faith" (ibid., 1:370). Or as he homiletically puts it, "Stained-glass windows glow only in the sanctuary" (ibid.; see *Meaning*, 53, 57; *Creed*, 218; *Modern Thought*, 451).

31. *Evangelical Faith*, 1:366.
32. Ibid., 1:375.
33. Ibid., 1:369.
34. Ibid.; italics added.
35. *God's World*, 217.

the need of faith.³⁶ Yet there is no neutral zone where both believer and unbeliever can meet and agree over the knowledge of God or interpretation of reality (see chapter 4). For this exact reason, as previewed in chapter 2, Thielicke will "go over" to the opposite side and "take a stand on the ground" of his dialogue partner for argument's sake.³⁷ Nonetheless, he categorically rejects the Logos theology because "there is no Confession and no theology, nothing at all that would have anything to do with *Logos* and '-ology,' which will defend us from [*faith-crisis*]."³⁸ The Christ who is the Son of the living God—the only One who protects from unbelief—must be revealed (Matt 16:17) and cannot be theorized by human reason or preconceived through philosophical speculation.

Classical Proofs

A recent apologetics textbook explains that the classical proofs for the existence of God, "as the term *classical* suggests, is the dominant approach to apologetics in church history, especially prior to the modern period."³⁹ The methodology follows the trail blazed by early and medieval theologians such as Augustine, Anselm, and Aquinas. Proponents of classical apologetics and authors of the popular book by that title argue that their approach is not merely legitimized by the history of the Church, but is still truly the only acceptable apologetic: "From the Apologists to the dawn of our own era, this has been the central tradition of the church, Eastern, Roman, Protestant, the teaching of the creeds and of the theologians."⁴⁰ As the tradition originated with the Church fathers who had turned from Greek philosophy—but nonetheless had not completely escaped its prioritization of human reason over revelation—the classical system stresses the rationality of the faith and seeks to demonstrate the truth of Christianity through philosophical arguments or "proofs."⁴¹

36. The idea of "common ground" is a significant factor in apologetic methodology, dealing with issues to which we shall return; "General Revelation" (ch. 4) and "Point of Contact" (ch. 5). Van Til agrees with Thielicke's rejection of the Apologists' method and the appeal to common ground: "The Apologists . . . tried to strike a bargain. They attempted to build theism with the Greeks in order to lead them on to Christianity from that common point" (*Christianity in Conflict*, in Bahnsen, *Van Til's Apologetic*, 292).

37. *Modern Thought*, 452.

38. *Between*, 27; translation mine, cf. *Zwischen*, 54.

39. Boa and Bowman, Jr., *Faith Has Its Reasons*, 49.

40. Sproul et al., *Classical Apologetics*, 210.

41. Craig, a contemporary vanguard of evangelical apologetics, ironically repeats Thielicke's complaint about apologetics in that it claims to remedy *faith-crisis*: "In times

Thielicke evaluates classical apologetics in the first volume of his dogmatics. "The proofs of God are not merely epistemologically debatable," he argues, "but in them God is usually the pale and unreal construct of thought, the 'God of the philosophers' (Pascal), whose intrinsic being is maintained but is not for me."[42] Following the French mathematician, Pascal, Thielicke believes that the theistic proofs merely arrive at the First Cause, Logos, or Unmoved Mover of Greek philosophy, but do not demonstrate the God of Abraham, Isaac, and Jacob whose higher thoughts have brought one into being that one might have a personal relationship with him. Moreover, Thielicke warns, "We cannot go back behind Kant" to "grasp God directly as the old proofs assumed."[43] For the Enlightenment philosopher from Königsberg, Immanuel Kant (1724–1804), "pulverized the arguments for God's existence."[44] In Thielicke's judgment, Pascal and especially Kant effectively ended any use of the classical proofs. The old arguments to which Thielicke refers are those that Kant considered to be the "three kinds of proof for the existence of God possible from speculative reason,"[45] specifically, the cosmological, teleological, and ontological arguments. Thielicke's censure of them naturally warrants a review of both the proofs and their critiques given by Pascal and Kant.

Cosmological Proof

The cosmological proof receives its name from the Greek term, *cosmos* (world), for the argument reasons from the existence of the world to the existence of God. The proof is based on the principle of causality, that is, for every effect there must be a sufficient cause. Though there are numerous formulations of the argument, including those provided by Islamic scholars,[46]

---

of *doubt*, we should not only seek the face of the Lord, but also strengthen ourselves by recalling these arguments" ("Classical Apologetics," 54; italics added).

42. *Evangelical Faith*, 1:97.
43. Ibid., 1:227.
44. Ibid., 1:266.
45. Immanuel Kant, *Critique of Pure Reason*, 563. The term *teleological* is used for Kant's "physico-theological." Later in his *Critique of Practical Reason*, Kant provides a moral proof for the existence of God. Yet Thielicke considers it futile since the God that Kant threw out the front door in his first *Critique* is merely smuggled "in through a side door in his ethics for pragmatic and sentimental reasons" (*Modern Thought*, 303; see *Evangelical Faith*, 1:271). Out of regard for his beloved servant Lampe who "must have a God or else he cannot be happy," Kant "resurrects the corpse of deism which pure reason had slain" (ibid.). So Thielicke maintains that the "God of Kant can indeed have no initiative or direct influence on our lives" (ibid., 1:275).
46. Craig reformulates the *kalam* cosmological argument given by the medieval

in the most basic form it "contends that no satisfactory explanation of the data of experience can be given without assuming the existence of a self-sufficient primary cause responsible for the world of phenomena."[47] Thus the argument runs: "The world is an effect. Therefore the world must have had a cause outside of itself and adequate to account for its existence."[48]

Aristotle articulates the earliest version of the argument which is that of motion. In the world there are things in motion or a state of change. Yet, anything in motion has been moved by something else. For anything that has the potential to move cannot actualize its own potential. It must be moved by some other thing in motion. The chain of motion, however, cannot go back to infinity because then there would be no first mover, and, consequently, no other motion. If there were no first mover, there would be no intermediate movers since they are put in motion by the first mover. To explain the motion in the cosmos, therefore, there must be an Unmoved Mover, "the eternal source of eternal motion."[49]

The cosmological proof received Christian formulations from the medieval theologian, Thomas Aquinas (1225–1274). He offers Five Ways, or proofs, for the existence of God, of which four are causal. For example, after using Aristotle's Prime Mover as his first proof, Thomas offers a second way where he reasons that "there is no case known (neither is it, indeed, possible) in which a thing is found to be the efficient cause of itself; for so it would be prior to itself, which is impossible."[50] In other words, for something to be self-caused, it must exert power on itself before it exists. It must exist and not exist at the same time, which violates the most basic law of logic, the law of non-contradiction. Yet, it is also impossible that there be an infinite regress of efficient causes, otherwise "there would be no ultimate effect."[51] If the causal chain continued backward into eternity past, then the present effect would never arrive. To put it simply, we would not be here. "Therefore," Aquinas maintains, "it is necessary to admit a first efficient cause, to which everyone gives the name of God."[52]

---

theologian, al-Ghazālī (*Reasonable Faith*, 80, 92–100).

47. *Oxford Dictionary*, 351.
48. Hodge, *Systematic Theology*, 1:208.
49. Copleston, *History Philosophy*, 1:314.
50. Aquinas, *Summa Theologica*, 1:13.
51. Ibid.
52. Ibid.

Teleological Proof

Aristotle claims that among the early Greek philosophers, "Anaxagoras uses Mind as a *deus ex machina* to account for the formation of the world."[53] In contrast to prior materialistic philosophers, Anaxagoras (b. 500 BC) posits the existence of a Mind that put pre-existent matter in motion. The Mind itself is material and does not create, yet it "is infinite and self-ruled . . . and it has all knowledge about everything."[54] The principle of Mind is that of an ancient cosmic computer which programmed or "set in order all things" such as the orbit of the planets and movement of the stars.[55] In other words, when considering the cosmos, Anaxagoras sees design. Though he fails to develop his principle of Mind into a complete metaphysical system, Anaxagoras is credited for introducing the idea of "teleology" to Greek philosophy. The term stems from the Greek word, *telos*, meaning "end." The science of teleology traffics in ends, goals, or final causes. It seeks to explain purpose or design.

The teleological, or design, argument was more extensively developed by later philosophical schools which reason from the evident design throughout the universe to an intelligent designer. After the advent of Christianity, the teleological argument was adopted by theology. Aquinas employs it as the Fifth of his Five Ways. Arguing from the operation of the world, he notes that all things are directed toward some end, even natural bodies which lack consciousness. Yet, no unthinking object can reach a goal unless guided by a thinking being. An arrow, Thomas illustrates, does not track its target unless aimed by an archer. Likewise, it is impossible for the world's operations to occur by chance. "But designedly, do they achieve their end . . . Therefore some intelligent being exists by whom all natural things are directed to their end; and this being we call God."[56]

The most famous version of the teleological argument was developed by William Paley (1743–1845) in his *Natural Theology*, which opens with the analogy of the watch found in a field. After inspecting its interlocking parts such as the coiled spring, chain, and gears, he infers the inevitable, "that the watch must have had a maker."[57] Paley then lays out the evidence

---

53. Aristotle, in Copleston, *History Philosophy*, 1:71.
54. Anaxagoras, in Copleston, *History Philosophy*, 1:70.
55. Copleston, *History Philosophy*, 1:69.
56. Aquinas, *Summa Theologica*, 1:14.
57. Paley, *Natural Theology*, 6.

for design in the universe and concludes, "Design must have had a designer. That designer must have been a person. That person is God."[58]

Ontological Proof

Anselm of Canterbury (1033–1109) "was one of the main contributors to Scholastic philosophy and theology."[59] At the request of friends he wrote an apologetic treatise, the *Monologium*, which contained various proofs of God including his own version of the cosmological argument. Yet his labor left him wanting. He wondered "whether there might be found a single argument which would require no other for its proof than itself alone; and alone would suffice to demonstrate that God truly exists."[60] The archbishop sought the ultimate argument which, in and of "itself," would prove the existence of God without any appeal to Scripture. The so-called ontological proof, contained in his *Proslogium*, is the result.

Anselm begins by praying to the "absent" or hidden God for understanding.[61] Yet, the understanding which he seeks is not a bare knowledge of the cosmic system. Rather, Anselm seeks to understand "that thou art as we believe; and that thou art which we believe."[62] He desires knowledge of what he already believes, namely, that God is and who he is. "For I do not seek to understand that I may believe, but I believe in order to understand."[63] What does he know about God? God is "a being than which nothing greater can be conceived."[64] If one conceived of something greater than one's conception of God, then *that* would be God, since by definition God is that than which a greater is inconceivable. Even those who reject God have in mind the concept of something than which nothing greater can be conceived. Yet, Anselm asks, what is greater, to exist only in the mind or to exist in reality? In answer, he offers the example of a rare painting. Prior to the artist's work, the masterpiece exists only in her mind. Though afterward the painting exists not only in her mind, but in reality as well, which is far greater according to Anselm. Likewise, were God to only exist in the mind, then something greater than that could be conceived, specifically, his existing not just in the mind but in reality as well. "Hence," Anselm reasons, "there is no doubt that there exists

58. Ibid., 246.
59. Copleston, *History Philosophy*, 2:161.
60. Anselm, in Edgar and Oliphint, *Christian Apologetics*, 1:370.
61. Ibid., 1:371.
62. Ibid., 1:373.
63. Ibid.
64. Ibid.

a being, than which nothing greater can be conceived, and it exists both in the understanding and in reality."[65] The ontological proof demonstrates not merely that God exists, but that God is a necessarily existent being since, as Anselm prays, "thou canst not be conceived not to exist."[66]

Pascal's Criticism

Thielicke's apologetic incorporates an approach influenced by "Pascal's Wager" (see chapter 6). It is worth noting that the apologetic work in which it is contained, the *Pensées*, reveals not only Pascal's loathing of the theistic proofs, but his disgust with philosophy in general. The famous mathematician enjoyed the social life of Paris until he discovered the "God of Abraham, God of Isaac, God of Jacob, *not of philosophers and of the learned.*"[67] Thereafter, Pascal — known for his "Pascal's Line" in geometry and his probability theory which laid the basis for infinitesimal calculus — continues to be committed to the supremacy of the mathematical method, yet he realizes its usefulness is limited and does not apply to all fields, especially metaphysics. He believes the "God of Christians is not a God who is simply the author of mathematical truths, or of the order of the elements; that is the view of heathens and Epicureans. He is . . . the God of Abraham, the God of Isaac,

---

65. Ibid., 1:374.

66. Ibid. Though Kant critiques the ontological proof, Thielicke does not consider it to be a strict proof in the modern sense: "For a proof makes the transition from what is uncertain to what is certain" (*Evangelical Faith*, 1:280). So in order to be able pray to God, e.g., the existence of God must first be proved. "Anselm, however, prays before he 'proves.' He obviously does not expect the proof to offer him either a basis or enhancement of certainty" (ibid.). Rather, the function of the proof is to help the understanding catch up with what belief already knows. For faith and reason are not synchronized. Believing is ahead of understanding. Therefore reason must overcome the lag and bring itself into line with faith that God might be loved "in all the dimensions of my being" (ibid.).

Nonetheless, though perhaps not a proof in the strict sense, Thielicke believes that the ontological argument has come to an end with the atheism of modernity. This is not due to external attacks or, as Nietzsche's madman declares, because God has been buried in a secular grave. Rather, Thielicke maintains that it is the inevitable result of Anselm's process: "The immanent logic of the process itself brought it to its end" (ibid., 1:286). In other words, "The faith which originally sought understanding has finally been dissolved in understanding" (ibid.). Faith seeking understanding ends in emancipated rationalism. Thielicke observes that "when faith ceases to define, to interpret, and to control the experience of reality . . . a process is set in motion which will necessarily lead in the long run to the proclamation of the death of God" (ibid., 1:295).

67. Pascal, "Memorial," http://www.ccel.org/ccel/pascal/memorial.i.html/; italics added.

the God of Jacob."[68] The God who revealed himself to the patriarchs is not some impersonal cosmic force of the philosophers, but the personal God who also is the "*Deus absconditus*" who has "hidden Himself" from unregenerate humankind.[69] Pascal exults in the hiddenness of God which defies subjection to mathematical theorems and proofs: "But we know neither the existence nor the nature of God, because He has neither extension nor limits. But by faith we know His existence; in glory we shall know His nature."[70] Human reason is unable to demonstrate God's existence. Rather, it is faith alone that assures us of his presence. This faith, Pascal emphasizes, is "different from proof; the one is human, the other is a gift of God";[71] therefore it "makes us not say *scio*, but *credo* [I know . . . I believe]."[72]

Nonetheless there are moments when it appears that Pascal contradicts himself since he offers proofs such as miracles, the person of Christ, fulfilled prophecy, and so on,[73] but the inconsistencies are easy to reconcile. Pascal has no problem with biblical proof. Rather what he takes issue with are the rational theistic proofs themselves. In his judgment, the "metaphysical proofs of God are so remote from the reasoning of men, and so complicated, that they make little impression; and if they should be of service to some, it would be only during the moment that they see such demonstration; but an hour afterwards they fear they have been mistaken."[74] Moreover, though the proofs are agreeable to believers already convinced that God is the source of all existence, they are worthless to atheists. Indeed, the attempt to dialogue with skeptics about "the course of the moon and planets" in order to persuade them with a teleological argument "is to give them ground for believing that the proofs of our religion are very weak. And I see by reason and experience that nothing is more calculated to arouse their contempt."[75] In other words, if the purpose of the philosophical proofs is to persuade unbelieving intellectuals, then they are counterproductive. So Pascal rails against their source: "If the greatest philosopher in the world finds himself upon a plank wider than actually necessary, but hanging over a precipice, his imagination will

---

68. Ibid., *Pensées: Thoughts*, 556 (citations refer to numbers in traditional arrangement, not pages).

69. Ibid., 194. Pascal is fond of quoting the prophet, "Thou art a God who hidest thyself" (Isa 45:15; see 242).

70. Ibid., 233.

71. Ibid., 248.

72. Ibid.

73. Ibid., 289.

74. Ibid., 543.

75. Ibid., 242.

prevail, through his reason convince him of his safety."[76] Philosophy is limited because human reason is influenced by the dominant faculty of human imagination. Moreover, philosophy blinds one to the internal contradictions of its own system, especially that of atheistic materialism: "Philosophers who have mastered their passions. What matter could do that?"[77] On the other hand, Pascal might qualify as one himself since "to make light of philosophy is to be a true philosopher."[78] Nonetheless Pascal reasons, "We do not think philosophy is worth one hour of pain."[79]

The reason for Pascal's rejection of the theistic proofs, however, lies on an even deeper foundation than the basis that they cannot prove the existence of God. For the knowledge of God that he has in view is that which is revealed in the Redeemer: "Jesus Christ is end of all, and the centre to which all tends. Whoever knows Him knows the reason of everything."[80] The mere knowledge of God as the Logos, First Cause, or Unmoved Mover, derived from philosophy, shows neither humanity's need of salvation nor the Savior. Herein lies its inherent danger: "The knowledge of only one of these points gives rise either to the pride of philosophers, who have known God, and not their own wretchedness, or to the despair of atheists, who know their own wretchedness, but not the Redeemer."[81] The philosophical proofs of God's existence are not only epistemologically defective, but useless since the knowledge of God grasped is void of Christ. In other words, philosophical theism cannot lead to salvation: "Had Epictetus seen the way perfectly, he would have said to men, 'You follow a wrong road'; he shows that there is another, but he does not lead to it. It is the way of willing what God wills. Jesus Christ alone leads to it [John 14:6]."[82] According to Pascal and then Thielicke following him, the theistic proofs are misleading.

Kant's Criticism

Thielicke agrees with the universal consensus among modern scholars that "Kant effected a basic Copernican Revolution" in epistemology.[83] What is

76. Ibid., 82.
77. Ibid., 349.
78. Ibid., 4.
79. Ibid., 79.
80. Ibid., 556.
81. Ibid., 556.
82. Ibid., 466.

83. *Evangelical Faith*, 1:265–66. Thielicke believes that Kant also triggered a "theological earthquake to the degree that *via* Ritschl and Hermann . . . unless we take Kant

this revolution by which he overthrows the reign of the theistic proofs? In contrast to the Enlightenment's emphasis on the authority of reason, "Kant made reason *itself* a question and the object of criticism,"[84] as is reflected in the title of his *Critique of Pure Reason*. Thielicke explains, "What is questioned is not some previous knowledge but the act of knowledge itself. This is what leads to a Copernican revolution in Kant."[85]

Thielicke reminds us that in Enlightenment philosophy prior to Kant, the mind was simply a "blank slate that simply receives impressions (cf. British empiricists like Locke)."[86] Just as a slate, or writing tablet, remains blank until inscribed, so the mind in its original state is empty until it receives "impressions" from the outside world, from which it gathers ideas. In other words, the mind functions in a passive role. There is no innate knowledge, rather all knowledge comes from empirical experience.

Yet Kant, convinced that the empiricists' view of cognition led to the radical skepticism of David Hume (1711–1776) which threatened the cause of modern science,[87] put forth a new hypothesis in which the mind is active in the constitution of knowledge. Kant reverses the order and assumes "that the objects must conform to our cognition, which would agree better with the requested possibility of an *a priori* cognition of them, which is to establish something about objects before they are given to us."[88] The mind forces upon the objects of sense experience its own forms of cognition. What we experience in the world—phenomena—are thus molded and shaped by twelve categories of the mind, which are constituted for conceiving the quality, quantity, relation, and modality of objects. Thielicke explains:

---

into account we can hardly deal properly with secularization or the secular interpretation of the Christian message" (ibid., 1:266). To evaluate the aftermath, Thielicke begins with the interpretation of Kant given by Heinrich Heine (ibid., 1:265–311; see *Modern Thought*, 302–5) since the latter "forges the link between the death of God concept and the this-worldliness of general consciousness which Kant initiated" (*Evangelical Faith*, 1:266) Thielicke does not accept Heine's conclusion that Kant is really the "initiator of the death of God concept" (ibid., 1:275), yet he does maintain that Kant's philosophy is ultimately inconsistent with its own presuppositions and fails. In sum—anticipating his counterquestion strategy—Thielicke asserts that "the summons: 'Adam, where art thou?' cannot be attributed to this [Kant's] God" (ibid., 1:275).

84. *Modern Thought*, 276.

85. Ibid., 276.

86. Ibid., 281.

87. The skepticism of the Scottish philosopher contained a "nihilism more chilling than that of any twentieth-century atheistic existentialist" (Livingston, *Modern Christian Thought*, 1:58). Hume denied not only the knowledge of miracles, God, the physical world, and the self, but the principle of causality which serves as the basis of the scientific method.

88. Kant, *Pure Reason*, 110.

> We thus have a union of sensory perception and a determinative element of rationality . . . Only as these two activities come together is there a sphere of transparent and controllable knowledge. What we experience, e.g., a book or desk, does not tells us about things in themselves. All that we encounter in the objective area is preformed by our ability to perceive and know.[89]

Thielicke understands Kant's philosophy as a synthesis of rationalism and empiricism. To illustrate, he uses the example of modern radar. For it "does not show me things themselves (ships, hills) but only things at they are worked over and electronically transformed."[90] A radar transmits a beam that intercepts an object, such as a ship, which bounces off the object and returns a signal to the radar receiver. The signal is then internally processed by the radar system and projected onto an electronic screen. The small image, or blip, on the screen is a combination of the ship as it really is and the operation of the radar's computer. In Kantian terms, as Thielicke translates, the radar then "as a subject is affected by outside impressions, puts them in its own categories, and then produces them in a form determined by the categories."[91] Accordingly, if there is no raw material of sense experience which trigger's the mind's radar, then knowledge of reality remains limited. Human understanding is consequently "restricted to the sphere of objective experience."[92] Thielicke summarizes, "Kantian thought, then, does not offer us any noetic possibility of making all reality the theme of empirical statements."[93]

Yet reality beyond the empirical—the existence of God—is allowed by Kant's epistemological program. For though pure reason alone cannot demonstrate God's existence, neither can it demonstrate his nonexistence. Objective knowledge of God cannot be proved or refuted as it is relegated to a sphere which transcends that of space, time, and perception. In the preface to *Critique of Pure Reason*, Kant justifies his method by explaining that he "had to deny knowledge in order to make room for faith."[94] So he preserves a place for faith by putting speculative knowledge of God beyond the limits of human reason. To this end, he attacks the theistic proofs.

---

89. *Modern Thought*, 280.
90. Ibid., 282.
91. Ibid.
92. Ibid., 280.
93. *Evangelical Faith*, 1:284.
94. Kant, *Pure Reason*, 117.

Kant begins his critique with the ontological argument. As seen above, it treats "that, than which nothing greater can be conceived,"[95] from which is inferred the existence of an absolutely necessary being. Kant rejects the argument since "*being* is obviously not a real predicate,"[96] and, therefore it cannot be a predicate of even a most perfect being. He realizes that merely providing a "definition of this concept is quite easy," since it is just "something whose non-being is impossible."[97] He argues, instead, that a simple definition does not make us any "wiser in regard to the conditions that make it necessary to regard the non-being of a thing as absolutely unthinkable,"[98] for such a definition is "taken only from *judgments* and not from *things* and their existence."[99] In other words, just because the concept of the perfect being contains the *concept* of existence does not mean that we can conclude that the perfect being exists.

Kant then turns his attention to the cosmological proof, for which he provides a simple definition: "Now I myself, at least, exist; therefore, an absolutely necessary being exists."[100] The argument—the minor premise ("I . . . exist") which is grounded on experience—is considered to be distinct from the ontological proof, which is built solely on pure concepts *a priori*. Yet the single step distinction of experience is merely a ruse, Kant argues, through which "it sets up an old argument in disguised form as a new one."[101] He therefore rejects it since he considers the cosmological proof merely a covert version of the ontological. "Thus it is really only the ontological proof from mere concepts that contains all the force of proof in the so-called cosmological proof."[102] Furthermore, a second problem is that the claim "an absolutely necessary being exists" lies on "the transcendental principle of inferring from the contingent to a cause,"[103] that is, the use of the principle of causality beyond the realm of sense experience when it cannot rightfully be employed to transcend that realm. Kant explains, "The principle of causality has no significance at all and no mark of its use except in the world of

---

95. Anselm, in Edgar and Oliphint, *Christian Apologetics*, 1:374.
96. Kant, *Pure Reason*; original emphasis in bold.
97. Ibid., 564.
98. Ibid.
99. Ibid.; original emphasis in bold.
100. Ibid., 570.
101. Ibid.
102. Ibid., 571.
103. Ibid., 572.

sense; here [in the cosmological argument], however, it is supposed to serve precisely to get beyond the world of sense."[104]

Of the three proofs, Kant has the most respect for the teleological argument as it "is the oldest, clearest and the most appropriate to common human reason,"[105] for when Kant observes the world he sees "an immeasurable showplace of manifoldness, order, purposiveness, and beauty."[106] Despite the eloquent and astonishing design, however, Kant argues, "We cannot on that account approve of the claims that this kind of proof may make."[107] What reason does Kant give for this rejection? At most, the proof can only "establish a highest *architect of the world*, who would always be limited by the suitability of the material on which he works, but not a *creator of the world*, to whose idea everything is subject, which is far from sufficient for the great aim that one has in view, namely that of proving an all-sufficient original being."[108]

Kant's epistemological refutation of the theistic proofs does not awaken within Thielicke any "ontological terror";[109] rather, he is convinced that Kant does faith a favor:

> Kant has thus helped to clarify the theological doctrine of faith by strengthening from a philosophical angle its conviction that there is no certainty about God outside faith, no certainty on which the possibility of faith might stand as a logical deduction. God may be found only in faith and not outside it. This call to faith to remember its own unique certainty is implied in Kant's destructive work.[110]

Though Kant's criticism was not intended to offer new opportunities for the certainty of faith, in Thielicke's view, his theological earthquake implicitly and indirectly leveled the land and prepared ground for a new apologetic.

Summary

Thielicke is convinced that the theistic arguments rooted in ancient Greek philosophy fail because "the knowledge of God does not stand under the

---

104. Ibid.
105. Ibid., 579.
106. Ibid.
107. Ibid., 580.
108. Ibid., 581; original emphasis in bold.
109. *Evangelical Faith*, 1:271.
110. Ibid., 1:309.

conditions of our thinking capacity, as in the classical proofs."[111] For the God who hides himself transcends the noetic limits of the existence which emancipates itself from him. Indeed, Thielicke asserts, "This is why the question [of God's existence] underlying the proofs of God misses God."[112] In other words, the superior being, causation, and design indicated by the classical proofs can just as well demonstrate that the world was begun by extra-terrestrials.[113]

Evidentialism

Evidence has long been used to prove the truth claims of Christianity. While defending the faith before the Roman governor and Jewish king, the Apostle Paul offered his own eyewitness testimony of the resurrected Christ (Acts 26:13–18; see 22:7–10). Augustine quoted fulfilled biblical prophecy and pointed to the exponential growth of the Church through and during the impossible situation of persecution.[114] In classical apologetics, evidence for Christianity is employed as a second step after a successful theistic argument. With the advent of modernity, however, the use of evidence has taken on a new role and has evolved into its own distinct apologetic approach. A helpful apologetics textbook suggests that the "impetus to the development of evidentialist apologetics was the rise of deism."[115]

During the scientific era, with the ever new discoveries of natural laws such as gravity and inertia, a picture of the universe began to emerge that depicted it as a complicated mechanism of invisible gears and pulleys that ran with the incredible precision of a cosmic clock. Theology

---

111. Ibid., 1:367.

112. Ibid., 2:95. The relentless counterdemonstrationism of Thielicke's cross-centered apologetic (ch. 4) will not allow him even to consider the theistic proofs as traditionally formulated; however, he does use them indirectly in order to push the *Anfechtung* antithesis. E.g., in the first sermon of an early apologetic series, he repackages the cosmological argument (*God's World*, 16–19) to show that causation without God—a random, accidental, unguided causal chain—"only ends in nihilism, the absolute futility of human existence" (ibid., 19). Van Til holds a similar view: "I do not reject 'the theistic proofs' but merely insist on formulating them in such a way as not to compromise the doctrines of Scripture" (*Defense*, 255). He believes that "when the proofs are thus formulated, they have absolute probative force" (ibid., 198).

113. Francis Crick, co-discoverer of the DNA code and Nobel Prize laureate, advocates the theory of "Directed Panspermia." The microscopic seeds of life "are supposed to have traveled in the head of an unmanned spaceship sent to earth by a higher civilization which had developed elsewhere some billions of years ago" (*Life Itself*, 15–16).

114. Augustine, *NPNF*[1] 2:337–60, 391–96.

115. Boa and Bowman, *Faith Has Its Reasons*, 139.

accommodated itself to the age and applied human reason and the scientific method to the knowledge of God. How else would God be viewed, Thielicke explains, except as the "clock-maker who makes the clock and sets it going, and then lets it run by itself with no further intervention"?[116] For God to adjust the gadgets of the cosmic machine would indicate that a mechanism had malfunctioned, which would defy the majesty of an all-glorious deity. Thus deism: and the doctrine of God was reduced. In short, God is locked out of closed immanence; limited, impersonal, disinterested, uncaring, and arguably evil.[117] God is a simply a Higher Power, a beginning to the otherwise infinite regress of causes in eternity past. So deism, as it were, is a road-stop enroute to the atheism of the secular age. Yet as Thielicke concludes, "apologetics, faced by modern science, was unready to accept the thesis of a closed system of natural forces."[118] In this context, evidentialism has emerged as its own apologetic model. It was a scientific enterprise which has developed empirical arguments to defend the supernaturalism of biblical Christianity. In short, the "idea was essentially to fight fire with fire—to show that a scientific approach to the Christian truth claims would vindicate their rationality."[119]

Stopgap Apologetics

Within his systematics, Thielicke begins his treatment of evidentialism by analyzing Dietrich Bonhoeffer's critique of the "God of the gaps" apologetic strategy.[120] According to Bonhoeffer, "We shouldn't think of God as the stopgap [Lückenbüßer] for the incompleteness of our knowledge."[121] During the modern era, the gaps in human knowledge which remained from empirical observation were filled with the "Working hypothesis: God."[122] The idea of God served as a theory to explain what science had not yet discovered. Thielicke believes the failure of this system is that "if we adopt

---

116. *Evangelical Faith*, 1:288.
117. Sire, *Universe Next Door*, 43–48.
118. *Evangelical Faith*, 2:68.
119. Boa and Bowman, *Faith Has Its Reasons*, 140.
120. *Evangelical Faith*, 2:65–72.
121. Bonhoeffer, *Letters and Papers*, 405–6.
122. Ibid., 425–426. Here Bonhoeffer follows French mathematician Pierre Laplace who is often quoted to support atheism and one to whom Thielicke frequently refers (*God's World*, 104–6, 110–11, 144; *Evangelical Faith*, 1:250, 252; 2:63, 65; *Human*, 168, 458; *Modern Thought*, 97, 438). Asked by Napoleon about where God fit into his scientific work, Laplace responded, "Sir, I have no need of that hypothesis."

this apologetic strategy, we condemn belief in God to a lingering death."[123] For, as Bonhoeffer explains, "When the boundaries of knowledge are pushed ever further, God too is pushed further away and thus is ever on the retreat."[124] The point is inevitably reached where God can no longer be meaningfully discussed. Thus in Thielicke's judgment this "specific form of apologetic which began in the Enlightenment . . . has undoubtedly come to an irreversible end."[125] His solution is the reformation of apologetics which shall never occur "if we do not demand a theologizing of the sciences and historical structures and are not so bold as to reverse the universal secular axiom, i.e., the axiom according to which the knowledge and mastery of the world can be achieved only on the presupposition that we start with self-enclosed immanence."[126]

Thielicke maintains that the climax of stopgap apologetics "was reached with the physico-theology of deism,"[127] which is a very detailed, empirically driven version of the teleological argument. In this approach, he explains, "the self-resting finitude of the world was seen under the sign of a teleology running through all being."[128] A teleology which corresponds to a theistic plan and purpose is that which fills the gaps in human ignorance. In other words, design is the proxy for God. The challenge to this design argument therefore is the unending threat presented by the continuous stream of

---

123. *Evangelical Faith*, 2:65; 1:251. Here the underlying reason for Thielicke's angst over stopgap apologetics surfaces. For the "God of the gaps" ideology—a degenerate view of the God of the Bible—is that which provokes Nietzsche's "God is dead" attack against Christianity: "Into every gap they put their delusion, their stopgap, which they called God" (*Zarathustra*, 92).

124. Bonhoeffer, *Letters and Papers*, 406.

125. *Evangelical Faith*, 2:66.

126. Ibid., 2:71–72. Bonhoeffer's solution differs. He thinks that we should "find God in what we know, not in what we don't know; God wants to be grasped by us not in unsolved questions but in those that have been solved" (*Letters and Papers*, 406). He is convinced that theology needs to start with the prevailing assumption that the human race has come of age and reached adulthood. The world has become self-conscious of its own existence and autonomy. Theology must adjust to this modern situation or face the absurdity of "trying to persuade this world that has come of age that it cannot live without 'God' as its guardian" (ibid., 426–27). The attack of apologetics against closed immanence Bonhoeffer considers as "pointless—because it appears . . . like trying to put a person who has become an adult back into puberty" (ibid., 427).

Though Thielicke wholeheartedly agrees with Bonhoeffer's negative thesis, he believes the lack of clarity in its positive implications—that is, to "find God in what we know"—can lead to a "new Docetism" (*Evangelical Faith*, 2:70), interpretative escapades as found in Bultmann's demythologization (ibid., 2:69), and Tillich's principle of correlation (ibid., 2:71).

127. *Evangelical Faith*, 2:66.

128. Ibid.

new empirical data. For if any phenomena are discovered that are seemingly purposeless then the whole system collapses. Eventually the question arose regarding the purpose for deep-sea fish if they were never seen by man, the telos of creation. So Gottfried Richter excitedly responded with a proof of God in his substantial *Ichthyotheologie* (1754) which showed that deep-sea fish stir the water with their tails and thereby prevent the ocean from becoming a polluted pond. Yet it is challenges of this kind, Thielicke asserts, "that threatened a crisis in teleology."[129] For if the data ever demonstrates even an exceptionally insignificant or meaningless fact, then the existence of the designer would be deniable. In other words, for the stopgap apologetic, the devil is in the details. Although Thielicke insists the greater theological problem with this stopgap defense is that, unsurprisingly, its "philosophical presupposition" avoids the experience of *Anfechtung*: "Whereas today the cosmic nexus with its unbroken autonomy brings theology under assault and *faith-crisis*, for deism the autonomy of the world (in the form of teleology) was the element of comfort which bore testimony to God and confirmed him in his immanent presence."[130] By seeking to demonstrate the designer, stopgap apologetics minimizes the *Anfechtung* antithesis of faith. The self-assertion of the unregenerate goes unchallenged, and they are left in the comfort zone of their own unbelief.

Creationist Apologetics

Thielicke continues his rejection of evidentialism with the "more serious . . . false apologetic switch in relation to the Darwinian theory of evolution."[131] What was bogus about the approach according to Thielicke is that it began a battle against the evidence since, in the mistaken view of the apologists, "the empirical data which as the basis of the evolutionary continuum supported the theory of descent had to be denied."[132] From such theologians "engaging in scientific controversy," Thielicke turns his nose since it is done "only with the inadequate resources of the dilettante."[133] So Thielicke bans theologians from fighting over the facts since such disputes are not only a betrayal of one's profession, but "remain within the jurisdiction of their opponent" and irresponsibly give the advantage to the challenger.[134]

---

129. Ibid., 2:66.
130. Ibid., 2:66; translation mine, cf. *Evangelische Glaube*, 2:79.
131. *Evangelical Faith*, 2:67.
132. Ibid.
133. Ibid.
134. Ibid., 2:68.

The apologetic concern began when Charles Darwin (1809–1882) introduced *The Origin of Species* (1859) to the world, in which he prophesied its impact would ignite "a considerable revolution in natural history."[135] The great naturalist would not have been disappointed, for his theory of evolution is indisputably the most influential idea of the secular age. Darwin proposed that the various species of life originated from a common ancestor from which they descended via hereditary modification. Genetic micro-mutations, or "variations" as Darwin prefers, incrementally changed and the process of modification eventually resulted in the transformation of species.[136] Given eons of time, for example, a fish could evolve into a frog. Darwin labels the mechanism for this evolution as "Natural Selection, or the Survival of the Fittest."[137]

To contextualize the creationist apologetics against which Thielicke protests, the theory of evolution must be understood in its relation to God. Although within *The Origin of Species* Darwin does mention "God" (once) and the "Creator,"[138] such references seem merely rhetorical for the sake of argument and should be interpreted in light of the radical deism of his time. The clockmaker-God is all the more glorious for creating a world that ticks away on its own rather than requiring any divine tinkering. So for Darwin, the grandeur of God is magnified by his complete absence from nature. Indeed Darwin quotes a "celebrated author and divine" to show just how his theory supports such view: "He has gradually learnt to see that is just as noble a conception of the Deity to believe that he created a few original forms capable of self-development into other and needful forms, as to believe that he required a fresh act of creation to supply the voids caused by the action of his laws."[139] And the reason Darwin enlists the approval of popular clergy to support his theory is because, as a sensitive person, he would not want his views to "shock the religious feelings of any one."[140] Whether it would also be a good public relations strategy to repeat such a narrative is a fair question. Nonetheless, though Darwin's argument is patient upon deism, it

---

135. Darwin, *Origin of Species*, 643.

136. Other naturalists, e.g., Huxley, put forth the idea of giant "leaps," known now as *macro-mutations*, to account for transformation of species. Darwin, however, would hear nothing of it, "For natural selection acts only by taking advantage of slight successive variations; she can never take a great and sudden leap, but must advance by short and sure, though slow steps" (*Origin*, 247).

137. Ibid., 108.

138. Ibid., 209, 227, 231–32, 251, 647, 649.

139. Ibid., 638.

140. Ibid.

has been widely accepted that his theory reflects rather atheistic premises.[141] Indeed, the purpose of his book implies just such a presupposition. Darwin writes to show that the view entertaining the idea "that each species has been independently created—is erroneous."[142]

Darwin's reference to "the Creator" is to be interpreted by corresponding comments indicating that the subject is "beyond the scope of scientific discussion" or "not a scientific explanation."[143] For Darwin, evolution not only provides evidence against the doctrine of creation, but any attempt to discover a divine design in nature would be unscientific anyway.[144] So the point of his theory, that nature as found is "utterly inexplicable on the theory of independent acts of creation,"[145] was firewalled against any counterattack, for such arguments would not be scientific. Although Darwin mentions "God," no place for God is found in his theory.[146] In *The Origin of Species*,

---

141. Princeton theologian Hodge answers, "It is Atheism," to the question entitling his book, *What is Darwinism?* (177). Darwin's personal belief about God, a separate and complicated question, seems to have evolved over time. Warfield provides insightful analysis by examining Darwin's personal papers ("Charles Darwin's Religious Life," 9:541–82). Though the former ministerial candidate professed to be an "agnostic" (ibid., 576) at the end of his life, Darwin's "inextinguishable doubt" (ibid.) of God's existence as well as his denial of the existence and immortality of the soul (ibid., 556) led Warfield to conclude that Darwin's spiritual life was a "long-continued atrophying of his religious conceptions" (ibid., 577).

142. Darwin, *Origin*, 23. In reflecting on his goal in *Origin*, Darwin later reiterates, "I had two distinct objects in view; firstly, to shew that species had not been separately created, and secondly, that natural selection had been the chief agent of change" (*Descent of Man*, 81). If wrong about the latter, his consolation is that "I have at least, as I hope, done good service in aiding to overthrow the dogma of separate creations" (ibid., 82).

143. Darwin, *Origin*, 251, 581. His antithesis between God and science is further stressed in the prohibition against accounting for any modification outside of a micro-mutation, which would be "to enter into the realms of miracle, and to leave those of science" (ibid., 316).

144. The deistic structure of *Origin* obscures Darwin's personal views about design. Yet he unquestionably sees evolution as a random, unguided process left to chance: "The old argument of design in nature, as given by Paley, which formerly seemed to me so conclusive, fails, now that the law of natural selection has been discovered... There seems to be no more design in the variability of organic beings and in the action of natural selection, than in the course which the wind blows" (*Life and Letters of Darwin*, 1:309. http://darwin-online.org.uk/content/frameset?viewtype=side&itemID=F1452.1&pageseq=327/).

145. Darwin, *Origin*, 491, 535, 545, 626, 629, 634, 636.

146. Recent editors of Darwin inform that while at the University of Edinburgh, the seventeen year old student "had come under the wing of a radical evolutionist Robert Edmond Grant. So we do not have to look hard for the dissident origins of Darwin's later leanings" (Moore and Desmond, intro. to *Descent*, xii). The popular account that Darwin remained unbiased until he "discovered" natural selection seems to be

Darwin concludes that God is unnecessary, and by the end of the century Nietzsche declares him dead.

To perceive Darwin's theory as an atheistic account of origins, then, highlights the concern of the early creationist apologists, at least as Thielicke understands the situation. Their angst was not merely over the discrediting of the biblical account of creation, but with Darwin's eviction of God from the cosmos. For if God was not in the cosmic scene, and the only forces that appear to be in operation were random mutation and natural selection, "then obviously God became irrelevant and his non-existence could be asserted," explains Thielicke.[147] In the face of this challenge, an attack was launched on the idea of closed immanence as demanded by Darwin's theory. This meant waging an empirical battle to call into question the claims of evolution.[148] Since Darwinism denied the existence of God, a fight over the facts is what was therefore needed to prove God's relevance. At this Thielicke complains, "We find once again an empirico-immanent disputing of the facts and a preoccupation with the 'missing link' in the evolutionary chain from animals to man, the idea being that this would scientifically disprove the fateful continuum."[149]

---

hagiographical. Decades before writing *Origin*, Darwin was "a materialist and evolutionist. Such heresies had to remain concealed for a generation, for they were thought subversive by upright society" (ibid).

147. *Evangelical Faith*, 2:67.

148. Thielicke cites Hermann Werner's apologetic that highlighted "phenomena which defied causal-mechanistic explanation, e.g., the peculiar properties of water which enable ice to float, or the relation between the height of land and the depth of the sea" (*Evangelical Faith*, 2:67).

Thielicke escapes the creation-evolution debate by subscribing to a doctrine of theistic evolution, as did many apologists of the modern era, including Van Til's distant mentor, Warfield (Noll and Livingstone, *Warfield: Evolution, Science and Scripture*); see also C. S. Lewis (*The Problem of Pain*, 61–78). Though theistic evolution brings to mind a wide range of interpretations, Thielicke's exact meaning is certain and could be classified as "BioLogos," as it has been recently christened by Francis Collins, the former director of the Human Genome Project and fervent theistic evolutionist (*Language of God*, 197–211). Thielicke believes that "Michelangelo's depiction of the creation of man on the ceiling of the Sistine Chapel is a profound interpretation of how man became man" (*World Began*, 83). At some point in evolutionary descent, a "half raised" hominid with a "dull and dreamy expression" is touched by the outstretched finger of the Creator, at which moment the "Lord God breathed into his nostrils the breath of life; and man became a living being" (ibid., 83). This *miracle*, as Thielicke envisions the encounter, is what bestows the image of God upon Adam so that he becomes fully human. Without this "miracle of the spark of the Spirit leaping from the outstretched finger" of God, he would remain "pre-man" (ibid.). Thus, in Thielicke's view, man's evolution "still remains a *miracle*, a real *creation*" (ibid., 86).

149. *Evangelical Faith*, 2:68. Thielicke considers an exclusive fact fight as ineffectual. This is due to his conviction that one's existential state, i.e., regenerate or unregenerate,

Intelligent Design

Thielicke's evaluation of stopgap and creationist apologetics is certainly relevant to theology's current conversation with science. For recently there has been a resurgence of very intricate, empirically based versions of the design argument enlisted in apologetic service for the battle against Darwinism, which opponents label as "god of the gaps" strategies.[150] Indeed, Thielicke could never have foreseen the rise of this movement known as Intelligent Design (ID) with its severe criticism of Darwinism as a sufficient explanation for the adaptive complexity of life.[151] Yet more unpredictable would have been the fact that those renewing the empirical fight against Darwin's theory are mathematicians, biologists, biochemists, biophysicists, philosophers, and even lawyers.[152] How would Thielicke inform the conversation today? Though he bans theologians from engaging in scientific controversy, what would he advise laymen whose vocations lead them into scientific fields, and in the tradition of the great Lutheran work ethic, seek to master the world by their work (Gen 1:28)?

The Intelligent Design movement identifies itself as a research program pushing science into a new paradigm. The iconic example of its cutting-edge work most commonly proffered to show evidence for an intelligent designer

---

determines how facts are viewed, which means they are never examined from a position of intellectual neutrality: "The facts cannot be known by the old self; they are non-existent for its 'mind' and 'heart' (1 Corinthians 2:9)" (ibid., 1:157). So faith is the proper interpretive paradigm; see ch. 4. Van Til heartily agrees that "brute facts . . . are mute facts" (*Defense*, 279). That is, a "brute," or uninterpreted, fact does not say anything self-evident but rather every fact is heard through a particular interpretative paradigm.

150. Intelligent Design proponents anticipate the "god of the gaps" criticism as seen in their own polemical spins of the phrase used to counter objections; see "The Chance of the Gaps" and "Darwin of the Gaps," in Dembski (*Design Revolution*, 116-26), and Wells (*God and Evolution*, 117-28), respectively.

151. Opponents of ID characterize it as "Creationism in a Cheap Tuxedo." Yet design theorists plead innocent to the charge and disavow any religious commitments or claims: "Intelligent design is not an evangelical Christian thing, or a generically Christian thing or even a generically theistic thing" (Dembski, *Design Revolution*, 25). ID scientists will not be heard pontificating about the origin of the universe, a young earth, or the geology of the Genesis flood. Instead their fundamental claim is "there are natural systems that cannot be adequately explained in terms of undirected natural forces and that exhibit features which in any other circumstance we would attribute to intelligence," whatever that may be (ibid., 27).

152. Denton, *Evolution*; Johnson, *Darwin on Trial*; Wells, *Icons of Evolution*; Hunter, *Darwin's God*; Dembski, ed., *Uncommon Dissent*; Flew with Varghese, *There is a God*; Berlinski, *Devil's Delusion*; Meyer, *Signature in the Cell*. Opposition to ID is found among theistic evolutionists, e.g., Miller (*Finding Darwin's God*); Giberson (*Saving Darwin*); and Collins.

is that of Michal Behe's *Darwin's Black Box*.[153] The biochemist reminds the reader of what Darwin perceived to be the gravest threat to his theory: "If it could be demonstrated that a complex organ existed which could not possibly have been formed by numerous, successive, slight modifications, my theory would absolutely break down."[154] So Behe takes up Darwin's challenge with biochemistry, a field about which the latter was totally ignorant. For Darwin, the living cell was a "black box" into which no scientist could see at the time. Yet now researchers know that the cell is a complex factory of connecting conveyer belts, each of which is made up of a group of protein machines which in turn are composed of interlocking parts. Though Darwin expressed his concern about complexity, for example, as with the eye, he had no idea about the amazing complexity of the single cell.

Behe analyzes the complexity of just one machine within the cell, the microscopic rotary engine known as the bacterial flagellum. The flagellum, with its whiplike tail, spins at twenty thousand revolutions per minute and propels the bacterium through its watery world. The machinery in this molecular motor is manufactured with over forty distinct protein parts including a rotor, stator, bushings, and drive shaft. The absence of any one of these proteins would result in the complete loss of motor function. Behe describes it as an "irreducibly complex" system which he defines as one "composed of several well-matched, interacting parts that contribute to the basic function, wherein the removal of any one of the parts causes the system effectively to cease functioning."[155] The biochemist illustrates with the humble mousetrap. It consists of five parts (the platform, hammer, spring, catch, and holding bar), of which if any were missing the trap would be totally non-functional. With four of the five parts in position, the device would not be just eighty percent efficient. Rather it would not operate at all. In other words, the mousetrap is irreducibly complex. It is either a complete mousetrap or completely useless. This means, according to Behe, that no irreducibly complex system can be produced by Darwin's requirement of "successive, slight modifications" of a precursor system. As he concludes, "It would have to arise as an integrated unit, in one fell swoop, for natural selection to have anything to act on."[156]

The probability that irreducibly complex mechanisms could suddenly come into being by blind chance instead of design is simply incalculable.

153. Behe, *Darwin's Black Box*. Behe identifies himself as a Roman Catholic (ibid., 239).

154. Darwin, *Origin*, 232; see Behe, *Darwin's Black Box*, 39.

155. Behe, *Darwin's Black Box*, 39.

156. Ibid. For a critique of Behe, the "poster child of ID," see Collins (*Language of God*, 192).

That does not necessarily function as a theistic apologetic, however, for the designer behind Intelligent Design, according to the leader of the movement, "need not even be a deity" but is "compatible with the watchmaker-God of the deists, the Demiurge of Plato's *Timaeus* and the divine reason (i.e., *logos spermatikos*) of the ancient Stoics"[157]—or perhaps ancient aliens whose pyramid design still dots the map of the earth.[158] That this apologetic could lead to "the god of the philosophers" instead of the God of Abraham, Isaac, and Jacob—who is the Father of Jesus Christ—is consequently the reason Thielicke would reject the approach as invalid.

Summary

Thielicke's criticism of evidentialism as seen in both stopgap and creationist apologetics adds an insightful contribution to the current conversation with Christian scientists who wish to engage in the task of persuasion. He equips them with the mindset that there can never be a "'presuppositionless' science."[159] In fact, he sees the modern enterprise as a "scientific atheism" which uses "the closed immanence of the world as a presupposition."[160] In other words, there is no neutral scientific method by which the raw empirical data is investigated and interpreted. Thus, for those engaging in Christian conversation with colleagues or the scientific community at large, God-talk must move beyond an empirical discussion of the facts to counterquestion the atheistic presuppositions behind the facts.[161] Chapter 5 shall examine this table-turning method which aims to strike one's hearer in the *imago Dei* below the radar of a person's consciousness which he or she tries to sup-

---

157. Dembski, *Design Revolution*, 25.

158. As seen above (n113), prominent scientists have proposed the idea that aliens are responsible for evolution. Dawkins does not dismiss the theory when interviewed by Stein (*Expelled: No Intelligence Allowed*, directed by Nathan Frankowski [Premise Media Corporation, Rampart Films, 2008], DVD).

159. *God's World*, 180.

160. *Evangelical Faith*, 2:65.

161. John C. Lennox provides an excellent example (*God's Undertaker: Has Science Buried God?*). The Oxford mathematician rightly emphasizes the role of presupposition in science from the first chapter, "War of Worldviews" (ibid., 14–29). He then ends the book by challenging scientists to "choose the presupposition with which we start" doing science (ibid., 179). Lennox was catapulted onto the apologetic stage and became instantly famous for silencing Richard Dawkins in recent debates. *The God Delusion Debate*, the exchange over Dawkins book (*God Delusion*), took place in Birmingham, Alabama (2007). Dawkins demanded a rematch, *Has Science Buried God?* which followed (2009) at Oxford University's Museum of Natural History, the location of the 1860 creation-evolution debate between Huxley and Wilberforce. Both debates are available on DVD by producer Larry Taunton (Fixed Point Foundation).

press (Rom 1:18, 25).[162] Without this offensive characteristic of Thielicke's approach, he would have scientists know that "all such apologies involve both improper means and improper objects . . . and cannot bring out what is distinctive in God."[163] They fail simply because they are a fight about the facts and "do not transcend the level of the empirical sciences."[164] Thus the inherent limitation of their approach is that of evidentialism in general. It is content to live in the dark cave of the immanent and never escape from it. "They are unable for this reason to bear witness to transcendence."[165]

Conclusion

Thielicke's loathing of traditional apologetics is rooted in his *faith-crisis* theology which, as seen, is elemental to a theology of the cross. "For Jews demand signs and Greeks seek wisdom, but we preach Christ crucified, a stumbling block to Jews and folly to Gentiles" (1 Cor 1:22–23). The cross condemns an apologetic of glory based on sign-seeking and wisdom, that is, science and philosophy. For faith does not come by either of these methods, the reasons for which we now turn.

---

162. *Between*, 26; *Ethics*, 1:169; *Modern Thought*, 452.
163. *Evangelical Faith*, 2:68.
164. Ibid.
165. Ibid.

4

An Apologetic of the Cross

IN THIELICKE'S REJECTION OF traditional apologetics, he complains about the faulty characteristic which "leaves no room for genuine offense because it seeks to *demonstrate* the Christian faith . . . and therefore confuses faith with sight and sets itself, not *under* the Word, but rather above it."[1] His allergy to demonstration, indeed, his counterdemonstrationism, is a product of his *faith-crisis* theology—component to a theology of the cross. "For Jews demand signs and Greeks seek wisdom, but we preach Christ crucified, a stumbling block to Jews and folly to Gentiles" (1 Cor 1:22–23). The cross repudiates a demonstrational theology of glory based on sign-seeking and philosophy (literally, *love of wisdom*); therefore, these two basic epistemological methodologies of emancipated humanity—empiricism and rationalism—are unreservedly abandoned by the cross-centered theologian in his venture to develop an apologetic of the cross that engages unbelief at a "theologically genuine level."[2] In other words, the method itself must be molded by the message.

To construct an apologetic of the cross, Thielicke shows, one begins with the "Nevertheless." He maintains that "the saying: 'Nevertheless I am continually with thee' (Psalm 73:23) which the devout say to the hidden God . . . recurs in a deeper and more radical form in the NT. The crucified Jesus utters this Nevertheless in his cry of derbeliction on the cross."[3] As seen in chapter 2, Jesus' complaint—"My God, my God, why hast thou forsaken me?" (Mark 15:34)—is not only a confession of his belief *in* God, but his belief *against* the antithesis, that is, the *Anfechtung* death of God conceptualized according to the "idolatrous image of reality."[4] His cry is

---

1. *God's World*, 216.

2. Ibid., 217. Guinness recognizes the urgency for an apologetic of the cross and makes a brilliant contribution to the cause with his *Fool's Talk: Recovering the Art of Christian Persuasion*. His conviction that "true to the cross of Jesus, Christian persuasion has to be cross-shaped in its manner just as it is cross-centered in its message . . . lies behind the choice of the title of this book: *Fool's Talk*" (28).

3. *Evangelical Faith*, 3:172.

4. Ibid., 1:229.

not a wail into the nothingness, but a prayer of the faithful (Ps 22:1) to the hidden God. Thus it is the "Nevertheless" of Psalm 73—as a foreshadow of Christ's "Nevertheless" confession—that prefigures an apologetic of the cross which divinely contradicts the preconceived epistemological paradigms of autonomous existence: "The Lord of history is not in fact manifest in his works. On the contrary, he is hidden in these works, so that faith in him can consist only in the protest of a Nevertheless against what the *senses see* and what *reason recognizes* to be the law operative in events of this kind (Psalm 73:23ff.)."[5] The "Nevertheless" apologetic of the cross operates antithetically to what the "senses see" and "reason recognizes," and it is thus both counterempirical and counterintuitive.[6] Here there is no demonstration of either scientific evidence or a cosmic philosophy, but only what is rejected as scandalous and foolish.[7] Intrinsic to a counterdemonstrational apologetic of the cross is the realization that there is no neutrality to the proof of God with respect to general revelation, miracles, resurrection appearances, eyewitness reports, or the function of human reason.[8] For what constitutes demonstration is defined by one's existential condition, that is, whether one's being is in truth or untruth (John 18:37).[9]

5. Ibid., 2:12; italics added.

6. Thielicke's broad use of the term *reason*, which includes basic human intuition, comports with Van Til's conviction that the distinction between intuition and reasoning should be minimized. It is often maintained, as in Scottish Common Sense Realism, that intuition is something more basic and thus purer than the conscious act of rational thought. Van Til argues that intuitions are sinful to begin with. "Reasoning is nothing but self-conscious intuition, and intuition is nothing but unconscious reasoning" (*Theology*, 163). We thus define what "reason recognizes" as *counterintuitive*. Trueman confirms that "the dark contradictions of the human predicament are connected to a number of Luther's antithetical distinctions. For example, the distinction between the two kind of theologian rests upon the *counterintuitive, counterempirical* nature of God's revelation and truth" (*Luther*, 125; italics added).

7. Montgomery states correctly that "apologetics fulfills its function only when it brings the unbeliever to the 'offense of the cross'" ("Once Upon an A Priori," 391). But does his understanding of "offense," i.e., "evidentially compelling," harmonize with the theology of the cross? (ibid.). Fee provides correction, "'Christ crucified' is a contradiction in terms, of the same category as 'fried ice'" (*First Epistle to the Corinthians*, 75). The offense of the cross—as God's ultimate contradiction of autonomous rationalism and empiricism—is the antithesis of evidentially compelling.

8. Penner claims that this flawed mindset is a function of "OUNCE," i.e., "objective-universal-neutral-complex" (*End of Apologetics: Christian Witness in a Postmodern Context*, 32).

9. This favorite theme is so important to Thielicke's apologetic agenda that he wanted to entitle his dogmatics as *Being in Truth*. Trepidation that the noun "being" might echo too much the sound of Heidegger restrained him otherwise (*Evangelical Faith*, 1:14).

Counterempirical

Hidden God

The "Nevertheless" presupposition of God's existence which confesses faith *against* what the "senses see" is deeply rooted in Luther's theology of a hidden God.[10] As seen in chapter 1, the hiddenness of God expressed in the *Heidelberg Disputation* reflects the prophet's confession, "Truly, thou art a God who hidest thyself" (Isa 45:15; RSV).[11] Isaiah's confession, in conjunction with yet another of Asaph's, "Thy way is in the sea, and thy path in the great waters, and thy footsteps are not known" (Ps 77:19; KJV), provides still more biblical and theological support for Thielicke's radical counterdemonstrationism.[12] The fact that God hides himself so that his traces may not be found shows that God "resists systematization and cannot finally be imprisoned in a system."[13] The radically distinct and transcendent Creator who created *ex nihilo* refuses to subject himself to the epistemological box of his immanent creatures. He dwells in a dimension of reality beyond the cosmic nexus and hence the activity of human observation. "God is beyond our power of perception," Thielicke teaches, "*not* because he is unreal, but because he is himself the upholder of reality . . . He therefore is not to be found within the world, because he is the Lord of the world."[14] God is not a link in the world continuum, rather the continuum is his creation and exists in him (Acts 17:28). He is simply "not objectifiable because he himself embraces the subject-object relation and hence cannot be drawn into it."[15] In other words, man-made empirical

---

10. Thielicke maintains that if the "Nevertheless" were not directed against what the "senses see," i.e., the empirical, one would be hard pressed to find faith on earth. He simply reminds of reality: "If the question depends on what we can 'see' and 'look at,' then the evidence seems to witness *against* God. Think of wars, mass graves, crippled children, flood disasters, and everything that we in our own lives see as meaningless cruelty. Not being able to see the sense of it, we can only have faith in him who knows its meaning. Here we have only the 'Nevertheless I am continually with thee'" (*Creed*, 59). Since the human and environmental misery that we "see" in the world testifies *against* the hidden God, then visible and verifiable evidence cannot be the apologetic fix for conquering the confrontation with *faith-crisis*.

11. Luther, "Proof of Thesis 20," *Heidelberg Disputation*, 44. Althaus explains: "Luther here once again repeats the thought—always so important to him—that the hiddenness of God's grace under the terrible reality of rejection creates room for faith and for its character as a risky 'nevertheless'" (*Theology Luther*, 283).

12. *Evangelical Faith*, 2:12, 74; 3:99, 152.

13. Ibid., 1:373.

14. *Nihilism*, 64.

15. *Evangelical Faith*, 1:367.

categories cannot contain God. When the apostle bears witness to what no eye has seen, nor ear heard, nor has it entered any human heart (1 Corinthians 2:9), Thielicke asserts, "this saying can mean only that the eye, ear, and heart do not have suitable criteria."[16] Creaturely standards are totally invalid when dealing with the Creator who lies beyond the horizon of human experience. Empiricism, then, as an epistemological method, is shipwrecked with respect to the hidden God. For empirical standards do not apply to that reality which cannot be empirically proven.

In the context of God's hiddenness, Thielicke commits himself to campaign for the apologetic cause that "God cannot be demonstrated."[17] For, he emphasizes, "the reality that we call 'God' transcends all immanent relations, can never be identical with them, and, unlike them, can never be objectified."[18] Indeed, Thielicke is so relentless about the non-demonstrability of God he argues that anything bearing on the God-world relation is itself not verifiable. For man and woman, created in the *imago Dei* who is the ground of life's meaning, "meaning does not manifest itself with demonstrable evidence."[19] Human freedom is "nonobjectifiable."[20] Even "the question what humanity is cannot be answered objectively."[21] With the human problem in mind, Thielicke adds that "sin, then, is not just something which I can empirically ascertain and demonstrate."[22] This non-demonstrability further implies that "there can be no possibility of finding objectifiable [salvation] history."[23] For example, in the conversion of Paul "the creative intervention of God stands in no demonstrable continuity with events of the secular plan, whether historical or psychological."[24] On the dark side of the spectrum of the God-world relation, Thielicke's thorough counterdemonstrationism compels him to declare that "in its nonobjectifiablity satanic power shares in the mysteries of God which also cannot be objectified and therefore cannot be demonstrated."[25] The total non-demonstrability of the

---

16. Ibid., 2:10; *Ethics*, 1:323.

17. *Evangelical Faith*, 2:95. Van Til defines demonstration as the "exhaustive penetration by the mind of man, pure deduction of one conclusion after another from an original premise that is obvious" and agrees with Thielicke that "such a notion of demonstration does not comport with the Christian system" (*Defense*, 198).

18. *Evangelical Faith*, 2:78.

19. *Evangelical Faith*, 1:33.

20. *Human*, 13.

21. Ibid., 7.

22. *Ethics*, 1:329.

23. *Evangelical Faith*, 2:36.

24. Ibid., 2:22.

25. Ibid., 3:453. As such evil cannot be explained objectively but can only be

spiritual realm is the reason the believer is called to live not by sight but by faith (2 Cor 5:7) in "a reality which I cannot prove and yet which exists without me, which enjoys objective givenness and yet which is not accessible to me in an objectifiable way."[26]

The Holy Spirit

In light of God's non-demonstrability, Thielicke finally states that "God controls the criteria" by which he is made known.[27] This truth which he tirelessly champions is expressed in his theology of the Holy Spirit:

> For the testimony of the Spirit tells us that it is God himself who creates the possibility of his being known. He thus discloses himself to the one who has no way of finding him (1 Corinthians 2:9f.). He himself gives the light in which we see him (Psalm 36:9). Hence the knowledge of God does not stand under the conditions of our thinking capacity, as in the classical proofs or natural theology. God himself grants the capacity through the gift of the Spirit, through his self-impartation.[28]

Thus, for Thielicke, the reformation of apologetics begins with the Trinity, specifically the *opera ad extra* of the Spirit.[29] His focus on the "Holy Spirit

---

encountered (*God's World*, 168–70). For some it is surprising to find an atomic era theologian of Thielicke's intellectual caliber that holds to a pre-modern view of a real devil. This outdated belief certainly caused quite a bit of laughter among other theologians. Barth, for one, makes sport, "Down in Swabia lives Thielicke, the man who has come face to face with the Devil. I expect the Devil got a nasty fright!" (*Notes*, 71). Yet Thielicke unwavering insists that "our theology is always a theology of temptation (*Anfechtung*) theology in the face of the open jaws of hell that would swallow us up" (*God's World*, 166–67).

26. *Evangelical Faith*, 2:309.

27. Ibid., 2:11.

28. Ibid., 1:367.

29. See "Theological Starting-Point in the Doctrine of the Holy Spirit" (*Evangelical Faith*, 1:129–37). Van Til teaches that apologetics must begin with the "ontological Trinity," i.e., "self-contained God," (*Apologetics*, 29–30, 39, 43, 97–98, 128) in order to emphasize God's eternal plan as the ultimate reference point in predication. As seen in ch. 2, Thielicke stresses that in the language of God's "higher thoughts." For Van Til's talk of the ontological Trinity, he is charged with philosophical abstraction and Idealism (*Defense*, 228–29). In response, he claims that some criticism is influenced by dialectical theology (ibid., 396–98). Thielicke is certainly no ally of Barth and provides a sober assessment of dialectical theology (*Modern Thought*, 546–61). Yet he is careful in his use of the descriptor, "ontological" Trinity, out of concern that an emphasis on ontology introduces the "temptation" ([*Versuchung*] *Evangelical Faith*, 1:371; see *Evangelische Glaube* 1:543) to erase the "ontological distinction" between God and the world

is for its part a protest against the Cartesian approach in theology."[30] The egocentric method exalts both the apologist's power to persuade and the hearer's receptivity to the message, neither of which are effectual though without the Spirit who works by the Word in the heart of the hearer.

Further highlighting the role of the Holy Spirit is that what can be known about God, Thielicke claims, is only "God's own knowledge of himself."[31] For only the Spirit searches the depths of God and knows what no eye has seen nor ear heard neither has it entered the heart of man (1 Cor 2:9–10). If, as the apostle says, "those who love him" are the recipients of the things that cannot be heard and seen, this means that God reveals himself so as to allow men to become sharers in his own self-knowledge. Thielicke asserts that this can only be explained pneumatologically: "God shares the Spirit in whom he knows himself. He does not heighten our natural knowledge nor extend the table of categories but sets us on another plane, where his Spirit tells us who he is and thus discloses to us what only he knows."[32]

This has significant impact on apologetic method (see chapter 5). Since the knowledge of God is disclosed through the miraculous work of the Holy Spirit, "theological statements cannot have the character of proof or demonstration. They will always be proclamation, address, and appeal."[33]

Certainty

Thielicke's unwavering conviction that God is not demonstrable does not at all imply that his apologetic reduces to an approach of "probability" as in mathematical theory. His renunciation of the objectifiability of God does not mean that after an encounter of Christian persuasion the unbeliever is left to conclude merely that God probably exists or that it is highly likely. For that would contradict "the *certainty* of the reality of God" which he relentlessly emphasizes in the "Nevertheless."[34] Indeed, the "Nevertheless" itself is an expression of the fact that the concepts of non-demonstrability and certainty are not at all incompatible. For the "Nevertheless" is a "confession of an absolute certainty by which a man lives, by which he stands

---

which is "the constant error of natural theology" (*Evangelical Faith*, 1:366), as seen in the Logos Apologist (ibid., 1:369), although this would not be applicable to Van Til. So Thielicke refers to the pre-temporal being of God by talking of the "essential" Trinity (ibid., 2:176–81).

30. *Evangelical Faith*, 1:132.
31. Ibid., 3:23.
32. Ibid.
33. Ibid., 1:211; *Conversations*, 43.
34. *Modern Thought*, 451; italics added.

or falls, yet which he cannot prove."[35] Thielicke illustrates this relation with a simple analogy. It "is rather like a child who believes with *absolute* certainty that his mother loves him, yet would be utterly confused if some intellectual brute were to say to him, 'Now show me why you assume that your mother loves you. Do you have any evidence?'"[36] In other words, the certainty with and about which Thielicke speaks is existential and not that derived from rational inquiry or empirical research.[37] Rather it comes via personal "encounter."[38]

General Revelation

The thorough counterdemonstrationism of Thielicke's apologetic of the cross applies to general revelation. According to orthodox Christian theology, God makes himself known in both general and special revelation. General revelation, as Thielicke explains the doctrine, is "a static transparency of the created world, while special revelation comes to be equated with the given thesaurus of holy scripture."[39] God reveals himself in two books, the book of nature and the Bible. The former reveals God's self-testimony as Creator and lawgiver, distinct from the latter which reveals his Son as Redeemer. The self-revelation of God in the book of nature, like Scripture, is perfectly perspicuous. God's attributes are clearly manifest in general, or natural, revelation. Thielicke asserts, however, that it would be pointless to seek to prove God by appealing to the evidence in creation. For the sufficiency of the proof in general revelation is a function of a specific existential perspective. In other words, it is objectively sufficient, yet subjectively

---

35. *Creed*, 3.

36. Ibid.

37. This is not outside of *Anfechtung* which Thielicke believes "can shatter only penultimate certainties and that when I let these go I come upon a solid and impregnable layer which—for Luther at least—cannot be shattered. This layer is the *certainty* about God . . . which I cannot establish *rationally*" (*Modern Thought*, 56; italics added).

38. *Evangelical Faith*, 2:302, 304–6, 370, 408, 443. In Thielicke's wide use of the term "encounter," he "baptizes" the language of Bultmann, the representative of existential theology, for an apologetic purpose. In Bultmann's program to demythologize the New Testament, he uses the rhetoric of "encounter" to rescue the Christ event from the confining ghetto of consciousness: "A vision is never purely subjective. It always has an objective basis. In the vision the encounter which precedes it attains fruition, so that the vision itself becomes a further encounter" (Bultmann, in Thielicke, "Mythology," 152). Thielicke turns the tables, "It is just the opposite: the resurrection is the only thing which creates a real encounter with Christ (ibid., 154).

39. *Evangelical Faith*, 2:8.

insufficient to the natural man.⁴⁰ As Thielicke stresses repeatedly, the facts of nature are ambivalent. One can read the evidence manifest in the book of nature either way—for or against God.

To make his case, Thielicke considers Psalm 104, replete with references to natural revelation. After reminding that the subject of the Psalm is the Creator and not the creation, he hastens to emphasize his point, "Nor is the Thou of this Creator known from nature . . . Nature in its indirectness is ambivalent. It does not make God manifest. It envelops him in mystery."⁴¹ Although general revelation shows that God is "stretching out the heavens like a tent" and "makes the clouds his chariot" (Ps 104:2, 3), Thielicke believes that nature "is also a parable of the corruptible, of the blatantly non-eternal, which sinks into nothingness when God withdraws his breath (Psalm 104:29)."⁴² Beside the cedars of Lebanon which stand to glorify God (Ps 104:17), one finds that "the grass withers, the flower fades" (Isa 40:7). In view of the facts, Thielicke asserts, the "grass bears witness to both life and death . . . It thus represents the ambivalence of all created forms and of all indirectness in which God appears."⁴³ Nature both reveals and conceals the existence of God. An apologetic attempt to prove God from the book of nature can just as easily end counterproductively.

The traditional apologist might object and insists that the "birds of the air and the lilies of the field" are certainly "pointers to the Lord of creation, who cares for all his creatures";⁴⁴ yet, from the unbeliever's perspective, Thielicke pushes the *Anfechtung* antithesis, they are "also figures of a world of nature that is dumb, nature that is silent to *me*, that goes on its way, careless of my concerns and my loneliness."⁴⁵ What of the celestial evidence then? Surely the planets are proof of God's existence, for "the heavens declare the glory of God, and the sky above proclaims his handiwork" (Ps 19:1). Thielicke, though, counterquestions such certainty, "Are the stars just symbols of an eternal order or are they not also a sign of orderly processes that go on quite indifferent to my lot? May they not chill me with the cold of

---

40. *Theologie Anfechtung*, 39. Calvin explains the Reformation's view of general revelation and would "let this difference be remembered, that the manifestation of God, by which he makes his glory known in his creation, is, with regard to the light itself, sufficiently clear; but that on account of our blindness it is not found to be sufficient (*Romans*, 71).

41. *Evangelical Faith*, 2:11.
42. Ibid.
43. Ibid.
44. *Waiting*, 11–12.
45. Ibid., 12.

cosmic space rather than make me feel the pulse-beat of a Father's heart?"[46] General revelation, as it is commonly known, is ambivalent, and thus natural theology problematic.[47]

Romans 1

To assess the ambivalence of nature, Thielicke turns to—from the very beginning of his theological work—the "central pericope of the New Testament" where his thinking is repeatedly drawn, "the Apostle Paul's analysis of heathen idolatry" in the Epistle to the Romans (1:18–25).[48] In orthodox doctrine, the text refers to "God's ontic revelation in the works of creation,"[49] which would seem to lend support to the possibility of the theistic proofs. As Thielicke quickly qualifies, however, the person who relentlessly stands in opposition to the truth "does *not see* God's invisible being, his eternal power and deity (Romans 1:20)."[50] This is not due to any epistemological limitations, as suggested for instance by Kant, but because the basic state of human self-assertion compels one to suppress the truth in unrighteousness. Rather than giving thanks to God, the natural person surrenders oneself to untruth, and lives in denial of the revelation of God. This exchange of the truth for a lie (Rom 1:25) excites within one an unbreakable addiction to untruth. Eventually, God gives a person exactly what one desires and abandons one to one's own noetic bondage. Thielicke continues, "As man opposes truth, God withdraws from him his revelation in creation. He

---

46. Ibid. The spectacles of Scripture are needed to see God's handiwork in the heavens. Commenting on Ps 19 which points to general revelation, Calvin writes "The same prophet, after he states, "The heavens declare the glory of God, the firmament shows forth the works of his hands . . . then proceeds to mention his Word" (*Institutes*, 1.6.4:73). The reason, according to Calvin, is "since God in vain calls all peoples to himself by the contemplation of heaven and earth, this [God's Word] is the very school of God's children" (*Institutes*, 1.6.4:73). Hence, it is the glasses of God's Word that allow the psalmist to see God's fingerprints all over the universe; see below.

47. When Calvin speaks of the "knowledge" of God in general revelation, explains his editor, he never means a "purely objective knowledge" but rather more what is equivalent to "existential apprehension" (Battles, in Calvin, *Institutes*,1.1.1:35–36n1). As Calvin explains, by "'knowledge' we do not mean comprehension of the sort that is commonly concerned with those things which fall under human sense perception" (*Institutes*, 3.2.14:559). Instead, he speaks "only of the primal and simple knowledge to which the very order of nature would have led us *if* Adam had remained upright" (*Institutes*, 1.2.1:40; italics added). Since the Fall, because of sin, a sound natural theology has been impossible.

48. *Theologie Anfechtung*, iv; translation mine.

49. *Evangelical Faith*, 2:6.

50. Ibid.; italics added.

delivers him up (*parédōken*, Romans 1:24, 26) to his opposition to the truth and hence hardens him in error."[51] Here, there is both revelation and concealment, yet the judicial hardening makes it impossible for the defiant to see any ontological evidence of a Creator from the fact of creation. Indeed, the person is blind to the perspicuity of general revelation.[52] As a result of one's spiritual blindness, one can no longer understand true reality and instead invents for oneself an alternative and delusional reality of a godless and self-existing world. Consequently, God remains concealed and hidden from him or her. For this person, God is silent and absent. Nature shrouds God's presence in mystery.[53]

Though natural revelation is objectively perspicuous, for fallen autonomous humanity the creation provides no subjective proof of God's reality. For the blind cannot escape the bondage of their willful blindness. Thielicke explains:

> Even though Romans 1:18ff. says that God's "invisible nature," "his eternal power and deity," may be seen in the things that have been made (*poiēmata*), there is no contradiction here . . . That this is so may be seen negatively from the failure of men to perceive God's creative work and their incurring thereby of the wrath of God. This blindness to the footprints of God in his creation is not an epistemologically conditioned lack of insight. It rests instead on an unwillingness to see. Men suppress (*katechein*) the truth that is held out to them because they do not want to understand themselves in their creaturelines. Since they aim at emancipation and autonomy they overlook the Creator who disturbs them in this attitude of theirs. In psychoanalytic terms, they "repress" him. Their blindness, then is in truth blinding.[54]

51. Ibid., 2:7.

52. Calvin maintains that the "mind of man is blinded; so that it may justly be pronounced to be covered with *darkness*" (*John*, 1:33). As the case is, fallen humanity gropes blindly (*Institutes*, 1.5.3:54) in the "dazzling theater" of the Creator's glory (*Institutes*, 1.5.8:61). Van Til employs a similar illustration: "The sinner has cemented colored glasses to his eyes, which he cannot remove. And all is yellow to the jaundiced eye" (*Apologetics*, 98). Moreover, "He cannot remove them because he will not remove them. He is blind and loves to be blind" (*Defense*, 317).

53. Van Til explains in the "hidden God" and "higher thoughts" language so crucial to Thielicke that "the perspicuity of natural revelation, then, may be said to have [its] foundation in the doctrine of the God who 'hideth himself,' whose thoughts are higher than man's thoughts and whose ways are higher than man's ways. There is no discrepancy between the idea of mystery and that of perspicuity with respect to . . . revelation in nature" (*Apologetics*, 78).

54. *Evangelical Faith*, 3:99. Calvin writes that Paul "had said before that 'they became

Thielicke will not leave Romans 1. In another place he returns to the God-question prompted by general revelation: "The question of God is wrongly put, finally, when the *question* of God . . . is changed into an *answer* according to the analysis in Romans 1:18ff."[55] Here—using his counter-question method (see chapter 5)—Thielicke provides a brilliant analysis of humanity's question about the existence of God. He reverses the "Where is God?" question to show that it is, instead, really a question about man and his existence. Still, considering the question as man puts it, Thielicke insists that "God is manifest to the 'Gentiles,' and is so in answer to the question contained in his works (*poiēmata*, v. 20) of creation."[56] Creation does indeed answer the God-question. Are God's attributes clearly revealed in nature so that his existence may be known? Yes; however, as Thielicke is quick to add, for sinfully emancipated humanity the question is closed. The reason is because autonomous man, "who curves in upon himself,"[57] has already answered the question. "The answer is not God. It is the idol, the likeness (*homoiōma*, v. 23)."[58]

Retrospection

God attributes are evidently manifest in natural revelation; however, as Thielicke insists, one can only "find traces of God retrospectively after the manner of the analogy of faith."[59] Herein lies the explanation for the ambivalence of general revelation. The difference in the ambiguity of nature for any given person is his or her existential condition, that is, whether he or she is a new creation from whose eyes the scales have been miraculously

---

futile in their thinking' [Rom. 1:21]. In order, however, that no one might excuse their guilt, he adds that they are justly blinded" (*Institutes*, 1.4.1:48). He adds, "Where Paul teaches that what is to be known of God is made plain from the creation of the universe [Rom. 1:19], he does not signify such a manifestation as men's discernment can comprehend; but, rather, shows it not to go farther than to render them inexcusable" (*Institutes*, 1.5.14:68).

55. *Evangelical Faith*, 2:75.
56. Ibid., 2:76.
57. Ibid.
58. Ibid. Calvin explains in the section, "The evidence of God in creation does not profit us" (*Institutes*, 1.5.11:63–64). For our blindness only allows humanity "rashly [to] grasp a conception of *some sort of divinity*" (*Institutes*, 1.5.11:64; italics added), i.e., an idol. Horton asserts that "if there were no general revelation, there would be no idolatry" (*Christian Faith*, 149).

59. *Evangelical Faith*, 2:74. Van Til agrees with Thielicke on his concept of analogy. In distinction from a Thomistic analogy of being, Van Til teaches that one must think analogically, that is, "to think God's thoughts after him" (*Apologetics*, 77n19, 131, 140).

removed so as to see clearly evidence of the Creator. In other words, the question of sin and faith is what determines one's perspective of natural revelation, for there is no neutral epistemological ground from which one can view the world.[60] To support his case, Thielicke often quotes the epistemological methodology of the psalmist, "In thy light shall we see light" (Ps 36:9; KJV).[61] It is the light of the knowledge of God that illumines the light of nature. The point of view from which one observes nature—in the light of God or the darkness of unbelief—is crucial. This means that "anybody who tries to discover God through the world sees only the distorted reflections of created things, a reflex of his own mind."[62] In the reverse approach, Thielicke explains, "we start with God and then learn to discover the world anew."[63] So explains the author of the Epistle to the Hebrews, "By faith we understand that the universe was created by the word of God, so that what is seen was not made out of things that are visible" (Heb 11:3).[64] The ability to perceive God as the Creator is a function of faith. This means that the traditional apologist who views the creation and rightly sees evidence for the Creator—which he or she would happily employ as proof of God—must realize that he or she views nature retrospectively only through the eyes of faith whereas the unregenerate cannot. The evidence for God in creation is only seen as a reflex of faith and never from a supposedly neutral vantage point.[65] Therefore an empirical fight over the "brute facts" of science is totally futile since the data will always be interpreted through one's epistemological paradigm—belief or unbelief. Thielicke argues that "the facts cannot be known by the old self; they are non-existent for its 'mind' and 'heart'

60. Thielicke's inherits his aversion to neutrality from Luther. The reformer opens *Bondage of the Will* with a review of Romans 1, from which he claims "the division he [Paul] makes leaves no one on neutral ground" (*Luther's Basic Theological Writings*, 180). Luther repeats that there is "no neutral ground . . . Otherwise, Paul's whole argument would come to nothing, since it presupposes this division" (ibid., 195). The way in which Thielicke takes up Luther's insights casts him as a kind of sower of presuppositionalism.

61. *Evangelical Faith*, 1:310, 367; 2:83, 121; 3:453. This perspective is also crucial to Van Til's method (*Apologetics*, 65, 140–41).

62. *Waiting*, 12.

63. Ibid.

64. Calvin states that the biblical author "means by this that the invisible divinity is made manifest in such spectacles, but that we have not the eyes to see this unless they be illumined by the inner revelation of God through faith" (*Institutes*, 1.5.14:68).

65. Thielicke asserts that "there is nothing in the world that is without theological significance. The methods of science and historicism may be 'atheistic' . . . but they still have a theological reference once we include in them the man who uses these methods" (*Evangelical Faith*, 1:368). There is no unbiased scientist who uses a neutral method of inquiry.

(1 Corinthians 2:9)."[66] The ambivalence of creation is only cleared away in theological reflection.

For Thielicke a new creation provides the difference in existential perspective. Since this miracle only occurs by the sovereign intervention of the Holy Spirit operating by his Word, then the Word is critical. Thielicke explains, "The Word, then, is the decisive basis of the revelation in creation."[67] Without it the natural man shall never find "a direct readability of the Creator from the creation."[68] Here Thielicke echoes the Genevan, John Calvin (1509–64), who asserts that one, therefore, needs the "spectacles" of Scripture to "read distinctly" about the Creator in the book of creation.[69] It is only through the eyeglasses of the Bible that one can see the fingerprints and footprints of God in nature. Thielicke therefore emphasizes, "His traces are ambiguous and unrecognizable apart from his efficacious and interpretive Word."[70]

For apologetic strategy, then, this means that general revelation, the book of nature, as proof of God "is in itself no use at all. Indeed, it confines and limits us to this introverted creation."[71] In this respect, general revelation is like a parable which, if not seen "from the point of view from which Jesus Christ, the *teller* of the parables sees it, the whole profundity of parabolic images turns into a confused labyrinth; for him the doors are shut instead of opened."[72] So the evidence of creation, Thielicke concludes, "is disclosed to us only in the great textbook of God—the Word in which he speaks to us and tells us who he is and what his purposes are."[73] General revelation is the predicate and possibility of special revelation or not at all.

---

66. *Evangelical Faith*, 1:157. As already noted, Van Til wholeheartedly agrees that "brute facts . . . are mute facts" (*Defense*, 279). That is, a "brute," or uninterpreted fact, does not speak in a vacuum. Like Thielicke, he "would not talk endlessly about facts and more facts without ever challenging the nonbeliever's philosophy of fact" (ibid., 257). C. S. Lewis holds a similar strategy, "The result of our historical enquiries thus depends on the philosophical views which we have been holding before we even began to look at the evidence. This philosophical question must therefore come first" (*Miracles*, 2).

67. *Evangelical Faith*, 3:99.

68. Ibid.

69. Calvin, *Institutes*, 1.6.1:70; see n46 above.

70. *Evangelical Faith*, 3:99. Thielicke adds that "creation was called into being by the effective Word of the Creator, his 'Let there be . . . ,' so that there can be no access to creation without access to this creative Word" (Ibid.).

71. *Waiting*, 12.

72. Ibid., 11. Calvin agrees general revelation is like a parable that "was attended by no advantage, because *seeing, they did not see*" (*John*, 1:33; see *Institutes*, 1.4.2:48). He is also fond of "labyrinth" language ("Subject Index," *Institutes*, 1676).

73. *Waiting*, 12.

Miracle

Thielicke's relentless counterdemonstrationism appears where least expected, in the autobiography written at the end of his life. Recalling his recovery from a terminal illness in youth, which he truly believes was a "miracle,"[74] Thielicke seizes this last opportunity to vent his rage against empiricism. "Even the New Testament never understood miracles as objectively demonstrable proof of the existence of God."[75] Many traditional apologists, perhaps patient with Thielicke's project to this point, would find such a statement outrageous since in their view "miracles are used by God throughout the Bible as evidence."[76] Based on this position, the appeal to miracles has historically held a significant place in the proof of Christianity. Indeed, the traditionalist maintains that "as far as apologetics is concerned, the visible miracle is indispensable to the case for Christianity which case would thereby be demonstrated sound."[77] Thielicke is aware of the militant resistance to his position, yet the extremity of his comments continues unabated. "No one has ever been brought to faith by a miracle."[78] Still intensifying his rhetoric, Thielicke claims that "never in his life did he [Jesus] perform a miracle in order to make it easier for men to believe."[79] Yet over the top, Thielicke asserts that Christ "even consciously kept the miracles he performed ambiguous."[80]

Message of Miracles

To develop his theology of miracles, Thielicke first considers their message. Where else would he turn but to a primary example of *faith-crisis*, that of the Baptizer and the *Anfechtung* question which he puts to the Nazarene, "Are you the one who is to come, or shall we look for another?" (Matt 11:3). Here Jesus does not reply with a direct: "Yes. I am the coming Christ, you need not expect another." Instead, Thielicke notes, "he points to his works: 'The blind see and the lame walk, the lepers are cleansed and the deaf hear, and the dead raised, and the poor have the gospel preached to

---

74. *Notes*, 65.

75. Ibid.

76. Sproul et al., *Classical Apologetics*, 285. For a straw-man argument against Van Til's presuppositionalism, and by implication Thielicke's, see their cheeky defense against "The Attack on Christian Evidences" (ibid., 276–86).

77. Ibid., 145.

78. *Creed*, 168; *Meaning*, 53.

79. *How Modern?* 54.

80. *Creed*, 107.

them' (Matthew 11:5)."[81] At first glance it might seem that Christ himself points to his miracles as isolated and demonstrable proof of his divine person, and the traditional apologist would most happily agree. Yet Thielicke is not finished and would have the reader see that "the saying in which the mighty acts are enumerated culminates in the preaching of the gospel to the poor. This preaching is the key to the miracles."[82] To understand the message of miracles, they cannot be isolated from the Word. In Jesus' reply to John, the drama in the list of miracles builds until it climaxes in that which is higher than the miracles, specifically, the poor receive good news. This Word transcends miracles and also provides their meaning. Thus Christ's Word and work are bound together. His Word and miracles "interpret one another."[83] This is why, Thielicke believes, "the answer of Jesus is couched in the words of Isaiah 35:5f."[84] The prophecy is a commentary on the One who quotes this passage, relates it to his own works and in so doing reveals himself as the fulfillment of the salvation event. The coming of God promised long ago is fulfilled in the Nazarene. That is the message of the miracles. "Hence," Thielicke concludes, "this person is always presupposed as the subject of its works."[85]

Meaning of Miracles

The healing of the paralytic (Mark 2:1–12), according to Thielicke, provides "a clear contrast between what we normally conceive of as miracle and what the Bible means by the miracles of Jesus."[86] It is therefore the paradigmatic event to which he turns to teach on the meaning of miracles since it appears to provide support for the prevailing conception of miracle as "proof."[87] The popular thought is that "in this miracle Jesus seems . . . to be seeking to get hold of a medical attestation. If he succeeds in securing this clear evidence, he will be officially accepted as a miracle-worker and therefore proved to be the Messiah."[88] The reason this seems so is because of the purpose statement, "But that you may know that the Son of Man has authority on earth to forgive sins—he said to the paralytic—I say to you, rise, pick up your bed,

---

81. *Evangelical Faith*, 2:333.
82. Ibid., 2:334.
83. Ibid.
84. Ibid.
85. Ibid.
86. *God's World*, 116.
87. Ibid., 113–30; *Creed*, 54–67; *Evangelical Faith*, 2: 335; *How Modern?* 51–52.
88. *God's World*, 116.

and go home" (Mark 2:10–11). So one might suppose that Jesus performs the miracle in order to prove his identity and silence his critics.[89] Yet Thielicke categorically rejects this view. Rather, he insists, "the purpose of this miracle is not to 'prove' and therefore be something 'more' than the Word, but rather to *expound* and *interpret* the Word."[90] The miracle is not intended to prove the Word of forgiveness, but instead serves to clarify it.[91]

Thielicke arrives at this position by noticing what Jesus does not say. Christ does not begin with a general doctrine of God to inform the paralytic of absolute morality and cosmic justice. For then he could be mistaken as just another theologian or philosopher. Instead something happens here that is categorically distinct from anything that has occurred in the history of philosophy or religion. Thielicke points out that "the moment Jesus said, 'Your sins are forgiven,' he was not 'teaching,' but 'acting.'"[92] This does not at all imply that Jesus relativizes the cosmic moral order or trivializes the principle of retribution. The law of guilt and punishment are definitely operative, the reason for which Jesus is left a mangled corpse at Golgotha after becoming a lightning rod to absorb the storm of God's wrath otherwise directed toward this man. Yet the text does not allow one to think that Christ is here giving a lecture about the nature of sin and forgiveness; rather, he accomplishes it. Jesus does not teach about forgiveness, he enacts it. So by healing the paralytic, Christ is not offering evidence of his authority to forgive sins in order prove his identity, rather he wants to say, according to Thielicke, "*When I call halt to this disease, this is an authoritative intervention in the course of natural law; and in exactly the same way, it is an authoritative intervention in the law of guilt and retribution when I say, Your sins are forgiven.*"[93] Thus,

---

89. On this basis, Montgomery believes that "our apologetic should be modeled on the Christ who offered objective evidence of his power to forgive sins by healing the paralytic" ("Once upon an A Priori," 390).

90. *God's World*, 123.

91. Lane strengthens Thielicke's theological position with immediate exegetical support: "The thought that the Lord affirmed his dignity and function before the scribes during his Galilean ministry is in conflict both with general probability and more particularly with Mark's testimony concerning Jesus' consistent refusal to reveal himself to the scribes, priests and elders who challenged his authority (cf. Ch. 11:33). To hold that he did so in Galilee contradicts the posture he assumed before unbelief throughout his earthly ministry" (*Mark*, 97). What then are we to think of the purpose statement, "But that you may know that the Son of Man has authority on earth to forgive sins" (Mark 2:10)? Lane continues, "Verse 10a is a parenthetical statement addressed by the evangelist to the *Christian* readers of the Gospel to explain the significance of the closing phase of the healing *for them*" (ibid., 98). After Mark's interjection he resumes the narrative, "he said to the paralytic."

92. *God's World*, 121.

93. *God's World*, 123.

the purpose of the miracle is to reveal that both healing and forgiveness are acts, "both are *interventions* in the iron forces of law."[94] This means that "here a 'stronger one' (Luke 11:22) is at work; here the Son of God is in the fray. *That's the meaning of the miracle, that and nothing else!*"[95]

The miracle then is an illustration of the fact that the spoken Word actually accomplishes what it proclaims. Thielicke continues, "Once he had called upon them to believe that he had silently broken the chains of sin, he opened the picture book to an illustration by saying to the paralytic . . . 'Stand up, take up your bed, and walk.'"[96] Thus as with the picture book of general revelation, God's Word interprets the work. To read about the Creator in the book of creation, one needs the spectacles of Scripture. Likewise, to perceive the identity of the Nazarene one must read the work of miracles through the eyeglasses of His Word. "Hence," Thielicke dogmatizes:

> The word which brings faith and the miracle which can be seen are not alternatives. They are tied to one another and expound one another. The word expounds the miracle as an act of God and sign of his dawning rule. The miracle for its part expounds the word as an active word, a deed-word.[97]

Obfuscation

Thielicke believes the apologetic appeal to miracle operates beneath the level of genuine theology since "miracles are in principle ambiguous."[98] For example, he reminds of the time when Jesus heals the blind and dumb demoniac (Matt 12:22–24). The reaction of the crowd is similar to that in the healing of the paralytic: total amazement. No one denies that something sensational occurred. For the evidence shows that the man could see, hear, and speak. Yet the Pharisees respond to the evidence by interpreting the proof according to the preconceived paradigm of unbelief, "It is only by Beelzebul, the prince of demons, that this man casts out demons" (Matt 12:24). The skeptics attribute the healing to the power of Satan and charge Jesus with guilt by association. Thus "this 'perfectly unambiguous' miracle," Thielicke polemically explains, "did not convince these people at

94. Ibid.
95. Ibid.
96. *How Modern?* 51. Thielicke also refers to miracle as "a sort of echo" of the Word and a "'visual aid' which in a new and different way, refers faith back to the one to whom faith had already turned" (*How Modern?* 53).
97. *Evangelical Faith*, 2:336.
98. Ibid., 2:335.

all, but actually drove them into extreme opposition."[99] The miracle itself is powerless to persuade, but remains ambiguous due to one's existence in truth or untruth (John 18:37).[100] In other words, there is no neutral pedestrian zone for unbiased spectators to gather in order to view Jesus and his miracles (Matt 12:30; Luke 11:23). So "the miracles remain ambiguous and, one might say, within an enigmatic code . . . But once we have taken a position in relation to Jesus Christ himself, we can interpret the miracles correctly, because then we understand them through *him*."[101]

Since the ambiguity of miracles functions according to the state of belief or unbelief, it does not pass away with the ancient world. Rather the "half-light . . . in which miracles are set may be seen also in modern skepticism with regard to miracles."[102] Of course, the question now is not whether God or Beelzebul is active, but natural causality. The miraculous can be explained merely as the coincidence of several causal chains.[103] As Thielicke insists, "miracle, then, lives and moves in a sphere of confusion."[104] This ambiguity, as established at the healing of the paralytic, separates the bystanders into two groups. For some the miracle brings greater illumination upon the previously spoken Word. For others it brings greater obfuscation. Just as parables function for those with ears to hear, so the miracle, like general revelation, provides clarity for those with eyes to see—yet more confusion for those who demand sight, so that, though seeing, they do not see (Isa 6:9; Matt 13:14; Mark 4:12; Luke 8:10; John 12:40).[105]

---

99. *God's World*, 124. The Ligonier apologists miss this when they insist that "miracles are visible and external and perceivable by both converted and unconverted alike, carrying with them the power to convince, if not to convert" (Sproul et al., *Classical Apologetics*, 145).

100. Thielicke confirms that "the mere facts of the works . . . which bear witness to him, are not enough (cf. Jn. 10:24–30). He who does not belong to the flock is deaf to his word and deed (v. 26)" (*Evangelical Faith*, 2:337).

101. *Creed*, 64. Elsewhere Thielicke confirms that "the half-light and confusion disappear only for those who relate miracles to the person of Christ and interpret them in terms of this person" (*Evangelical Faith*, 2:336).

102. *Evangelical Faith*, 2:336.

103. Van Til notes that according to "the 'scientific method' [as autonomously interpreted] we must allow that it is quite possible that at some future date all the miracles recorded in the Bible, not excluding the resurrection of Christ, may be explained by natural laws" (*Christian-Theistic Evidences*, in Bahnsen, *Van Til's Apologetic*, 646). Even so, Thielicke's counterdemonstrationism persists: "Seeing in the conjunction of such causal sequences the miraculous acts of God cannot be objectified either by observation or deduction. What means certainty for faith is thus uncertain in the objective sense" (*Evangelical Faith*, 2:336).

104. *Evangelical Faith*, 2:336.

105. *God's World*, 126.

No Proof

Thielicke provides still more theological support to his rejection of the idea that miracles serve as proof. First, it contradicts the nature of faith, which by definition "always stands opposed to the immediacy of sight and possession. It is the basis (*hypostasis*) of what one hopes for, the demonstration (*elenchos*) of things one cannot see (Hebrews 11:1)."[106] Thielicke is even radical enough to assert that "this kind of objective proof of faith actually destroys faith."[107] The basic tone of the Bible is that "we walk by faith, not by sight" (2 Cor 5:7; Heb 11:2–40). So "if the miracle were to be understood as 'proof,'" explains Thielicke, "this would mean that Jesus, by performing miracles, was putting *sight* in the place of *faith*."[108] Indeed the day will come when faith shall end and see what it has believed, and unbelief, too, "will be *compelled* to see what it has *not* believed."[109] Until then, however, it has not been granted Christians to see the beatific vision.[110] For now, they are still in the condition of faith and pilgrimage waiting for the moment when they shall lift up their heads to see God face to face. It would be entirely unbiblical to think that the purpose of miracles is to replace faith with sight. Thus, Thielicke is convinced, "we must be on the wrong track when we interpret the miracle as a proof that would make faith superfluous."[111]

Second, the conception that Jesus would perform a miracle as proof contradicts his own attitude about providing miracles for just such verification. Thielicke points to the episode in which the scribes and Pharisees approach the Nazarene and say, "Teacher, we wish to see a sign from you" (Matt 12:38). The implication is that if Jesus performed a miracle then they would have the empirical evidence required to believe in him. But he absolutely refuses the request in the most exasperated way: "An evil and

---

106. *Evangelical Faith*, 3:29. Not to mention that the "miracle is relativized when with its help we try to get behind the Word and to evade faith" (ibid., 2:36). Faith is trust in God's presence in his Word, or as Thielicke polemically defines in the terms of Kant's famous phrase, faith takes the Word as the "thing in itself" (ibid., 2:35). This means that we cannot look beyond the Word to proof or verifiable history in order to help confirm the Word.

107. Ibid., 1:270. For it reduces faith to practical obedience and eradicates the need of the inward illumination of the Holy Spirit which grants access to the brute facts (Ps 36:9) by opening the eyes and ears.

108. *God's World*, 116.

109. *Waiting*, 48; *God's World*, 117.

110. Thielicke loathes the thought that God is "all at once to be so cheapened and demoted to the bargain basement that a person has only to open his eyes in order to see him" (*Creed*, 59).

111. Ibid., 60.

adulterous generation seeks for a sign, but no sign will be given to it except the sign of the prophet Jonah" (Matt 12:39; Mark 8:12; Luke 11:16, 29). Christ's shocking response questions the method of traditional apologetics. For if proof is all that these empiricists need to be convinced then why would he withhold it and, moreover, condemn them for requesting it? Thielicke answers that "Jesus sees in these people who demand a sign a peculiarly nasty, craven type of human being who does not take the Christ question seriously."[112] For all their talk of the scientific method and rational inquiry they are the most closed-minded, totally unwilling to believe what does not fit into their preconceived formula. In other words, what prevents them "from arriving at a clear and certain faith is not reasons, arguments and intellectual doubts, but sin."[113] They explain away the proof according to their own autonomous criteria (Matt 12:24) and remain personally uncommitted to Christ, in which case "signs lose their transparency and will simply harden us in our wickedness and rebellion."[114]

Thielicke sees the proof seekers as spectators at an arena only interested in show. For example, the crowd in attendance at the bread event (John 6:1–15) have their stomachs temporarily filled, but the whole while their hearts remain empty of the bread of life which the miracle denotes (John 6:26–35). Those who plead for proof are the type of people who want to remain distant bystanders, escape personal decision, and not commit themselves to Christ in a venture of faith (see chapter 6). Jesus consequently has no interest in becoming a circus celebrity who entertains them with miracles, for he knows such spectacles will never effect people in the *imago Dei* at the center of their being. Sure they might, as Thielicke portrays, "stand there for a moment in astonishment, but then the spiritual fireworks subside and the shadows of night close in again about the heart."[115] Yet, this is exactly what Jesus demands—one's whole heart and not just the tingling in one's fingertips. Thielicke also thinks that proof can become a false prop for faith. These bystanders may witness the miraculous healing of the paralytic, but the sight of the Son of God hanging on a gallows will not be very convincing. This brings the counterdemonstrationism of Thielicke's cross-centered strategy into sharp focus since "whoever allowed himself to be impressed only by miracles, only by the 'show,' would certainly have been thrown into confusion by the pitiful sight of Golgotha."[116] He assures, therefore, Jesus

112. *God's World*, 120.
113. Ibid., 119.
114. *Evangelical Faith*, 2:335.
115. *God's World*, 120.
116. *How Modern?*, 54.

"wants a miracle to be anything but a visual proof which makes the commitment of faith superfluous."[117]

Decision

The ambiguity of miracle leaves the unbeliever with a decision to make about the Nazarene. Thielicke concludes, "Jesus is not trying to *prove* anything by his miracles; his purpose is rather through his active, effectual Word to compel us to personal decision."[118] As the miracle operates in a sphere of half-light and confusion, it forces one to decide what one thinks of the historical Jesus of Nazareth. Everyone, including the Pharisees, scribes, and skeptics at the healing of the paralytic, as well as those today who hear of the account must make up their minds about the identity of Jesus. Each must determine whether one sees in him the God who created *ex nihilo* and possesses the sovereign power to rule over the cosmic order and intervene in the causal sequence of natural law. Each must decide whether one will see him as the Son of Man bringing the kingdom of God, or as a sorcerer, gifted with dark, demonic power—or even as the spawn of Satan.

Sure to incite the ire of traditional apologists, Thielicke argues that this personal decision cannot be aided by the empirical analysis of miracles. For no matter how incontrovertible the miracle is, no matter how attested by scientific observation via eyewitnesses—or video and DNA testing—the decisive question of the initial skeptics still remains open: "By what authority are you doing these things?" (Matt 21:23). Is it from God, the devil, or is it simply a freak, random accident of nature? "*That*," Thielicke stresses, "is the sinister question that persists and that no miracle can answer."[119]

Empty-Tomb Empiricism

The radical counterdemonstrationism of Thielicke's cross-centric apologetic is brought to the fore with the resurrection of Christ, which he treats from the lectern to the pulpit in an apologetic conversation with Friedrich Schleiermacher, Wilhelm Herrmann, Rudolf Bultmann, and the

---

117. *Creed*, 61. In this vein, Thielicke sees that in the parable of the Rich Man and Lazarus, Jesus has Abraham refuse the rich man's request for the ultimate sign to be given his unbelieving brothers (Luke 16:27–31). For "he never loved public miracles," Thielicke preaches, "and that's why the five brothers, the representatives of mankind, are not granted, even today, the miraculous spectacle of a messenger from the dead" (*Waiting*, 50).

118. *God's World*, 126.

119. *Creed*, 65.

historico-critical scholars in search for the historical Jesus.[120] The apologetic engagement immediately draws attention to the sublevel theology on which are based the traditional approaches to the resurrection. For, Thielicke plainly states, "the hitherto unstated presupposition of every attack on Christianity is the conviction, frequently taken for granted, that Christ never did rise from the dead."[121] That modern theology harbors this unspoken presupposition against the resurrection is the reason Thielicke develops a "new" apologetic approach to expose and attack a person's paradigm of unbelief (see chapter 5).

This epistemological presupposition of autonomous humanity highlights the reason why Thielicke argues that the resurrection cannot be demonstrated. "Only he who is in the truth . . . hears the voice of the empty tomb. Apart from this situation of faith Easter is not in fact verifiable."[122] Just as with general revelation or miracle, the proof of God in the resurrection of Christ is that which only the believer can perceive and "is in principle non-objectifiable."[123] It is therefore a methodological mistake to think that one can approach the empty tomb in order to investigate the evidence from a neutral standpoint. Thielicke asserts that "the NT does not offer a neutral and noninvolved affirmation of the resurrection events."[124] Naiveté to the myth of neutrality results in the attempts of "popular apologetics," that is, traditional methods, to argue that the resurrection "is the best attested fact in the history of antiquity."[125] Yet the brute fact is a mute fact which does not speak to deaf ears. Because of the human need of radical regeneration, "those who have no relation to the risen Lord . . . cannot accept the resurrection as either possible or factual."[126] So Thielicke stresses from the pulpit, *"The resurrection is a fact that takes place only for believers."*[127]

---

120. Ibid., 148–87; *Evangelical Faith*, 2:423–52; *Letters*, 87–97. In the context of this critical scholarship of the German academy, Thielicke would have the world know what he believes of the resurrection of Christ, *"Without Easter Christianity simply could not exist"* (*Letters*, 88).

121. *Evangelical Faith*, 2:426.

122. Ibid., 2:431.

123. Ibid., 2:432.

124. Ibid., 2:434.

125. Ibid., 1:270; 2:434.

126. Ibid., 2:434. This is totally lost upon Craig who considers it "stupefying that while most New Testament critics who have written on these subjects accept the facts which, at least in my opinion, furnish inductive grounds for inferring the resurrection of Jesus, they do not themselves make that inference" (*Will the Real Jesus Please Stand Up?*, 161–62).

127. *Creed*, 170.

Eyewitness Evidence

Thielicke explains the resurrection appearances that are seemingly presented as evidence by turning to the classical passage where traditionalist find warrant for such evidentialism, the Apostle Paul's argument for the resurrection in his first letter to the Corinthians. Here the apostle provides a list of eyewitnesses of the risen Lord, which culminates in a crowd of five hundred believers who witness the resurrected Christ, "most of whom are still alive" (1 Cor 15:6). Gordon Fee thinks that "the clear implication of v. 6 is that the eyewitnesses were around to be consulted" if anyone remained skeptical about the reality of the Easter event.[128] This would seem to justify an apologetic approach which employs the eyewitness reports as proof. Thielicke, however, argues that "the 'proofs,' which even externally are localized as introductory observations (vv. 1–8), simply serve as a preamble to the true argument" and not as a model for apologetics.[129]

Thielicke believes that the heart of the Paul's argument and its theological import lies in verse 12 following where he pushes the *Anfechtung* antithesis of a dead Christ. As already seen in the discussion of nihilism, the apostle argues that if Christ was not raised then the hopeless abyss of nothingness unavoidably yawns before one. For if Christ was not raised from the dead, then no one shall be raised the dead (1 Cor 15:13–14). This tragedy would then invalidate God's promise of the resurrection, expose Paul as a false witness (1 Cor 15:15), and prove God to be a self-contradictory and thereby nonexistent. Faith would be meaningless and those who had believed would be the most pitiful of all the deluded (1 Cor 15:19). The nihilistic case is summarized in the Epicurean proverb, "Let us eat and drink, for tomorrow we die" (1 Cor 15:32), a confession that all reality is reduced to absurdity. Thielicke is convinced that "for Paul then, the point of the resurrection is not that it discloses and demonstrates but that it puts in force."[130] In other words, the resurrection has not just noetic significance for the Christian message, but ontic significance for reality.

With the apostle's true argument in view, Thielicke perceives that Paul does not produce the eyewitnesses as "proof" of the resurrection. The reasons for his view are the same as those, that bear repeating, for which he sees that Jesus' miracles are not performed as proof. First, "all miracle is ambivalent."[131] The receptivity to miracle is a function of faith. Those with

---

128. Fee, *First Corinthians*, 729.

129. *Evangelical Faith*, 2:424. Craig thinks otherwise ("The Resurrection of Jesus," *Reasonable Faith*, 255–98).

130. *Evangelical Faith*, 2:426.

131. Ibid., 2:435.

eye to see the risen Christ worship the Lord of glory. Those without eye to see him interpret the empty tomb according to the paradigm of unbelief: "His disciples came by night and stole him away" (Matt 28:13). Though some receive the eyewitness testimony with rejoicing, those who suppress the truth (Rom 1:18) simply deny it. The reports are explained as a conspiracy theory or the hallucinations of his demoralized followers, and it is precisely here, Thielicke shows, that evidentialism meets its final end. He can imagine a scenario where a skeptic actually grants the *fact* of the resurrection, but refuses its *message* and *meaning*. The person honestly comes "to the scientific conclusion that the historical documentation for the resurrection of Jesus was without loopholes of any kind and beyond all doubt."[132] He or she, however, is not convinced of the deity of Christ. Rather he or she categorizes it as a mere "historical anomaly."[133] For in a godless world governed by chance, weird things happen.[134] Perhaps shortly after burial, lightning struck the tomb, causing an electric shock to resuscitate the body. So even in this most extreme case of an unbeliever who grants the facticity of the resurrection, the miracle still remains ambivalent and demands a decision, in this instance against Christ. Second, Thielicke insists, that if the eyewitness testimony were presented as evidence for faith, then faith would be replaced by sight. "Belief in this case would be subsequent subjective assent to what is first known objectively in proof of the credibility of what is to be believed."[135] He is convinced, however, that this is both soteriologically and epistemologically impossible and moreover "would make it [faith] a function of human cooperation."[136] In all this there is still to mention that appealing to eyewitness testimony in order to satisfy autonomous preconditions for belief contradicts Christ's own attitude about such empirical verification and falls under his condemnation of sign-seeking (Matt 12:39).[137]

132. *Creed*, 185.

133. Ibid. So the fact of the empty tomb has of itself "no convincing power in the sense of forcing us to the conclusion: Therefore" (*Evangelical Faith*, 2:340).

134. Van Til also conceives of such a case. His skeptic answers, "I have accepted the resurrection as a fact now for some time. The evidence for it is overwhelming. This is a strange universe . . . So why should there not be some resurrections here and there?" (*Defense*, 325; *Apologetics*, 190). Evidential apologetics meets its demise here, for the neutral ground on which it argues opens and swallows it. All that remains is the unbelief of the hearer which the method establishes rather than challenges.

135. *Evangelical Faith*, 2:431.

136. Ibid.

137. Thielicke confirms that "to seek historical facticity as such at a historical distance and with disinterested objectivity, and in so doing to cherish the expectation that this will furnish a basis for faith and a diagnosis of salvation events, is to come under the verdict of trying to get behind the Word by seeking after signs, and hence of evading

Thielicke argues that the apostle does not present the eyewitnesses as proof of the resurrection event, but rather as a prolegomenon to his resurrection theology. As such, he grants a twofold purpose for the reports. First, they function to keep the conscience of the church historically healthy. Second, they protect the event-ness of the resurrection by serving as a "prophylactic against spiritualizing, i.e., against interpretations which depict the event as purely subjective," for example, in psychological talk.[138] In this light, the relevance of the eyewitness reports is immediately recognizable for both the apostolic Church and modern Christianity which contends against critics that deny the historicity of the resurrection of Christ—from ancient Gnostics to modern existential theologians.

For this reason, Thielicke strongly advocates historical critical research of the Easter event. His rationale, however, is categorically distinct from that of the evidential apologist; to prove the message or buttress faith.[139] Rather, Thielicke's concern is "counter-criticism," that is, "contending against historico-critical presentations that might rob Easter faith of its historical basis."[140] The task of apologetics, with respect to the resurrection, is to attack the pseudo-history in modern theology's search for the historical Jesus. This means that apologetics' "primary concern will be whether the historicism against which it does battle does not rest on a defect in epistemological approach."[141] Such unexposed errors would "be found in the presuppositions of such historical-critical considerations—errors like that which we called the bias of 'imprisonment,' which then are condensed into definite methodological axioms."[142] The task of apologetics—to expose and counterquestion unbelief rather than answer its questions—applies most notably to the historicity of the resurrection.[143] Thielicke assures, "if there were no Easter, the cross would be meaningless."[144]

---

the faith which is engendered by this Word" (ibid., 2:37).

138. Ibid., 2:425.

139. For Thielicke is convinced that "faith can never be an 'aha' experience on the basis of historical findings" (ibid., 3:198).

140. Ibid., 2:437.

141. Ibid.

142. *Easter*, 83.

143. As mentioned, the similarities between Thielicke and Van Til are striking, as seen in the following statements. Commenting on the task of countercriticism, i.e., "historical" apologetics, Thielicke admits, "As a systematician, my responsibility is more to define and limit the scope of the task, while the actual resolution of this question falls in the realm of my colleagues in the New Testament studies" (*Easter*, 86). Van Til states this almost exactly, "I would therefore engage in historical apologetics. (I do not personally do a great deal of this because my colleagues in the other departments of the seminary in which I teach are doing it better than I could do it.)" (*Defense*, 257). As a theologian, each considers that his responsibility is to develop a new apologetic method and leave the historical-critical details to their colleagues in biblical studies.

144. *Letters*, 89.

The appeal to the eyewitnesses is what actually, and surprisingly, strengthens Thielicke's position regarding the non-verifiability of the Easter event. For, he reminds, "only those who had been in touch with the earthly Jesus witness the resurrection."[145] No enemy of Christ is ever produced as a witness. To make the testimony more plausible to the general public, and to dismiss the objection that it is biased by belief, "there would surely have been great interest in neutral witnesses 'outside faith' if objectifiability had been regarded as legitimate or possible."[146] According to Thielicke, however, it is not even a consideration. For the disciples who witnessed the miracles of Christ already know that the miracle is basically non-verifiable. Instead, the resurrection, as a "miracle demands faith and withholds itself from objectifying knowledge."[147] It is therefore never the concern of the New Testament writers to show the verifiability of the resurrection by producing neutral witnesses. For the One who wrought miracles gave enough instruction to make it clear that neutrality is impossible (Matt 12:30).

Fundamentally, for Thielicke, the resurrection of Christ is an "event which took place in time and space even if it cannot be explained in terms of time and space."[148] In other words, though an objective event, it is not objectifiable. Moreover, the two concepts, the ontic facticity of the resurrection and the noetic inquiry of it, are to be strictly divorced from each other as the history of epistemology has shown by their otherwise continual confounding. Hence when talking of the resurrection, Thielicke eschews the term "objectivity" because of its epistemological baggage, that is, "because it is usually understood as the presupposition of a possible objectifiability."[149] So when speaking of the "objectivity" of the resurrection he prefers to talk of "transsubjectivity." He maintains that "its non-objectifiability comes to expression in the NT in the almost complete absence of statements about the manner of the resurrection. Its transsubjectivity comes to expression in the solid testimony that is given to the fact of it."[150]

Proof for Doubting Thomas

The evidentialist would hold that Thielicke's counterdemonstrationism is completely undermined in the resurrection appearance to doubting Thomas

---

145. *Evangelical Faith*, 2:432.
146. Ibid.
147. Ibid.
148. Ibid., 2:424.
149. Ibid., 2:432.
150. Ibid., 2:433.

(John 20:24–29).[151] In anticipation of such criticism, Thielicke considers this unique example of *faith-crisis* to evaluate the role of empirical proof for apologetics. On the evening of the first Easter, the resurrected Lord appears to the disciples huddled together in the Upper Room (John 20:19). Thomas, however, is not there and remains thoroughly unconvinced of the disciples' reports. The skeptic refuses to believe what cannot be empirically proven: "Unless I see in his hands the mark of the nails, and place my finger into the mark of the nails, and place my hand into his side, I will never believe" (John 20:25). The next Sunday evening Jesus appears again, and Thomas' demand for empirical verification is granted. After calming the group (John 20:26), the Lord addresses his doubting disciple, and unpetitioned, does the totally unexpected. He caters to Thomas' conditions for faith: "Put your finger here, and see my hands; and put out your hand, and place it in my side. Do not disbelieve, but believe" (John 20:27).

Since throughout his ministry Christ condemns sign-seeking—and here blesses blind faith, "Blessed are those who have not seen and yet have believed" (John 20:29)—what he does is totally unpredictable.[152] Even though faith is independent of observable verification, Christ freely condescends to the doubter that he may doubt no more. Jesus' concession does not threaten Thielicke's counterempiricism, but rather confirms his theology. He explains comfortably that theologically "Jesus didn't act properly one might say. He didn't act in conformity with the prescriptions laid down in dogmatic textbooks under the heading 'Christology.'"[153] Thielicke therefore rejoices in the sovereign agency of the Son of Man who "is not only lord of the sabbath (Mark 2:28); he is also lord over dogmas, and, even more, over the methods of handling those dogmas."[154] Indeed while preaching on this event Thielicke triumphs over the fact that "Holy Scripture is always greater than our minds, even greater than our theology, and that an explosive power lurks within it."[155] Nonetheless, with the apostolic assertion that God freely "has mercy on whomever he wills" (Rom 9:18), Thielicke indicates that the text never mentions any examination of the evidence upon the

---

151. Montgomery asserts, "Our apologetic should be modeled on the Christ who offered objective evidence . . . and who convinced unbelieving Thomas that he was God and Lord by the undeniable presence of his resurrected body" ("Once upon an A Priori," 390).

152. "This does not mean," Thielicke states, "that faith is, or ought to be, intellectually blind" (*Evangelical Faith*, 2:269). For the role of regenerate reason, see below.

153. *Creed*, 183.

154. Ibid. So in apologetics Thielicke would rather have us "lay the responsibility of proof upon him" (ibid., 180; see chapter 6 for this apologetic venture).

155. Ibid., 174.

part of Thomas. Thus he questions "whether Thomas acted on Jesus' offer at all, that is, whether he *really* placed his hands in the woundprints."[156] To the contrary, Thielicke happily insists that "Thomas' belief does not rest on seeing and touching,"[157] for if so, then Thomas' modern colleagues in skepticism would be helplessly condemned "since we obviously can no longer perform the fingertip test."[158]

To understand what it is that brings Thomas to his knees in worship, Thielicke digs below a superficial reading of the text. The theologian notes "if it had been the experiential touching and seeing, then he would have come up with something like a medical diagnosis: 'Yes, it all fits. The nail prints are discernible and they are genuine. He is the one. He is actually risen and alive.'"[159] In this case, Thomas would have spoken of Jesus in the third person: "He is alive." That is precisely, however, what he does not do. Instead, he speaks in the first person. Thomas' response is a personal expression of shock and astonishment: "My Lord and my God!" (John 20:28). A clinical, detached, empirical inquiry does not evoke such an intimate confession of faith. No, Thomas' faith does not come by sight, rather, as Paul later explains, "faith comes from hearing, and hearing through the word of Christ" (Rom 10:17). In the encounter with the Risen One, it is Jesus' words that bring conversion. For his words reveal omniscient knowledge of Thomas' prior demand for evidence, leaving the freethinker overwhelmed with shame and amazement, that is, believing. So Thomas, Thielicke is

---

156. Ibid., 184. Morris confirms that "at the sight of Jesus all his doubts vanished and he did not need to apply any of his tests" (*John*, 753).

157. Ibid., 185.

158. Ibid. On this theme of historical distance, Thielicke shows solidarity with his hearers by articulating Lessing's skepticism of the miracle reports. "Miracles that I see with my own eyes and have an opportunity to test personally are one thing; miracles that I only know through *history*, that others claim to have seen and tested, are quite another" (*Believe*, 65). Thielicke quotes Lessing again to emphasize that "it is one thing to experience a miracle; it is quite another thing merely to receive a report about a miracle" (*God's World*, 118).

In this vein, Bahnsen cautions that "Christian apologists are not in the same position as Christ or the apostles with respect to presenting empirical evidence. Their hearers were presented with miracles, while our hearers are presented with reports of miracles. This important difference has tremendous epistemological implications for the way in which a person defends, or even can defend, the person and claims of Christ" (*Van Til's Apologetic*, 642n193). He indicates that an evidentialist like "Montgomery is also wrong to assert that, at least at the time of direct eyewitness encounter with a miracle like Christ's resurrection, the presence of Christ was 'undeniable.' Montgomery has apparently not given sufficient epistemological consideration to the implications of Matthew 28:17—'but some doubted'" (ibid.).

159. *Creed*, 184.

convinced, "recognized the Lord by his love and not by physical characteristics, just as Mary had probably done on Easter morning."[160]

As in the miracles of Christ, considered above, the resurrection appearance is a Word-deed revelation. The two are inseparable and interpret one another. The Word expounds the appearance, and the appearance expounds the Word. After this Word-deed event, Christ meets Thomas' question with a counterquestion, as per his *modus operandi* for dealing with unbelief: "Have you believed because you have seen me?" (John 20:29).[161] The heart-searching question—with its implied answer in the negative—brings further conviction, directing the doubter back to the non-verifiable source of faith, that is, the mysterious and powerful activity of the Word (Heb 4:12). Here the words of Christ, which clearly denounce empiricism, inform apologetic methodology: "Blessed are those who have not seen and yet have believed" (John 20:29).

Summary

Thielicke's unyielding counterempiricism reflects the conviction that the Nevertheless "presupposition of faith's indifference to historical differentiation is that the basic facticity of miracles and signs is accepted."[162] On the other hand, "the closed immanence of the world as a presupposition"—as conceived by atheistic humanity—categorically rejects the idea of God, nonetheless any proof of him in the creation, miracles, resurrection appearances, or eyewitness reports. For this reason, the rich man's brothers would not "be convinced if someone should rise from the dead" in order to persuade them (Luke 16:31). This means that for apologetics the role of evidence is totally ineffectual since it will never be presented to a neutral jury but can only take the witness stand either in the court of belief or unbelief.

Counterintuitive

The "Nevertheless" apologetic of the cross operates not only *against* what the "senses see," but what "reason recognizes" and is thus counterintuitive

160. Ibid., 185.

161. Thielicke actually does not point out Christ's counterquestion, which is totally inconsistent with his interpretation of Christ's conversations that forms a key characteristic of his apologetic (see ch. 5). This, however, can be excused since he uses Luther's translation, which in the original and 1912 revision translates as a statement, as do most English versions (unlike our ESV preference). In *The Greek New Testament* it is a question (Aland et al., 403).

162. *Evangelical Faith*, 2:340.

to autonomous rationalism.[163] The front lines of the antithesis form between "higher thoughts" and human thoughts. As seen in chapter 2, the former is the eternal plan of God by which he freely brings the future to pass. "For as the heavens are higher than the earth, so are my ways higher than your ways and my thoughts than your thoughts" (Isa 55:9). In view of these two drastically different noetic categories, Thielicke explains that "the *faith-crisis* against which one must believe" arises "because the autonomy of reason is not prepared to give up its normative rank or to renounce the role of being itself the criterion of those higher thoughts."[164] As it is urgent for the apologist to recognize this conflict between opposing epistemologies, Thielicke reformulates the antithesis, "the *faith-crisis* which is posed by Adamic reason forms the front 'against' which faith believes."[165]

In view of this antithesis, Thielicke, as a neo-Lutheran, cannot resist quoting the reformer "when he says that if the light of reason wants to explain for itself the acts of God it is blind and stupid."[166] Indeed, Luther employs quite a few choice epithets to describe autonomous reason, namely, "Frau Hulda."[167] The seductive madam of natural reason, Luther explains, "is the devil's prostitute and can do nothing else but slander and dishonor what God does and says."[168] This bold and "often misunderstood saying,"[169] to which Thielicke wholeheartedly subscribes, has solicited untold confusion and caricature of Luther.[170] Indeed, he continues to be depicted as a "naïve literalist, a dogmatic obscurantist, an anti-intellectual—in short, a 'fideist.'"[171]

---

163. Ibid., 2:12. As seen above in n6, Thielicke's wide use of the term *reason* ranges from that which recognizes immediately, i.e., intuition, to self-conscious rational thought. Van Til agrees that "reasoning is nothing but self-conscious intuition, and intuition is nothing but unconscious reasoning" (*Theology*, 163).

164. *Evangelical Faith*, 2:52; translation mine, cf. *Evangelische Glaube*, 2:63. As noted in ch. 2, these "higher thoughts" are also key to Van Til's apologetic. Describing autonomous reason, he states that man "would not think God's thoughts after him; he would instead think only his original thoughts" (*Apologetics*, 80).

165. *Evangelical Faith*, 2:60; translation mine, cf. *Evangelische Glaube*, 2:73.

166. *Evangelical Faith*, 2:52.

167. *LW* 40:174. Luther's editor explains that in Germanic mythology, Frau Hulda is the ringleader of a group of elfin creatures believed to instigate human activity to good or evil. She is "a personification of order and clever reasoning" (ibid.n134).

168. *LW* 40:175.

169. *Modern Thought*, 136.

170. *Ethics*, 1:325; *Human*, 279. Complicating the problem, according to Althaus, is that "Luther speaks of 'reason' without defining it and without differentiating its various manifestations and possibilities. He always speaks of reason as a totality" (*Theology Luther*, 64).

171. Janz, "Whore or Handmaid," 48.

To this point, professional atheist and contrarian, Christopher Hitchens, opens a chapter of his bestselling *God is Not Great* with Luther's statement about "the Devil's harlot" in order to show how religion is fatally opposed to reason, and therefore, as the subtitle suggests, "poisons everything."[172] In the face of this misrepresentation, Thielicke hastens to the reformer's defense: "It is a stupid if common misunderstanding to see antirationalism in this thesis. The complaint here is not against reason but against the way it can be used, or misused, as an instrument. The issue is the existential area of motivation behind the arguments."[173] A contemporary theologian simplifies, "it is not *reason* that is opposed to faith but the *reasoner*."[174]

Before considering the reasoner, we should see Luther's depiction of reason as the "Devil's prostitute," or "whore," in the context of his otherwise exalted view of reason which he considers as an invaluable gift of the Creator. Althaus contends that "Luther speaks very forcefully of this gift of God and of its glory."[175] Indeed, the reformer believes that reason itself is the *imago Dei* in which humanity was originally created and is that which distinguishes people from the animals.[176] By the use of reason, the man and woman fulfill the cultural mandate given to them on the first page of human history (Gen 1:28). In this aspect Luther sees that "reason is the most important and the highest in rank among all things and, in comparison with other things of this life, the best and something divine. It is the inventor and mentor of all the arts, medicine, laws, and of whatever wisdom, power, virtue, and glory men possess in this life."[177] Reason is all that people need to subdue the world and administer civil matters. Luther teaches:

> In temporal, human affairs human judgment suffices. For these things we need no light but that of reason. Hence God does not in the Scriptures teach us how to build houses, to make clothing, to marry, to wage war, to navigate the seas, and so on. For these our natural light is sufficient.[178]

---

172. Hitchens, *God Is Not Great*, 63.
173. *Human*, 279.
174. Horton, *Christian Faith*, 142.
175. Althaus, *Theology Luther*, 64.
176. *LW* 1:63.
177. *LW* 34:137.
178. In Janz, "Whore or Handmaid," 48.

Reason leads to technological innovation, which, if used to the glory of God, should not be despised, particularly the printing press which Luther "praises as the highest and final gift of God before the end of the world."[179]

Rebellious Reason

In contrast to the exalted role of reason, at the Fall of humanity there is a change in its state or condition, and this is where Frau Hulda struts onto the scene of intellectual history. Luther does not mean that at this point humanity forfeits its rationality. To the contrary, he explains, saying, "nor did God after the fall of Adam take away this majesty of reason, but rather confirmed it."[180] As the physical endowments of humanity are not destroyed, likewise humanity's reason with its cognitive ability remains intact. Nonetheless, at this juncture, reason "shares man's fall,"[181] Thielicke states. Consequently, "reason is in no position to perceive God as the basis, meaning, and goal of world occurrence."[182] The explanation for this limitation lies beyond the epistemological restrictions of reason policed by Kant; rather, human reason is tied to the conditions of human existence. The human state of self-determination causes reason to "suppress the truth" and "exchange the truth about God for a lie" (Rom 1:18, 25). Reason is enslaved to the sinful nature of humanity and is thus compelled to serve the self-assertion and self-glorification of autonomous man. In this sense reason becomes the Devil's whore, Thielicke illustrates, and "offers the body of its arguments to its inferiors" to be used, bent, and laid in whatever position one fancies.[183]

On this ground, Thielicke argues that "reason as the organ of knowledge which has to do with finding the truth is never isolated, then, but it is always to be seen in conjunction with the existence within whose framework and in whose name it acts."[184] Reason, as the data processor of the

179. Althaus, *Theology Luther*, 65.

180. *LW* 34:137.

181. *Evangelical Faith*, 2:57. Thielicke explains that "by his fall," there is "not a quantitative loss of reason in the sense that he sinks to the level of the irrational creatures, but a qualitative alteration in the sense that reason now serves only to make him 'even more brutish than the beasts'" (*Ethics*, 1:163).

182. *Evangelical Faith*, 2:56. Calvin agrees that "we conceive that there is a Deity . . . but our reason here fails, because it cannot ascertain who or what sort of being God is" (*Romans*, 71). As it is, Calvin writes, "by that guidance of their reason they do not come to God, and do not even approach to him" (John 1:33–34).

183. *Modern Thought*, 136. Van Til uses a less offensive illustration to describe unregenerate reason, that of a buzz-saw adjusted to the wrong setting. Despite the keen intellect of the carpenter, "every board he saws is cut slantwise" (*Apologetics*, 93).

184. *Evangelical Faith*, 2:56.

mind, is never impartial. It operates according to the being of the person whom it serves, that is, either in a state of rebellion or redemption. This is a vital point for Thielicke's apologetic and, therefore, one to which he returns. "There is no such thing as reason in the sense of a neutral, timeless, *a priori* faculty divorced from the actual state of man's existence."[185] The idea of raw reason found in a natural state of neutrality is the invention of fallen reason which cannot see itself objectively. For there is "only rebellious reason which makes itself the measure of all things, or receptive reason which thinks the thought of faith after it."[186]

This is why Thielicke maintains that "reason is incapable of the knowledge of God."[187] The existence of God cannot be demonstrated by the use of reason simply because it exists and operates in a state of denial. "Reason belongs to the flesh," he reminds, and "'holds down in unrighteousness.'"[188] Reason does not want to think its way to the right knowledge of God, nor is it even able, "the mind that is set on the flesh is hostile to God, for it does not submit to God's law; indeed, it cannot" (Rom 8:7). The mind of man, in fixed epistemic hostility toward God, can only "provide man's autonomy with arguments" against God.[189] Reason functions to defend unbelief and therefore invents endless arguments which "are simply an intellectual excuse or cover" for its rebellion against God.[190] If there is a God, reason thinks, he would not allow the wicked to prosper while children suffer. So reason creates certain postulates about God. Then reason forms certain postulates of operations which agree with this postulate of God. In other words, Thielicke suggests, "reason, on the basis of its own inventory of norms, tells God who he has to be and how he must act."[191] The role which reason gives itself here mirrors the role which man gives himself over against God. He wants the knowledge of good and evil so that he can be like God (Gen 3:5).

Yet the contrast between who reason wants God to be and who he really is, is only magnified once the idol of God is fashioned in the human mind. "The question here," Thielicke puts, "is whether the Christian view of God does not contradict itself to the degree that rationally intolerable antinomies

---

185. Ibid., 2:60. So he continues, "Reason is not a neutral intellectual organ" (*Human*, 276).

186. *Evangelical Faith*, 2:269.

187. Ibid., 2:57.

188. Ibid.

189. Ibid. Thielicke states that "man's *reason*, at all events, is of *no* assistance in overcoming temptation [*Anfechtung*]. On the contrary, it easily yields to temptation [*Anfechtung*] and even invites it" (*Temptation*, 2328).

190. *Human*, 278.

191. *Evangelical Faith*, 2:52.

are concealed in it."[192] For example, how is the total omnipotence of God to be reconciled with the total impotence of the creature? Would not total impotence negate any responsibility upon the part of man? Furthermore, though man is conscious of the moral law, it seems rather unreasonable to reason that God would demand of us what is impossible to fulfill. Reason also hypothesizes insoluble tensions in the faith, for example, between Law and Gospel or judgment and grace, but as Thielicke shows, the "so-called antinomy arises out of the same autonomy of reason" which "runs according to the norms of reason."[193] Thus, reason posits distorted ideas of God which involve contradictions, and then wields them to cast God in its own image instead of viewing God as he defines himself, "I AM WHO I AM" (Exo 3:14). One can conclude that "it is no surprise, then, that reason, being grounded in an alienated existence, necessarily sees as a contradiction and even an absurdity the God who does not originate in its speculations but who manifests himself to us as the wholly other."[194]

This is where apologetic method comes into focus. For the inadequacy of traditional approaches based on rationalism, Thielicke believes, "may be seen in philosophy as the representative of reason."[195] Reason deals with the visible and apparent sphere of reality. In this realm offered to the senses, reason can see formal and material causes. Phenomena can be pictured and related causally, but reason cannot perceive the efficient and final cause of the phenomena. Hidden from reason, then, are their origin and meaning. "This means that God, who is their origin and meaning, is also hidden from it."[196] If reason tries to predicate their basis and meaning, however, then, as Kant critiques, it trespasses in illegal territory beyond the epistemological border. It does not matter whether the term God is used or not, as in Hegelian pantheism on the one hand or Marxist atheism on the other, reason invents "a cosmic formula which will elucidate the basis, goal, and meaning of all immanent being and occurrence."[197] Yet the God whose thoughts are higher than those of humanity refuses to be compared to the idolatrous image that reason makes of him, and thus reason leads itself into a situation of "*faith-crisis* when what it knows, or thinks it knows, comes into collision with faith in the God of the Bible."[198] So the failure of rationalism is that it can

---

192. Ibid., 2:52–53.
193. Ibid., 2:53.
194. Ibid., 2:57.
195. Ibid., 2:55.
196. Ibid.
197. Ibid., 2:56.
198. Ibid.; cf. *Evangelische Glaube*, 2:67.

only think its way to the "god of the philosophers," on which ground the theistic arguments for God's existence are rejected, as we saw in chapter 3. Further review of these "first fruits" of philosophy is not needed, but only to repeat Thielicke's assertion that "the knowledge of God does not stand under the conditions of our thinking capacity, as in the classical proofs."[199] In addition, there is no neutral public square where philosophers can gather in order to reason their way to God unbiasedly, as witnessed in the bankrupt approach of the Logos Apologists.

Regenerate Reason

In light of these different aspects of human reason, Thielicke reminds that Reformational theology "makes a distinction between reason before and after the fall and also between the reason of the natural and regenerate person."[200] Since the Fall, human reason is found in a state of depravity hardened by untruth (Rom 1:18–25; Eph 4:17–18), and before conversion in bondage to the will opposed to truth (Rom 8:7; 1 Cor 2:14).[201] Reason in this postlapsarian condition, "does not think that it needs redemption."[202] Indeed, in its fallen state enslaved to untruth, it is impossible for reason even to recognize that it is in need of miraculous renewal, for as the intellectual tool of man's epistemological rebellion: "reason sees only what it wants to see, what serves the self-will of man, and what opens up the possibility of self-affirmation."[203] Thus, assesses Thielicke, reason remains tied to the vicious cycle in which it moves and finally "curves in upon itself."[204]

What is needed to change reason involves far more than intellectual improvement or brainwashing. For reason to be brought to reason requires nothing less than radical regeneration. "New birth means being brought to the level of rationality. It is a redemption to objectivity."[205] Reason by itself, however, cannot find its way back to this objectivity, for it cannot break

---

199. *Evangelical Faith*, 1:367.

200. Ibid., 2:56. In his repudiation of the "Shadow-Art of Apologetics," Thielicke asserts that "'Reformed' theology has always known and proclaimed that rationality and its reasons do not say anything that is new in principle, but always merely express and clothe in words and thought symbols what man really is" (*Between*, 27).

201. In *Bondage of the Will*, Luther ties reason and the will together (184, 185, 186, 214–17, 219).

202. *Evangelical Faith*, 2:57.

203. Ibid.

204. Ibid., 2:57, 58.

205. Ibid., 2:58. Objectivity here is "restriction of reason to its proper place," i.e., "to the area of formal and material causes."

free from the centripetal force of the vicious circle in which it operates. Moreover, and on soteriological ground, "its struggle for soberness would be a form of work-righteousness which cannot succeed."[206] Yet reason, corrupted and ruined by the Fall, cannot conceive of any other way of justification. So it ever seeks to offer new epistemic accomplishments. Reason, however, cannot reason its way to the true knowledge of God and thereby achieve its own salvation, for flesh and blood cannot reveal this knowledge (Matt 16:17; 1 Cor 2:14). The regeneration of one's existence, and, with it, alienated reason, only comes by the mysterious and miraculous operation of the Holy Spirit. Regenerated reason can then believe the Word, which reveals truth like the fact that man is *simul justus et peccator*—at one and the same time righteous and a sinner—which is beyond rebellious reason's ability to grasp; indeed, which it finds offensive. Thielicke clarifies the situation: "The triumph over *faith-crisis* is achieved because the autonomy of reason is broken and the antinomy which it produced in the idolatrous image of God is overcome. The resolution of the antinomy, and the defeat of the *faith-crisis* which it causes, is not then an epistemological phenomenon; rather, it is an existential event."[207]

In this regeneration, reason no longer controls the relation between God and the person. God himself now determines who he will be for humanity, the God of love and forgiveness who draws near in the Crucified. This is scandalous and foolishness for rebellious reason (1 Cor 1:23), for the God which it invents is the God of glory; yet, in the cross God executes his judgment against rebellious reason, *against* which regenerate reason is engaged in a constant struggle. It believes against the distortion. Whereas reason was formerly antithetical to and antagonistic toward faith, now it serves faith as an aid to reflection, and in the Anselmian tradition, assists "faith seeking understanding."[208] If this reflection "were left out," Thielicke claims, "Christ would be left standing at the gate of reason and would not be Lord of every area of life."[209]

---

206. Ibid., Moreover, as seen above with evidence, "reason damages faith by trying to ground it objectively in a sphere outside itself" (Ibid., 1:274).

207. Ibid., 2:55; translation mine, cf. *Evangelische Glaube*, 2:66.

208. *Evangelical Faith*, 1:97, 196–97, 270, 276–77, 280–82, 285–95; 2:95, 269. Van Til's presuppositionalism, explains Edgar, also finds "its distant roots . . . in the Anselmian soubriquet, 'faith seeking understanding'" (*Apologetics*, 3).

209. *Evangelical Faith*, 2:306.

Summary

Christ is the sovereign Lord of all, even all thought. Thus the task of apologetics is to "take every thought captive to obey Christ" (2 Cor 10:5), and this in view of the greatest commandment which requires one to love God with all one's mind (Matt 22:37). The challenge this presents to apologetics then, Thielicke stresses, is to seek "to include the doxology of reason within the doxology of faith."[210]

Conclusion

Thielicke's "Nevertheless" apologetic of the cross is constructed with a rigid counterdemonstrationism which mortifies the autonomous methodologies of sign-seeking and philosophy (1 Cor 1:22–23). This crucifixion to empiricism and rationalism (Gal 6:14) results in a *pure* presuppositionalism, Thielicke's "new way" to accomplish the apologetic task at a "theologically genuine level,"[211] that is, a method that serves the message itself.

---

210. Ibid., Luther thus includes reason in his famous defense at the Diet of Worms, "Unless I am convinced by the testimony of the Scriptures or by clear reasons . . . my conscience is captive to the Word of God" (*LW* 32:112, in Janz, "Whore or Handmaid," 49).

211. *God's World*, 217.

The Apologetic Method of Christ's Conversations

THIELICKE'S VENTURE TO REFORM apologetics aims to "take over the task of previous apologetics in a *new way*," that is, to reverse the "characteristic of [traditional] apologetics" which "proposes to give Christian answers to human questions."[1] For the direction is completely backward from that of Christian persuasion which rightly "attacks the world with *its* questions and forces it to face them."[2] This basic confusion regarding its task, which lends to a defensive rather than its offensive role, was only compounded in the apologetics of Thielicke's day. He complains that "its function consists in giving talks and answers. It has flooded the book stores with countless brochures which are all entitled 'Answer to . . . ' or 'Christianity and . . . Natural Science,' 'Christianity and . . . Myth of the 20th Century,' 'Christianity and . . . Anthroposophy,' etc."[3] Yet as important as such arguments are, in his view the "pathos of the 'answer'" is completely disastrous,[4] for it does not at all foster a neutral mode of thought as assumed. It allows, rather, an autonomous mindset to control the conversation, gives the initiative over to the unbeliever, who then can dictate the rules of engagement for the intellectual and spiritual battle waged in God-talk.

Thielicke, therefore, abandons what he disparages as "Question-and-Answer Game" apologetics to search for a new way of Christian persuasion,[5] which he discovers, or, more precisely, rediscovers, in the conversations of Christ. Christ's style is new in that, long forsaken by traditional apologetics, it is essentially extinct today. Thielicke reintroduces the way in an early theological work, indicated by the title, *Questions Christianity Addresses to*

---

1. *God's World*, 217; italics added.
2. Ibid.
3. *Fragen*, 3; translation mine. Edgar also agrees that "apologetics is not an encyclopedia of answers but a wise approach to the art of persuasion" ("Foreword," in Oliphint, *Covenantal Apologetics*, 20).
4. *Fragen*, 3; translation mine.
5. Ibid., 4; translation mine.

the Modern World.⁶ Here he surveys Christ's counterquestion style modeled in his conversations, which Thielicke approaches in view of its foreshadow in God's first conversation with fallen humanity:

> For factual reasons, the Bible virtually reverses the direction of the question. The first occurrence of the question between God and man, at any rate, is not: "God, where are you?"—so that man would possess the initiative of the question—rather it is reversed: "Man, where are you?"—and that is the question of God, which of its own initiative attacks men, and attacks so much that man must hide himself and completely go over into defense.⁷

Apologetic Initiative

God's initiative in the first postlapsarian conversation with Adam is that which frames Thielicke's thought from his early theological work to the end of his career.⁸ For example, when introducing the apologetic goal of his systematic theology, Thielicke considers "how far Christian truth radically concerns and strikes man, or, more precisely, modern man."⁹ To discuss Christian persuasion in the space age, he therefore returns to God's initiative in the stone age dialogue with Adam:

> There is in fact a correlation between the questions man puts and the Christian answer, and conversely a correlation between the questions Christian truth puts to man and his need to put these questions to himself . . . (Note that the first correlation of question and answer in the Bible is God's question to Adam, not Adam's question to God [Genesis 3:9].)¹⁰

This theme of the divine initiative is a distinctive feature of Thielicke's apologetic, which Holger Speier captures to entitle his book on the subject,

---

6. Translation mine. Speier also sees Thielicke's approach reflected in the title (*Initiator*, 167n317).

7. *Fragen*, 4.

8. This includes references to its formulation in the counterquestions of Christ (*Waiting*, 161; *World Began*, 9, 19, 36, 167, 208; *Nihilism*, 103; *Silence*, 39; *Depths*, 14, 31, 53–56, 65–66, 89; *God's World*, 217; *Mount*, 59, 66, 192–93; *Conversations*, 3, 102; *Trouble*, 108; *Ethics*, 1:38, 99, 361; *Creed*, x; *Evangelical Faith*, 1:59, 89, 275, 342, 353; 2:31, 75–78, 96, 193, 271–72, 288, 3:312, 322, 348; *How Modern?* 17; *Death*, 119; *Believe*, 121; *Letters*, 59, 62, 100, 145; *Human*, 32, 101, 110; *Modern Thought*, 33, 454).

9. *Evangelical Faith*, 1:24.

10. Ibid., 1:24.

God as the Initiator of the Question.[11] To Thielicke, God's initiative in questioning humanity indicates that the apologist, as one speaking about God on his behalf, should likewise take the initiative in Christian conversation.[12] Instead of merely providing answers, one should ask questions that strike the hearer in the core of his or her being; probing questions that challenge the hearer's unbelief and disturb his or her existence in untruth. Questions are more appropriate for this task because they have a subversive quality that an answer does not possess. Unlike answers, which one can ignore, questions engage. In the postlapsarian encounter with our first father, God does not ask "Where are you?" because he is actually unaware of Adam's location.[13] Rather, God asks the question to draw him out of his hiding place and confront him. The question calls him to give an account for the transgression that he knows he has committed. The question forces him to face the truth, which he would otherwise suppress, that he is without excuse (Rom 1:18, 20). Yet, the same truth formulated in the answer "You are not here"—which man already knows—he could just continue to evade, but the question "Where are you?" exposes him. In short, the answer allows for escape. The question arrests.[14]

God takes the initiative to question humanity in conversations throughout redemptive history—and shall, Thielicke preaches, until "the graves open and the sun is darkened, and when God for the last time will cry, 'Adam, where are you?'"[15] The most relevant case to Thielicke's concern is Job, another example of *faith-crisis*, which he frequently puts forth.[16] In

---

11. Translation mine. Speier attends it in "Apologetics as the Initiative of God in the Person and Language of the Proclaimer" (*Initiator*, 113–23; translation mine) and "Apologetics as a Question to Secular Mankind" (ibid., 164–70; translation mine).

12. Van Til thinks similarly, although his view of God's initiative focuses on the doctrine of salvation broadly and not as narrowly on the initial post-Fall conversation: "The Reformed believer knows that he himself has been taken out of a world of misinterpretation and placed in the world of truth by the *initiative* of God. He has had his own interpretation challenged at every point and is ready now, in obedience to God, to challenge the thinking and acting of sinful man at every place" (*Common Grace*, 7, in Bahnsen, *Van Til's Apologetic*, 556; italics added; see Oliphint, *Covenantal Apologetics*, 41).

13. The reason for which God asks the question is "not that He was ignorant of his hiding-place, but to bring him to a confession of his sin" (Keil and Delitzsch, *Commentary*, 1:61).

14. *Depths*, 53. Hamilton suggests that "the Lord addresses a question rather than a command to the secluded man, for God 'must draw rather than drive the man out of hiding'" (*Genesis*, 1:192–93).

15. *World Began*, 19.

16. Thielicke sees Job's *faith-crisis* as the theological twin of Asaph's (Ps 73). Thus it is a narrative to which he is repeatedly drawn, even "one which makes me reach for Job

response to Job's "Where is God?" question, God does not provide a consoling answer, nor any answer at all for that matter. Instead, God reverses the direction of questioning and puts Job on trial, announcing His initiative in the interrogation from its start: "Who is this that darkens my counsel with words without knowledge? Brace yourself like a man; I will question you, and you shall answer me" (Job 38:2-3; NIV; see 40:7). Then God unrelentingly asks the man over fifty questions in the category of "Where are you?" until Job repents in dust and ashes (Job 42:7).[17] Space will not allow for a survey of the prophets to notice God's initiative in the conversations spoken through them, although a glance at Isaiah allows one to see God questioning the nations (Isa 1-39), then the coming Servant takes up the role as prosecutor: "But when I look, there is no one; among these there is no counselor who, when I ask, gives an answer . . . Behold my servant" (Isa 41:28; 42:1). This Servant, to become the Suffering Servant (Isa 52:13—53:12), is fulfilled in Christ Jesus (Acts 8:32-35). Thielicke can say that through Christ "God asks: 'Adam, where art thou?' (Gen. 3:9), 'Saul, Saul, why persecutest thou me?' (Acts 9:4), 'Whom seekest thou?' (John 18:4)."[18] Christ possesses the divine right to initiate the question. Thus returning to the former and first question addressed to humanity, Thielicke claims, "Jesus Christ too is calling to us, saying the same words. He too is searching for us behind the bushes and calling, 'Man—my brother and my sister—where are you?'"[19]

Christ's style of persuasion, as the initiator of the question, stands in stark contrast to the defensive, answer-giving mode of traditional apologetics. In view of renewing this method, Thielicke insists that the task of apologetics is "something which is always on the offensive and, far from giving ready-made answers to the doubtful questions of men, *turns the tables* by putting questions on its own account—aggressive, violent, radical questions—and striking straight to the hearts of men."[20]

---

again and again on ocean journeys" (*Diary*, 12). He also considers Job's *Anfechtung* in his dogmatic work (*Evangelical Faith*, 1:89, 229, 231, 380; 2:82, 238; 3:173-75, 400-401; *Modern Thought*, 35, 37).

17. Frame notes God's initiative in the conversation with Job (*Apologetics: Justification*, 175-76, 190) and devotes a chapter to "Apologetics as Offense" (189-206). He does not develop his system on the counterquestion initiative, however, and instead focuses on providing answers.

18. *Depths*, 54.

19. *World*, 167.

20. *Between*, 26; italics added. The apologist should never operate from a defensive position, Thielicke claims sarcastically, "as if faith were something that could be defended by us" (ibid., 26). This book originally appeared in resistance to Nazi tyranny (ibid., v). Its 1938 date shows Thielicke as an early reformer of apologetics in the twentieth century.

Turning the Tables

The paradigmatic model for this table-turning strategy is the "pastoral conversations of Christ" which Thielicke considers "the reversal of apologetics."[21] He explains in a vital text by that title—translated idiomatically as "turning the tables on apologetics"[22]—which polemically questions the theological legitimacy of traditional approaches. Veteran apologist Os Guinness proves the relevance of Thielicke's reform by coincidentally calling for a table-turning style modeled after Christ's conversations. He provides an invaluable contribution to the cause and emerges as a dialogue partner in his timely, *Fool's Talk: Recovering the Art of Christian Persuasion*, certainly to become a milestone on the road to developing an apologetic of the cross. From the first chapter, Guinness hosts a brilliant discussion of "turning the tables,"[23] and in a later chapter by that title he provides detailed analysis of "the broadly negative strategy of 'table turning'":

> This strategy turns on the fact that all arguments cut both ways. It therefore proceeds by taking people seriously in terms of what they say they believe and disbelieve, and then pushing them toward the consequences of their unbelief. The strategy assumes that if the Christian faith is true, their unbelief is not finally true, and they cannot fully be true to it. At some point the falseness shows through, and at that moment they will experience extreme cognitive dissonance, so that it is no longer in their best interest to continue to persist in believing what they believed until then. When they reach this point, they are facing up to their dilemma, and they will be open to rethinking their position in a profound way.[24]

This subversive style of persuasion, in which the apologist allows the conversation partner to be "hoist by his own petard,"[25] to use Guinness' words, is what Thielicke explains using similar imagery: "For the question as

---

21. *Fragen*, 5; translation mine ("Die seelsorgerlichen Gespräche Jesu. Die Umkehrung der Apologetik").

22. This is the preferred translation in context of the former "turns the tables" quote (*Between*, 26) where *umkehren*, the verb form of *Umkehrung*, is used (*Zwischen*, 52).

23. Guinness grabs the reader's attention with a colorful account of the controversial chauvinist, Norman Mailer, in order to show that "the *style* in which he communicated was closer to Jesus than many of us who are followers of Jesus," i.e., "*to people predisposed to reject what he had to say, he communicated in a way that made them see his point—despite themselves*" (*Fool's Talk*, 22).

24. Ibid., 109; see "Turning the Tables," 107–29.

25. Ibid., 23–25, 26.

posed is subtly formulated to make the person questioned hang himself."[26] Guinness also labels the style as "prophetic persuasion," and claims that "this approach was demonstrated most brilliantly of all by Jesus."[27] Here a significant apologist in the Van Tilian tradition recognizes the need to advance a Reformed method by following Christ and employing his model of conversation.[28] Indeed, as indicated in the subtitle of "*recovering* the art," Guinness reiterates Thielicke's point—the way in which Christ communicates his message with those predisposed to reject it has been lost. Christ's "model of Christian persuasion," Guinness argues, "revives a way of persuasion that was powerful in the Bible and persistent down the Christian centuries, but largely forgotten today."[29] The now forgotten approach is essentially foreign to traditional apologetics, as Thielicke complains; thus, Guinness aims to reintroduce the method and thereby joins the reformation of apologetics that Thielicke initiates in the early twentieth century.

Pushing the Anfechtung Antithesis

The convergence of Guinness' recovery of Christian persuasion with Thielicke's reformation of apologetics only serves to underscore the latter's cause. This comes to fore in Guinness' explanation of the negative function of table-turning, where he makes a subtle distinction between evangelism

---

26. *Believe*, 155.

27. Guinness, *Fool's Talk*, 26. He shows this was the strategy used by the Old Testament prophets and traces the approach through the confrontations of both Micaiah and the unnamed man of God with King Ahab (23–26), and Nathan with King David (153–55).

28. Guinness attended L'Abri, a community established by Francis A. Schaeffer, by whom he was profoundly influenced. As Schaeffer studied under Van Til (1936–37), Frame considers Guinness as one of "Van Til's grandchildren" (Frame, *Van Til*, 396). For the differences in these patriarchs of presuppositionalism, see Edgar, "Two Christian Warriors: Cornelius Van Til and Francis A. Schaeffer Compared," 57–80.

Frame notes Christ's table-turning method, "Jesus, after refuting several questions intended to entrap him, *turns* on his critics" (Frame, *Apologetics: Justification*, 189–90, 191; italics added), yet does not renew Jesus' negative strategy. Seeking to mediate between traditionalists and presuppositionalists, in characteristic charity, he revises Van Til's emphasis on negative argument (ibid., 83–85) and does not capitalize on the subversive quality of questions; see below. Frame's proof has, in his judgment, "the force of TAG [transcendental argument for God], though it is formulated in positive rather than negative form" (ibid., 96).

Bosserman sees that presuppositionalism is a table-turning approach. He claims that Van Til's "presuppositional argument *turns the question around*, and involves asking the unbeliever how he supposes himself able to *get out* from under the biblical interpretation of himself" (*Trinity and Vindication*, 95; first italics added).

29. Guinness, *Fool's Talk*, 26.

and apologetics. His intention is not to separate the two into neat categories, but to draw attention to their respective roles as he understands them, and this in order to showcase the need of a table-turning method. "Evangelism," he broadly defines, "is the sharing the good news" with those who know they need salvation.[30] On the other hand, "apologetics is pre-evangelism in that it addresses those who do not realize they are in a bad situation."[31] To expound, he quotes John Wesley's advice to young preachers: "Preach the Law until they are convicted, then preach Grace until they are converted."[32] Using this Reformational Law-Gospel dialectic, Guinness likens the role of apologetics to the Law and evangelism to the Gospel. The table-turning function of apologetics, then, is to fulfill the negative function of the Law. For people closed to the truth, the Law-like role of apologetics means "pushing them out toward the negative consequences of their own beliefs."[33] In Van Tilian style, Guinness tirelessly stresses the need of this role which "drives people . . . to the logic of their own bad choices."[34] Its function is "to push them toward the false faith that was bound to be falsified by reality."[35] So the apologist should "push people toward the logical consequences of their unbelief" and "push them gently but firmly toward the place where they can see the unwelcome logic of their position,"[36] or, in Thielicke's idiom, the apologist is to push the *Anfechtung* antithesis of faith. As seen in chapter 1, *faith-crisis* "becomes the opposite pole of the Gospel," an application of the Law, which "initiates the flight from God and to God" along "the boundary line of nihilism."[37] One is forced to face the terror and despair of nothingness on the dead-end road of a "complete absurdity which cannot be sustained any longer, which cannot be lived out."[38] The negative function of turning the tables, therefore, is to push the hearer to the unlivable point of *Anfechtung* because, as Luther states, "whoever has not yet reached the point of being nothing, of him God can make nothing."[39]

30. Ibid., 110.
31. Ibid.
32. Ibid.
33. Ibid., 115.
34. Ibid., 116.
35. Ibid., 117.
36. Ibid., 121, 126–27.
37. *Temptation*, 2328–29.
38. *Evangelical Faith*, 1:258. Guinness confirms, "*While no thoughts are unthinkable and no argument is unarguable, some thoughts can be thought but not lived*" (*Fool's Talk*, 114).
39. *Temptation*, 2329.

Counterquestion

Christ's table-turning approach causes Thielicke to make "the following observation: Where people on their own initiative put a question to Jesus . . . Jesus never answers directly. Usually, he even puts a counterquestion with the goal of engaging the opposing person in a conversation and correcting the first question in the conversation as originally put."[40] Here Thielicke draws attention to the vintage characteristic of Christ's style of conversation that influences the art of apologetics. Whenever Jesus is questioned, accused, attacked, or exposed to entrapment, He typically responds with a counterquestion.[41] Accused of breaking the Sabbath, Jesus counters: "Have you not read in the Law how on the Sabbath the priests in the temple profane the Sabbath and are guiltless?" (Matt 12:5). At Caesarea Philippi with his disciples, Christ questions the question of his identity: "But who do you say that I am?" (Mark 8:29). When some disciples quit following him during the Galilean crisis, Jesus presses the twelve with the question: "Do you want to go away as well?" (John 6:67). To the lawyer seeking to save face, Jesus counters: "Which of these three, do you think, proved to be a neighbor to the man who fell among the robbers?" (Luke 10:36). Christ's critics question whether one should pay taxes to Caesar trying to entrap him. Jesus demands a coin and counters: "Whose likeness and inscription is this?" (Matt 22:20). When questioned about his authority, Jesus turns the tables: "The baptism of John, from where did it come? From heaven or from man?" (Matt 21:25). Repeatedly in his earthly ministry, Christ responds to his questioners with counterquestions until they are silenced: "And no one was able to answer him a word, nor from that day did anyone dare to ask him any more questions" (Matt 22:46). So Thielicke summarizes, "God has asked the question—consequently man can only be silent."[42] Christ's table-turning style, Thielicke conceives, is not without theological rationale:

> Jesus reacts to them with counterquestions. This is an indication that he will not let himself be known on the level of human judgment. He will let himself be known only when people are ready to allow their previous views to be revised as they listen, to

---

40. *Fragen*, 5; translation mine.

41. Thielicke repeats, "The questions put to Jesus do not remain unaltered. They are amended by counter-questions" (*Evangelical Faith*, 1:353).

42. *Fragen*, 2; translation mine. Thielicke stresses that "Christ is actually the one who prompts the real questions, and that by no means does he accept as binding upon him the questions men put to him and then proceed to answer them" (*God's World*, 217).

experience a total surprise which throws all the hermeneutical presuppositions to the winds.[43]

Jesus refuses to be imprisoned within the presuppositions of unbelief. Nor will he forfeit the initiative in the conversation which would allow it to be controlled by hermeneutical criteria of autonomous humanity; therefore, he seldom gives a direct answer. For, Thielicke explains, "such an answer would stand under the control of a given and as yet unredeemed line of questioning. Since this would be the line of questioning of the 'old' existence, an answer within its framework could not bear appropriate witness to God. Hence instead of a direct answer we usually find a counter-question."[44] The counterquestion, he maintains, does not always have to be externally packaged as such, but instead may be put indirectly in Socratic fashion. Its purpose, though, is to always bring forth something, that is, to expose "the inappropriateness of the disposition of existence out of which the original question springs."[45]

Quality of Questions

Christ's counterquestion style stands in stark contrast to the "assertive style that is customary in [traditional] apologetics."[46] The answer-giving mode of historical apologetics makes assertions. The strategy is based on the mistaken notion of human nature which assumes that every unbeliever is open and interested in the message. For those whose hearts and minds are closed to the truth, however, Christ takes the initiative to question them, which, as seen from the Fall of the human race, is God's own way to challenge unbelief. Thielicke, therefore, returns to the original postlapsarian interrogation in order to highlight the quality of questions. "This is the question by which we are *arrested* and must suddenly stand still and look God in the eyes."[47] Questions arrest attention and expose sin. In other words, questions possess a subversive quality that assertions do not.

Guinness elaborates: "Statements can be subversive, especially if the information they carry is explosive. But in most cases, questions carry a

---

43. *Modern Thought*, 33. In the Gospels, Thielicke explains, "Christ is never the answer to a given question; he does not fit neatly into the intellectual framework of the one who puts the question. He himself is the one who puts the questions, calling the question itself in question" (*Evangelical Faith*, 2:288).
44. Ibid., 2:97.
45. Ibid.
46. *Modern Thought*, 454.
47. *Depths*, 53; italics added.

subversive power that statements cannot match, because a statement always has the quality of 'take it or leave it.'"[48] For those with no stake in the information asserted or awareness of its relevance to them, the statements are simply uninteresting. For example, the weather report forecasting severe tornados will be received differently by those in their path than by those far removed from their danger. For those unconcerned with the information, the assertion is simply irrelevant. By contrast, questions are powerful for two reasons according to Guinness:

> For one thing, they are indirect. Whereas it should be crystal clear what a statement is saying and where it is leading, a good question is not so obvious, and where it leads to is hidden. For another thing, questions are involving . . . It invites us, challenges us or intrigues us to get into it and follow it to see where it leads. In short, even a simple question can be a soft form of subversion.[49]

Answers assert. Questions subvert. So Thielicke holds forth the powerfully subversive quality of Christ's counterquestions. If one examines them in

> the conversations of Jesus, one will note that they always end in an *arrest*, in a sudden termination of the circular [evasive discussions]. Without exception they end in a '*Hic Rhodus, hic salta*' [Here you must leap or retreat]. They end at the steep escarpment of a message which cannot be avoided by any detour.[50]

Rich Young Ruler

Thielicke does not leave his students in the rarified and chilling atmosphere where much apologetic discussion breathes. Time and time again he offers Christ's conversation with the rich young ruler as the classic model of Christian persuasion (Mark 10:17–22).[51] The meeting is not a trap planned by the enemies of Christ to catch him in a contradiction and thus incriminate himself. Rather, the aristocrat's appearance, posture, and respect with which he addresses Jesus—not to mention the embarrassing scene that he causes—indicate to Thielicke that "a man doesn't decide to do something like that

---

48. Guinness, *Fool's Talk*, 162–63.
49. Ibid., 52.
50. *Creed*, x; first italics added.
51. *Fragen*, 5–6; *Depths*, 55–56; *Evangelical Faith*, 1:144; 2:92–97; *Believe*, 101–3; see Speier, *Initiator*, 100.

unless it is a matter of life and death."[52] The substance of the inquirer's question confirms his sincere earnestness. He asks, "Good Teacher, what must I do to inherit eternal life?" (Mark 10:17).

About this seeker one should first notice that, according to Thielicke, "the presuppositions of his conduct were wrong."[53] The ruler has deluded himself into thinking that eternal life can be *achieved*, in contrast to Jesus' teaching that it must be *received* as a gift of God in one's total helplessness (Mark 10:15). This fundamental flaw is molded by a mistaken assumption of God's nature and person. For the man does not take God radically, Thielicke explains, but just "'incidentally' as a kind of eleventh commandment alongside the familiar ten commandments" or "as an elixir of life that would shake him loose from the boredom of the wealthy and give him some inner excitement."[54] God is the means to an end, but not the end himself. It is clear that the ruler's "question as posed misses God altogether, or, better, that God stands apart from this line of questioning and transcends it."[55] Yet Jesus will not allow the conversation to be framed by a fallen mindset, so he takes control of the conversation with a counterquestion.

Technique for Apologetics

Before considering the content of Christ's question, it would behoove one to notice what the place of the counterquestion itself shows about Christian persuasion. Thielicke wants to show that, in contrast to traditional apologetics, Christ's approach does not play into an apologetic game which simply allows for a memorized repetition of the philosophical proofs indicating superior being, causation, or design, nor does Christ's style call for a rehearsal of astronomical data captured in DVD titles such as "Cosmic Evidences for Christ."[56] Rather, Christ addresses his hearer's specific question. He meets the rich young ruler where he is individually in his own existential context. Traditional apologetics misses this vital connection and has earned an intolerable reputation for always giving answers to questions which no one is asking, indeed, about which the hearer is unconcerned or even unaware. Instead a table-turning approach meets the hearer precisely where one is in the unbelief of one's particular situation in life. Whether one's question is about eternal life, morality, justice, the problem of evil, truth, or comedy, it

---

52. *Believe*, 104.
53. *Evangelical Faith*, 1:144.
54. Ibid., 2:93; *Believe*, 112.
55. *Evangelical Faith*, 2:92.
56. Reasons to Believe, http://shop.reasons.org/.

counters by asking for an account of the intelligibility of the presuppositions embedded in the God-question. There is thus no need for the apologist to answer with a "Well, let's back up to the . . . 'Big Bang' . . . or . . . 'reliability of the eyewitnesses'" assertion. The hearer's question about any fact in the universe is countered by asking for one's ultimate reference point that makes the interpretation of that fact intelligible.

Jesus addresses the unique question of a unique person. In this respect, he never has the exact same conversation twice. Thus, Christ's personalized counterquestion style questions whether a one-size-fits-all or cookie-cutter approach comports to Christian conversation.[57] This means that what apologetics desperately needs—as Thielicke claims from the beginning of his reformation—is not a better technique or technology, but a better theology. Of course, this is not to suggest that Jesus does not have a technique, for ultimately he does; but, his work is done in his way which is not modeled after the wisdom of the world (1 Cor 1:21). Rather his method serves his message.[58] His way is shaped by his Word: an apologetic of the cross that counterquestions the premises of unbelief.

Attack of Apologetics

Christ turns the tables on the rich young ruler's falsely put God-question by asking, "Why do you call me good? No one is good except God alone" (Mark 10:18). In this counterquestion, Christ steps over onto the man's own ground for the sake of persuasion. This ground is his conception of the "good" by which he addresses Jesus.[59] For the aristocrat's understanding of

---

57. Oliphint makes this point by appealing to Aristotle's *trivium* of persuasion, particularly the *pathos* of the audience, in order to determine whether it would be "wise or appropriate, therefore, simply to approach every situation with some kind of premade apologetic 'template'" (*Covenantal Apologetics*, 197). Guinness minimizes the criteria of classical rhetoric since "*Christian persuasion is a matter of cross talk, not of clever talk*" (*Fool's Talk*, 39).

58. Van Til states that "the method by which a Christian develops the content of his faith must not be denied by the method he uses to defend that content" (*Jerusalem and Athens*, 15).

59. In Christ's conversation with the Sadducees (Mark 12:18–27), he likewise argues on their own ground. They grossly mock the idea since they can find no reference to the resurrection of the dead in the Pentateuch. Thielicke claims that "Jesus meets them on the basis of the same canon. After dismissing their question and showing how absurd it is, he takes them to the Pentateuch . . . and shows them what the resurrection means" (*Evangelical Faith*, 3:404). Guinness sees Christ's style following that modeled by the prophets like Elijah, who "knew that pious calls to return to God would have fallen on deaf and divided ears. He had to mount the challenge on their grounds" (*Fool's Talk*, 117).

the good, Thielicke explains, is "a kind of ethical quantum along the lines of a principle of achievement" rather than as it is in God who is the source of goodness."[60] According to his idea of goodness, defined by ethical performance, he undoubtedly regards himself as a "good" man and indeed insists that he has been since adolescence. Yet he wants confirmation for the sake of assurance and therefore seeks to discover from another "good" man exactly what measure of goodness meets the standard for eternal life. For "the rich young man sees Jesus as some sort of *teacher* who has certain patent recipes at his disposal which can help the man out of his life's uncertainties."[61] Indeed, Thielicke continues, "Jesus is a sort of 'Dear Abby' for him."[62] But Jesus refuses to be lowered to the level on which good advice is offered and thus rejects the title "Good teacher."

Jesus steps over onto the ruler's own ground of goodness, Thielicke shows, and in characteristic style "*attacks* the world with *its* questions and forces it to face them."[63] On the opponent's ground is thus where, as seen above, the counterquestion "initiative *attacks* men, and *attacks* so much that man must hide himself and completely go over into defense."[64] Thielicke evokes the martial imagery of "attack" in order to underscore the offensive rather than defensive role of apologetics.[65] In the European context of a continent ravaged by centuries of sectarian violence, however, Thielicke should not be misunderstood by his use of this militant language. For the attack is not a physical onslaught against the man himself, assault on his personality, or polemical insults against his intelligence; rather, the attack is spiritual warfare against the idolatrous presuppositions of his question which originate from his existence in unbelief. To avoid any confusion, Thielicke gives

---

60. *Evangelical Faith*, 2:93.
61. *Believe*, 105.
62. Ibid.
63. *God's World*, 217; first italics added.
64. *Fragen*, 4; italics added. Guinness stresses that "in strong contrast to this insistence on God's *initiative*, our human role is always a humble, supportive and subservient part" (*Fool's Talk*, 59; italics added), which thought he coins in "God is his own best apologist" (ibid., 51, 142).
65. Van Til agrees with the aggressive task of apologetics which is to "*attack* him [the unbeliever] in his philosophy of fact, as well as on the question of the actuality of the facts themselves" (*Theology*, 242; italics added). This offensive task shapes Thielicke's entire theological enterprise: "The task of Christian *ethics* must consist exclusively in putting questions to the secular understanding of reality, in demanding responsibility from it, and in showing it to be a system by means of which man hopes to protect himself against the divine *attack*" (*Ethics*, 1:38; italics added).

a precise description of it: "The *attack* itself consists of one single sentence: 'One thing you yet lack for perfection; go and sell all that you have.'"[66]

With this demand, Jesus does not implement an unrealistic economic system for a new world order, nor does he introduce an extra-biblical commandment revealing that poverty merits eternal life.[67] This demand rather is a specific application of the Tenth Commandment for this particular individual in his own existential situation, for the man lives in utter self-deception and is totally blind to his idolatry and covetousness. He is convinced he has taken the God-question seriously. He has kept the commandments perfectly, he claims, while not even realizing that they are not limited to external behavior but apply to the emotion and intellect as well (Matt 5:21–28). Perhaps he has restrained himself from murdering investors who embezzle his money, but that would have hardly quenched his anger with them. Maybe he does not pay for the sexual services of an escort, but he has undoubtedly experienced lust.

So "with his demand for the selling of everything," Thielicke writes, "Jesus destroys as it were the way of the commandments or the ethical way. He does this again in a 'Socratic' manner, forcing upon the young man an experiment in thought."[68] The experiment forces him to decide whether eternal life and God are really unconditional for him. It asks whether this aching void in his life, which though troubling, is tolerable, or, in this search for meaning whether he is dealing *radically* with the question of ultimate destiny and existence. He must decide what it is that he cannot live without; his wealth, which provides his popularity and life-style, or eternal life and hence God himself. Jesus' thought experiment is not ineffectual, for, unable to deny himself, the rich young ruler's worldview is shattered as he is pushed toward the negative conclusion of his own belief and suddenly "comes to know himself as one who is questioned by God."[69] Thielicke shows, therefore, that Christ's conversation with the ruler rewinds to the initial postlapsarian encounter and the man's "question: 'Where is God?' is replaced by the counter-question, or rather the prior question: 'Adam, where art thou?'"[70]

---

66. *Believe*, 109; italics added.

67. In fact, "scribal legislation prohibited the giving away of all one's possessions precisely because it would reduce a man to poverty which is 'worse than all the plagues of Egypt'" (Lane, *Mark*, 367n46).

68. *Evangelical Faith*, 2:92.

69. Ibid., 2:97.

70. Ibid.

Attitude for Apologetics

The aggressive and threatening application of the Law in turning the tables requires a particular attitude upon the part of the apologist in order to prevent one from needlessly alienating his or her conversation partner. Thielicke again points to Christ and stresses that when he "thus leads the *attack* against the rich young man, we must watch it against the background of this *other* word: 'Jesus, looking at him loved him.'"[71] Christ's attack on the rich man's false presuppositions is an expression of his love for the aristocrat. Indeed, the Law of God itself reflects his love for defiant humanity, which Christ lovingly enacts in his counterquestion style. Love is the motivation and manner of a table-turning apologetic. Sadly, some Christians are known for anything but love when expressing their faith. To this concern, the task of apologetics itself appeals to a certain personality type drawn to debate and controversy, which introduces a potential hazard for Christian persuasion. A contentious apologist with an obnoxious attitude does more to discredit the cause of Christ than commend it, yet Christ's love for the rich young ruler adjusts the attitude for apologetics. His example challenges apologists to examine their own motives to determine why they are in the business, whether it is because they love others, or love to hear themselves; whether they are truly arguing for Christ, or whether they are satisfying a psychological need to argue.

Love is required for the art of Christian persuasion and encoded in its apostolic mandate. Peter writes to suffering Christians and exhorts them to be loving apologists in the face of their hostile antagonists: "Always being prepared to make a defense [apologia] to anyone who asks you for a reason for the hope that is in you; yet do it with gentleness and respect" (1 Pet 3:15). One exhibits a loving attitude by treating one's conversation partners gently and respectfully. Does Peter here recall when Christ called him to become a disciple and apologist? "Follow me, and I will make you become fishers of men" (Mark 1:17). It is men and women who are to be won and not arguments. As many have witnessed, a quarrelsome apologist can win an argument but lose his audience, but the offensive task of apologetics is not a call for the apologist to be personally offensive. There is no need for an apologetic courtroom to prosecute one's hearer nor an apologetic backroom to interrogate via enhanced techniques. The enactment of the Law in the counterquestion is threatening in and of itself, which calls the apologist to be all the more loving and authentic in order to win his or her hearer. This is

---

71. *Believe*, 109; first italics added.

the reason why Thielicke insists that, as seen in chapter 2, for persuasion to be effectual, the apologist must display an attitude of *Anfechtung*:

> Consequently the dialogue with those outside can be carried on only if it has first taken place within myself as a monologue, that is to say, as a dialogue of the spiritual man within me with the natural man within me. And to that extent this dialogue is carried on, not in certainty and security, but in *Anfechtung*, in faith assailed and tempted by doubt and despair.[72]

A humble and vulnerable *faith-crisis* attitude allows the apologist to build solidarity with one's hearer, which contributed to Thielicke's own success in persuasion. This approach was confirmed, he recalls, "when neopagans told me that I had understood them and sometimes asked me if I was one of them."[73]

One must emphasize, however, a loving attitude upon the part of the apologist does not imply a weak apologetic. Thielicke wants us to see that in Christ's conversation with the rich ruler, "Jesus can also be hard, that he gives us opposition; and that he is not at all like the feminine, coiffeured male fitted out with a halo that popular Christian art has made him."[74] Precisely because Christ loves the ruler he therefore applies the Law to the man in the form of a counterquestion, steps over onto his ground in order to attack his unbelief, and obliterates his epistemological paradigm:

> In this manner Jesus handles people with their questions. Before they know it, they themselves are the ones being questioned. Their question about God and his kingdom bounces back at them with incredible force. They believe that they can enter the God-zone out of their own interest and according to the spiritual or pious mood. By doing it, however, they enter into an electrical force field, and the shock of God touches them. So it really is: It is not the world that questions God, rather God questions the world.[75]

---

72. *God's World*, 218.

73. *Notes*, 79.

74. *Believe*, 109. Van Til agrees that apologetics should be "mild in manner, strong in matter" (Oliphint, *Covenantal*, 260).

75. *Fragen*, 6; translation mine. Guinness describes the effect of the table-turning style: "As the speaker asks a question, unfolds a story or plays out a drama, an *expectation* suddenly builds up in one direction until, suddenly—through the wham of the punch line—an effect is brought about in an entirely different direction. The method acts like a spring-loaded trap that promises cheese but delivers a *coup de grace* to the unsuspecting mouse. The sudden switch between the expectation and effect triggers a complete revolution in seeing that both *reverses* the original way of understanding and

Outcome of Apologetics

After Christ's conversation with the rich young ruler, "he went away sorrowful, for he had great possessions" (Mark 10:22). The man rejects Christ, and walks away. His reaction is puzzling and has generated considerable speculation regarding the aristocrat's final destiny. Special attention is given to the kind or degree of Christ's love for the young ruler. The Greek verb is a conjugation of ἀγαπάω, which when used in reference to God can describe his covenantal love reserved for those whom he predestines, justifies, and adopts as children (Rom 9:13). This term is seen in contrast to Φιλέω, the word usually employed to describe affection, which when used of God could refer to God's love for humankind in general.[76] If the verb choice does indicate the man's election, his response is all the more surprising since he refuses to follow Christ. Here some commentators are tempted to spy into God's eternal decree in order to see whether the ruler stands among the redeemed. Though fully aware of their human inability to divine his destiny, they still fall prey to vain speculation, which often results in unfortunate discrimination against him.[77] Thielicke, however, will only hold out hope for Christ's conversation partner until his very end: "We don't know what happened to him after that. Did the One who saw him and loved him one day catch up with him? Was his leaving perhaps a last attempt at flight which he later gave up?"[78] Thielicke's wise pastoral practice provides encouraging guidance to any apologist in similarly bleak scenarios. In Christian persuasion, the apologist does not have to look for immediate conversion or worry oneself wondering whether one's conversation partner has been predestined according to the *secret* counsel of God. Instead one can focus on taking the

---

reveals an entirely new way of understanding. The effect of this revolution in thinking is a paradigm shift" (*Fool's Talk*, 42).

76. Lenski argues that Christ's "love is far beyond mere affection" indicating its highest purpose in the ruler's salvation (*Mark's Gospel*, 436). Hendriksen disagrees, "In the NT the verb ἀγαπάω is gradually pushing out the verb Φιλέω" so that in some cases "the two verbs are used interchangeably" (*Mark*, 395n475).

77. Here Calvin distinguishes between the "degrees" of God's love, e.g., fatherly love for his elect compared to the Creator's love for his human creatures. In the latter sense, he can explain that "God *loved* Aristides and Fabricius, and also *hated* them" (*Harmony Evangelist*, 2:399). Though he resists the temptation to place the ruler in this category, he finally conjectures "with probability, that his covetousness kept him back from making any proficiency" (ibid., 2:400).

78. *Believe*, 113. Lenski believes so: "He left Jesus, but the words of Jesus did not leave him. The fact that he was not changed on the instant need cause no surprise. The change would cause a struggle, and this might be severe and prolonged" (*Mark's Gospel*, 439).

initiative in the conversation and turning the tables on the premises of his or her unbelief and then leave the hearer in the hands of a loving God.

Summary

The conversations of Christ, according to Thielicke, turns the tables on apologetics as the task was known in his day. To this table-turning strategy he thus returns in order to renew the art of Christian persuasion and effectually advance the message of Christ:

> So we see how wrong the view of "apologetics" is, if it always understands itself only as the Answerer and not the Questioner. The Church of Jesus Christ, in the name of God, has much more to ask the world than it has to answer. The Christian faith is by no means a simple or straightforward answer to the life problems of religious people. Jesus does not respond, so to speak, rather he first of all poses the deepest questions. And this mode of the counterquestion approach should also preserve our message.[79]

What Thielicke says in this last statement is what we have seen from the introduction of this book. A supposedly neutral apologetic approach dis-integrates the message by segregating it from the method. For the reformation of Christian apologetics then, the art of persuasion must re-integrate the method with the message in order to be true to the message itself. In short, the Lord's Word must be advocated in the Lord's way.

Point of Contact

The table-turning conversations of Christ are utterly distinct because of the peerless person and sovereign agency of the God-Man. The finite limits of human knowledge cannot compare to his divinely penetrating insight. The limitation in human discernment compels the apologist to seek solidarity with his or her hearers and personally share *faith-crisis* existence with them. Then perhaps he or she can finally come to the moment of applying the counterquestion, which raises the difficult issue, where exactly are the tables turned? Or—as is often asked in apologetic discussion—what is the "point of contact"?

---

79. *Fragen*, 7; translation mine. Again Thielicke stresses, "Christianity is not, as we supposed, an answer to our questions, and is therefore not a direct answer to the question 'Where is God?' On the contrary, it is Christianity that asks the serious questions and therefore teaches us what true questioning is" (*Depths*, 55).

The concept of the point of contact is a controversial one that Thielicke would rather avoid. Indeed, he is resistant to the term itself and only uses it out of necessity: "'Point of contact' is a borderline concept, a figure of speech to help our understanding; we use it only in the way a school teacher uses chalk on the blackboard, to make a point and then to rub it out immediately what he has written."[80] Essentially, the issue is whether there is a neutral zone of knowledge about God and reality that is accessible to both unbeliever and believer over which they would both agree. Thielicke elaborates, "The question is whether and how far there are elements in our natural consciousness (or conscience) which make God's Word intelligible to us, which go to meet it, and which are thus the presupposition of possible appropriation of it."[81] The first issue is more narrowly apologetical, the second straightforwardly soteriological, and Thielicke deals with the two issues in tandem. The question of communicating knowledge of God apologetically is related to the fundamental question of how it is possible for humans to have knowledge of God at all. The "problem," as Thielicke refers to the "point of contact,"[82] gives rise to the historic controversy between Thomistic and Reformation theology about nature and grace.[83] In this context, Thielicke rejects the Roman Catholic conception of the point of contact in order to revise it according to Reformational theology.

In Thomism, the point of contact is expressed in the analogy of being. Thielicke explains, "Still lying dormant in the ground of the existence of the goodness of creation is a direct *point of contact* for revelation, on which it builds straightforward and unbroken . . . That is the secret of the *analogia entis* [analogy of being]."[84] The *analogia entis* is that which provides the point of contact for the Gospel. As seen in the evaluation of Logos apologetics, the analogy of being—rooted in Aristotelian metaphysics—is a method of predication that uses the creaturely language of our finite experience to

---

80. *Ethics*, 1:324; *Evangelical Faith*, 1:146.

81. *Evangelical Faith*, 1:139.

82. See "The Problem of the Point of Contact," *Theologie Anfechtung*, 35–49; translation mine.

83. The subject was re-popularized in the famous Barth-Brunner debate (*Natural Theology*). Thielicke is very sympathetic to Brunner's emphasis on "responsibility," upon the part of both the hearer and *apologist* (*Evangelical Faith*, 1:147–50: see Brunner, 31, 56–58). Speier is convinced that Thielicke pursues an apologetic goal similar to that of "Brunner's 'eristic' or 'missionary theology'" (*Initiator*, 230; translation mine).

84. *Theologie Anfechtung*, 39; translation mine. Spencer confirms the accuracy of Thielicke's view of the Roman Catholic doctrine. For in Thomistic metaphysics *being* is analogous—not equivocal—otherwise there would be "no point of contact between the infinite being ascribed to God and finite being ascribed to the creature" (*Analogy Faith*, 172).

explain how we can have any knowledge of the infinite Creator. Specifically, it is a continuum, or scale of being, that ascends from undifferentiated matter at the bottom to God at the top. For beings on the same level of the scale, knowledge is related univocally, or identically. Yet, with respect to God, this veers toward pantheism and is unthinkable because of the infinite distance between the Creator and creature. For beings at distant levels, knowledge is related equivocally. The direction toward which this veers is skepticism, meaning there could be no knowledge of God. True knowledge is accessible to beings on a closer level analogically. Thus, God is accessible in that the relationship between God's knowledge and God's being is proportional, or analogical, to the relationship between human knowledge and human being. In short, this means that the natural person can basically read reality correctly. The Fall of humanity only affected original righteousness and does not entirely corrupt the human will or reason. Human volitional and intellectual powers remain largely intact. In other words, the natural person's self-consciousness and understanding of the world is totally intelligible without reference to God. Believer and unbeliever both share the same view of reality. God's light is not necessary to see light (Ps 36:9). In redemption, the latter needs more information, not radical regeneration.

In the discussion of general revelation and human reason, as seen in chapter 4, the Apostle Paul presents a sharp contrast regarding how the unregenerate person sees and thinks about God and the world. His thinking is futile, and he suppresses the truth in unrighteousness (Rom 1:18, 21). His warped reason brainwashes belief and blinds him to the evidence of God in and around him; consequently, it is "at this point of the *analogia entis*, the direct line of contact," Thielicke emphasizes, "Reformation thought rises steeply and abruptly."[85] Thus he rejects the Thomistic point of contact and instead offers a Reformational version of the concept.[86] To illustrate his revi-

---

85. *Theologie Anfechtung*, 39; translation mine. Barth vehemently rejects "the *analogia entis* as the invention of Antichrist" (*CD* 1/1:xiii). Van Til also rejects "the main motif of Romanism, that of the *analogia entis*" (*Defense*, 187) and agrees that a Reformational apologetic "stands over against the *analogia entis* idea of Romanist theology" (ibid., 177).

86. The urgency of Thielicke's apologetic venture is underscored in that many Reformed theologians, amazingly, do not utilize a Reformational apologetic. For Hodge, the point of contact is unregenerate reason: "Reason must judge of the evidence by which a revelation is supported" since "faith without evidence is either irrational or impossible" (*Systematic Theology*, 1:53). Sproul et al find a point of contact in three "basic" and "nonnegotiable assumptions" which "are held by theists and nontheists alike" (*Classical Apologetics*, 72): The validity of the law of noncontradiction; the validity of the law of causality; and the basic reliability of sense perception.

Arminian evangelicalism holds a similar anthropology to that of Rome and thus a similar point of contact. As ultimately it is the individual person who decides in

sion, Thielicke evaluates the anthropological themes of consciousness of the moral law and the *imago Dei*.

Conscience

Not a few prominent apologists advocate appealing to the innate awareness of morality—embedded within the human conscience—as a point of contact in order to argue for the existence of God.[87] For, as the apostle clearly teaches, when the heathen who are unacquainted with the moral law of the Decalogue behave lawfully, it shows that *"the law is written on their hearts, while their conscience also bears witness, and their conflicting thoughts accuse or even excuse them"* (Rom 2:15). Since every human being is conscious of the Law of God, it follows that this moral God-consciousness provides the point of contact to which the apologist can appeal in Christian persuasion.

Thielicke believes that because of this innate awareness of moral law, "we cannot avoid the idea of a point of contact as a borderline concept."[88] So for didactic purposes he writes the idea on the chalkboard, entertains it for a while, and then erases it. Thielicke agrees "that if there is in us a point of contact for God's revelation it will be found in the waiting, questing, receptive conscience as described in the categorical imperative."[89] In mentioning the categorical imperative, Thielicke refers to Kant's famous moral philosophy from which he derives his proof for the existence of God. As Kant "had to deny knowledge in order to make room for faith" in his *Critique of Pure Reason*,[90] he returns to argue for the knowledge of God in his *Critique of Practical Reason*. In this he seeks to demonstrate that just as there are *a priori* categories of mind which assure scientific knowledge, so are there certain *a*

---

salvation, the point of contact is found in unaided human reason. For Van Til (*Apologetics*, 63n9, 100, 124, 143, 189n25) the historic representative of Arminian apologetics is Bishop Joseph Butler (1692–1752). His book, *Analogy of Religion*, is an attempt to show the analogy between nature and religion. The common ground approach was once the "most successful and popular work of apologetics for well over a century, and inspired a proliferation of apologetic works emphasizing inductive reasoning analogous to that used in science" (Boa and Bowman, *Faith Has Its Reasons*, 140).

87. Brunner believes that "what the natural man knows of God, of the law and his own dependence upon God . . . is the necessary, indispensable point of contact (32–33). Van Til is "assured of a point of contact in the very fact that man is made in the image of God and has impressed upon him the law of God" (*Apologetics*, 120). C. S. Lewis employs the sense of "ought" as a point of contact in his moral argument (*Mere Christianity*, 3–32).

88. *Ethics*, 1:330.

89. *Evangelical Faith*, 1:143.

90. Kant, *Pure Reason*, 117.

priori propositions which constitute the moral order or the sphere of value. From these Kant focuses on the categorical imperative, namely, "Act only on that maxim through which you can at the same time will that it should become a universal law."[91] Though a version of the Golden Rule (Matt 7:12), its "metaphysical basis" is "You ought therefore you can."[92]

Thielicke believes that Kant is trapped in "the illusion that if he ought he can."[93] For the "ought" of God's unconditional command—to love him with all your heart, soul, mind, and strength and to love your neighbor as yourself (Mk 12:28–31)—does not limit itself to the radius of ethical action, but rather questions "man himself in the very form of his existence, including his constitution and character."[94] Instead, as Thielicke provides correction, "I ought but I cannot."[95] The reason for which he cannot is because "I am what I am." That is, a human being can only amend one's behavior, not one's nature. The "I am" is what determines the "I will" and hence provides no hope for salvation based on performance. The "I will" cannot alter the "I am." Since, however, the "ought" demands that one ceases to be oneself, that one should transcend one's own existence, it seems nonsensical to the natural person, for action cannot be expected that is impossible in principal to achieve. As the contradiction does not harmonize with a person's self-understanding, he or she cannot at all regard it as a real demand or "ought," and thus dismisses it as illusion.[96] So one confuses reality with illusion and envisages oneself as the subject who commands, invents one's own norms, and defines one's own obligations and abilities.[97] Thielicke thus concludes, "The reality of man, e.g., his ethical reality, cannot be a systematic point of contact because it is a perverted and mythicized reality rather than the true one, because it is an illusion."[98]

Still Thielicke will not leave the matter, for he insists, the "point of contact" itself is "an improper term because it secretly suggests the 'how,'"

---

91. Ibid., *Practical Reason*, in Copleston, *History Philosophy*, 6:324.
92. *Evangelical Faith*, 1:141.
93. Ibid., 1:143.
94. Ibid., 1:142.
95. Ibid.
96. Dawkins locates the sense of morality in a lower Darwinian origin (*Delusion*, 209–26).
97. Van Til describes this emancipation using "higher thoughts" language so crucial to Thielicke, "When man fell, he . . . assumed that he was autonomous; he assumed that his consciousness was not revelational of God but only of himself . . . He would not think God's thoughts after him; he would instead think only his original thoughts" (*Apologetics*, 80).
98. *Evangelical Faith*, 1:144.

which cannot be objectified.[99] What Thielicke is describing here is what he means as regeneration, which occurs by "the great disrupting of the presupposed illusion of the 'You ought and therefore you can' which thus serves as a contact."[100] He explains that since the Law of God is addressed to the conscience of the natural man, this means that "man by nature, by innate conscience, already has knowledge of an 'ought,' of obligation, of, e.g., the categorical imperative (cf. Romans 2:14f.)."[101] When God summons a person, he makes contact with the pretended "ought" with its illusion "You ought, and therefore you can"—which Thielicke portrays as a "'collision' of revelation with our consciousness."[102] The conscience is disturbed by God's Law, not because it is aware of not having met, or having been able to meet its own standards, but because it fears that those criteria are illusory. This is illustrated in the question the rich young ruler puts to Jesus (Mark 10:17). His conscience was not merely plagued because he had not fulfilled the Law, for he imagined that he had. What disturbed his conscience was the haunting question whether the criteria for the Law's fulfillment, according to his own definition, were defective. This, then, is the secret dread of the natural conscience when confronted with God's demand: "If it acknowledges this demand—and of course it can refuse to do so—the presuppositions of its very existence are questioned."[103] It fears that the safety wall of the "You ought, and therefore you can," which it has erected against the attacking Law of God will be breached by its "You ought, but you cannot" which assaults man in his existence in untruth. For the manufactured "ought" with its illusion of autonomy—"You ought, and therefore you can"—is merely a refuge from the reality of theonomy—"You ought, but you cannot." In short, there is no neutrality with respect to the conscience's awareness of God.

99. Ibid., 1:146. This is because it is a "miracle of the Holy Spirit, which is why we can know nothing of 'how' this break takes place" (*Ethics*, 1:324–25). Thielicke's mention of "how" is in dialogue with Brunner regarding his concern that "a pastor might . . . go to heaven on account of the What but go to hell on account of the How" (Brunner, *Natural Theology*, 58). Brunner therefore believes that just because "there is a false apologetic way of making contact does not mean that there is not a right way" (ibid.). Though Thielicke resists the notion of objectifying "how" the Holy Spirit regenerates, he advocates "how" to persuade with respect to the human responsibility of the apologist; see below.

100. *Evangelical Faith*, 1:145.

101. Ibid., 1:144.

102. Ibid., 2:132. The imagery of "collision" is a favorite which Thielicke also employs to describe the *Anfechtung* conflict of reason and faith (ibid., 2:56; *Modern Thought*, 36). Van Til also expresses the point of contact in this manner: "If there is no head-on *collision* with the system of the natural man, there will be no point of contact with the sense of deity in the natural man" (*Apologetics*, 127; italics added).

103. *Evangelical Faith*, 1:144.

"Conscience," Thielicke states, "cannot be regarded simply as a neutral container for natural *and* divine law. On the contrary, conscience has always to be understood either as alarmed and on the defensive or as vanquished and comforted."[104] This means then that the "point of contact" in the presupposed "ought" is where people "suppress the truth" and exchange "the truth about God for a lie" (Rom 1:18, 25). Thus, the point of contact is really an attempt to break off all contact with God.[105]

Thielicke insists, therefore, "We cannot speak of a constant point of contact which may be located in the reality of the natural man and which forms a steady continuum."[106] He sees rather that contact is dialectical. "God makes contact with man at the point where man digs in against him, at the nerve of man's curving in upon himself. The contact is thus a new creation and a new birth, and as such it is a transcending of the actual point of contact."[107]

Imago Dei

The notion of appealing to the *imago Dei* as a point of contact in apologetic dialogue finds it biblical foundation at the beginning of human history, "Then God said, 'Let us make man in our image, after our likeness'" (Gen 1:26). Precisely what this divine likeness means almost escapes definition. A simple search shows that "many theories have been advanced to explain in what the *Imago* consists," such as human freewill, reason, the immortality of the soul, or the body itself.[108] Thielicke believes that the lack of explicit definition in the creation account indicates "that there is something ineffable about the *imago Dei*. It cannot be made the subject of concrete statements."[109] This is not the result of methodological or linguistic complications. Rather he suggests that the ineffability of the *imago Dei* is due to the very nature of the question itself, that is, the mystery of God which veils the image of God in man.

Despite its indescribability, Thielicke believes that the *imago Dei* merits theological treatment since its discussion has an important place in ethics,

---

104. *Ethics*, 1:329. Thielicke emphasizes that "this uncompromising either-or necessarily involves rejection of the view that conscience is a middle thing, a link between two stages, an empty and neutral vessel" (ibid., 1:330).

105. This is what Thielicke means by "The Impossibility of Conscience as a Point of Contact for the Law of God" (ibid., 1:321-31).

106. *Evangelical Faith*, 1:145.

107. Ibid., 1:146.

108. *Oxford Dictionary*, 692.

109. *Ethics*, 1:159.

for an attack on the *imago Dei* warrants the institution of capital punishment (Gen 9:6). To this end, he stresses the impossibility of providing an ontological definition of the *imago* in terms of such qualities as personality, freedom, dignity, conscience, and responsibility. In line with Luther, he states that "if these powers are the image of God, it will also follow that Satan was created according to the image of God, since he surely has these natural endowments, such as memory and a very superior intellect and a most determined will, to a far higher degree than we have them."[110] The *imago Dei* is not an ontological concept, but a covenantal one as Thielicke perceives it. The covenantal, that is, relational reference of the divine likeness is two dimensional. First, there is a vertical direction toward the Creator. Second, there is a horizontal direction toward the fellow creature.[111]

Thielicke glosses his favorite parable through which he views the Gospel, the Prodigal Son (Luke 15:11–24), to develop his idea of the *imago Dei* as a point of contact. He sees the prodigal's sonship, his biological relation to the father "as a symbol of man's divine likeness."[112] Instead of using the term "point of contact," however, Thielicke prefers to frame the discussion in terms of "identity." For the comparison between the *imago Dei* and the prodigal son is "that man as a son and partner stands in a position of privileged identity in his relation to God and all God's dealings with him have this presupposition as their point of contact."[113] The identity of the prodigal is persistent and not lost during his alienation. It has an indelible character and is therefore permanent, yet paradoxically, it is not fixed. In other words, the returning son can no longer appeal to this ontic quality.[114] Twice the prodigal confesses, "I am no longer worthy to be called your son" (Luke 15:19, 21). He is the son, and then again, he is not. In forfeiting his claim to sonship, he expresses, "I am no longer a son for thee." The father confirms the fact, "This my son was dead" (Luke 15:24). In other words, "He was dead for me." So on one hand, the prodigal's identity is not lost, and yet on the other hand, there is no discernible continuity is his identity. Arguably his self-alienation was so magnified that he would have been unrecognizable to his former neighbors. Thielicke asserts, "They could no

---

110. Ibid., 1:162; see *LW* 1:61.

111. For more, see *Ethics*, 1:147–70.

112. Ibid., 1:146–47.

113. Ibid., 1:147.

114. Thielicke employs the paradox of identity to express what Brunner intends with his distinction between the "formal" and "material" *imago Dei*. The former is "the concept of the human, i.e., that which distinguishes him from the rest of creation" (Brunner, *Natural Theology*, 23). The latter is *justitia originalis*, which is "completely lost" (ibid., 24).

longer 'identify' him."[115] So he is both son and not son. This paradox of identity is best exemplified by the paradox of Paul's "It is no longer I who live, but Christ who lives in me" (Gal 2:20), which can only be explained by the miracle of regeneration. "This miracle," Thielicke explains, "is not a creation out of nothing for it is performed on the old self that still keeps it identity. Yet there is no discernible continuity between the former 'living soul' and the present 'life-giving spirit.'"[116] Regeneration is not a creation *ex nihilo*, rather a creation *ex contrario*.

Thielicke realizes that the paradox of identity intended to express one's "responsibility and addressability . . . is obviously limited. It is dubiously ambivalent."[117] He would retain the ambivalence, however, in order to stress that the forgiven and restored son symbolizes a new creation regenerated by the non-demonstrable operation of the Holy Spirit. The *opera ad extra* of the Spirit, which works by the Word, cannot be charted on the grid of addressability. Rather, "God's Word creates its own hearer."[118] Yet in emphasizing this non-demonstrability, Thielicke would not want this statement to be taken "one-sidedly and nondialectically."[119] For as a preacher of the Word, who feels the task's "heavy burden of responsibility," he believes that "the aim of the sermon, after all, is to *create* something living and set it in motion."[120] An apostolic example of this dialectic of contact occurs at the riverside in Philippi when "the Lord opened her heart to respond to Paul's message" (Acts 16:14; NIV). According to God's "higher thoughts" (Isa 55:9), that is, his eternal plan, the Word creates its own hearer in the person of Lydia, but the Word creates its response through the means of an apologist engaging in Christian preaching and persuasion.[121]

---

115. Ibid., 1:151.

116. Ibid., 1:149.

117. *Evangelical Faith*, 1:150.

118. Ibid.

119. Ibid., 1:139. In stating that "God's Word creates its own hearer," Thielicke agrees here with Barth whom he believes Brunner takes "one-sidedly and nondialectically" (see Brunner, *Natural Theology*, 48, 59).

120. *Notes*, 291.

121. Guinness believes that "the two words *preach* and *persuade*, and the two ideas behind them, are indissoluble—most prominently in the tireless work of St. Paul, who was an apologist everywhere he went. He preached and he persuaded" (*Fool's Talk*, 112).

Summary

In both his preaching and persuasion, Thielicke aims to touch the center of being affected by the conscience of his hearers.[122] "My goal," he reflects, "had to be above all to ensure that everyone could say afterwards (because he had been personally *touched in the center of his being*), 'I was the subject of this sermon, he meant me.'"[123] Thielicke appeals to that "something" which is below the radar of a person's consciousness, in the sense of deity that one seeks to suppress and deny (Rom 1:18, 25).[124] To reach this center of being requires that apologetics "*turns the tables* by putting questions on its own account—aggressive, violent, radical questions—and striking straight to the hearts of men."[125] Simultaneously though, this "contact"—in contrast to the Thomistic analogy of being—is a divine miracle which "escapes all systematizing."[126] The actual point of contact, therefore, cannot be seen as a "neutral antenna" to receive transmission from heaven[127]—for otherwise man would not conspire to sabotage it.[128]

---

122. Thielicke targets "that aspect of human nature that is common to *all* human beings, that *center of their being* in which—each in his own different way—human beings are moved by fear and hope, by their finitude, by ambition, desire, the search for meaning, by the burden of guilt and torment of *conscience*" (*Notes*, 292; second and third italics added). Van Til agrees that "a method of apologetics that meets the requirements of the hour" is that which "challenges the natural man in the very citadel of his being" (*Reformed Pastor*, 30–31, in Bahnsen, *Van Til's Apologetic*, 39n12).

123. *Notes*, 292; italics added.

124. Thielicke states that "we cannot ascribe to this 'something' any content, nor can we describe the manner in which it is changed" (*Ethics*, 1:330).

125. *Between*, 26; italics added. Van Til also employs combative imagery to describe the appeal (*Apologetics*, 120).

126. *Evangelical Faith*, 1:146.

127. Ibid. Using a similar analogy, Thielicke imagines a hedonist who wants to escape being plagued "with interruptions on the intercom called 'conscience'" (*Believe*, 15).

128. The Barth-Brunner debate over *Natural Theology* is contextualized by Calvin's position on the matter. He writes, "There is within the human mind, and indeed by natural instinct, an awareness of divinity" (*Institutes* 1.3.1:43). This term, *divinitatis sensum*, the reformer uses synonymously with the "seed of religion," states his editor, both of which "refer generally to a numinous awareness of God, and are closely related to conscience, which is a moral response to God" (Battles, in Calvin, *Institutes* 1.3.1:43n2). However, this innate knowledge of God is insufficient for salvation, since it is "either smothered or corrupted" (Calvin, *Institutes* 1.4.1:47). As a result, Calvin believes that "scarcely one man in a hundred is met with who fosters it [the seed of religion], once received, in his heart, and none in whom it ripens" (ibid.).

The New Apologetic

Thielicke never writes a book on apologetics; rather, the art of persuasion is part and parcel of his entire theological enterprise. For Thielicke, theology is apologetics and apologetics is theology. Preaching is persuasion and persuasion is preaching.[129] His *Anfechtung* apologetic of the cross is that which turns the tables on unbelief, in enactment of the Law, following Christ's initiative to counterquestion the world with its questions. At the end of his career, however, toward the back of *Modern Faith and Thought*—his textbook on modern theology and the last of his dogmatic work—Thielicke summarizes his approach in a *how* section on apologetics, that is, "how to conduct a relevant dialogue with those who contest Christian truth."[130] For it is one thing to observe the conversations of Christ, yet quite another to apply Christ's style to one's own conversations. He thus models the table-turning method in the appropriately entitled text, "The End and New Beginning of Apologetics."[131] Here there is no virtual conversation with a straw-man. To the contrary, Thielicke attempts to persuade Ludwig Feuerbach (1804-1872).[132] The simple reason for the choice of this conversation partner is "because here we have the most radical questioning of Christian truth in intellectual history."[133] In his attack on Christianity, Feuerbach "shows us our own deepest *faith-crises*."[134]

Conversation with Ludwig Feuerbach

Feuerbach studied at Berlin under the greatest of the German Idealists, G. W. F. Hegel (1770-1831), but broke from his teacher's philosophy since he perceived it as "a fantastic Docetism, an undermining of reality."[135] What he seeks is a flesh and blood reality. Since even the act of thought itself is a product of physical matter, the brain, Feuerbach moves toward a materialistic dialectic and rejects speculative Idealism. Yet a more radical reason for

---

129. Van Til agrees on the apologetic task of preaching: "Preaching is confronted with the same dilemma as apologetic reasoning" (Van Til, *Defense*, 168).

130. *Modern Thought*, 451.

131. *Modern Thought*, 449-57.

132. The title of the text itself indicates that Thielicke's view of apologetics extends beyond the pulpit to include *personal* persuasion.

133. *Modern Thought*, 457. Speier believes that in "Thielicke's view the argument with Feuerbach's projection theory serves as a good example of how fundamentally important the following method is" (*Initiator*, 168; translation mine).

134. Ibid.; translation mine, 559.

135. Ibid., 444.

which he parts company is that "Hegel is the last of a long line of Christian apologists" defending Christianity against the atheism of modernity.[136] Feuerbach, "a pious atheist,"[137] complains that "Hegelian philosophy is the last place of refuge, the last rational prop of theology."[138] So in search for reality, Feuerbach decides to invert Hegel. "It suffices to put the predicate in place of the subject everywhere, *i.e., to turn speculative theology upside down*, and we arrive at the truth in its unconcealed, pure, manifest form."[139] Speculative theology is truth turned on its head which Feuerbach attempts then to set on its feet. Hegel posits the human subject as God in his self-alienation; therefore, Feuerbach inverts the idea, and—in religious service to humanity—suggests that God is the human subject in its self-alienation. "The true statement is this: man's knowledge of God is man's knowledge of himself, of his own nature."[140] This means that the concept of God is simply a projection of human self-consciousness. In the evolution of human consciousness, humanity projects its own being into the idea of God, attributes that it both possesses and those for which it wishes. This objectification of wishful thinking, that is, God, inversely expresses basic human desires for value and meaning. Heaven becomes therapy for humanity in its misery here on earth. Basically, the concept of God is a pipe-dream projection, indirectly expressing either human hope or fear. God is thus created in the image of man, instead of the reverse, and theology becomes anthropology.[141] The anthropological course that Feuerbach charts is immediately recognizable as that taken by Sigmund Freud and Karl Marx. In fact, the latter exalts Feuerbach's place in intellectual history by using a pun on the German meaning of his name. For anyone aspiring to become a serious thinker, "there is no other road to truth and freedom for you than through the 'brook of fire' (Feuerbach)."[142] The world remembers Feuerbach, according to Thielicke, as an "anti-theologian" who "posed the most consis-

---

136. Livingston, *Modern Christian Thought*, 1:222.

137. *Evangelical Faith*, 3:318.

138. Feuerbach, *Works*, 2:239, in Copleston, *History Philosophy*, 7:298.

139. Ibid., *Kleine Philosophische Schriften*, 56, in Livingston, *Modern Christian Thought*, 1:222.

140. Ibid., *Essence of Christianity*, 230, in Livingston, *Modern Christian Thought*, 1:222.

141. Feuerbach applies his psychogenetic method to Christian dogma to showcase how it indirectly expresses anthropological concerns, e.g., the resurrection reveals human desire for "personal immortality as a sensible, indubitable fact" (*Essence*, 135, in Livingston, *Modern Christian Thought*, 1:222).

142. Marx and Engels, *Historische-Kritische*, 1.1:175, in Livingston, *Modern Christian Thought*, 1:229.

tent antithesis to religion."[143] In other words, Feuerbach is a direct ancestor of the New Atheists.[144]

Thielicke responds to Feuerbach's radical attack upon Christianity by categorically rejecting any defensive and "frantic apologetic attempt to find in the sphere of religion *details* which cannot possibly be attributed to mere projection."[145] Even though Feuerbach's "*detailed* references from the Bible and church history might be contested at every point," Thielicke is convinced that a traditional "apologetic patchwork" fastened "on points of *detail*" does not lend to conversion,[146] for when considering the evidence for God in general revelation, the details are never viewed from a neutral no-man's land, as we saw in chapter 4. Common epistemological ground is a mirage. The evidence is always viewed through the eyes of belief or unbelief rendering a debate over the details completely ineffectual.[147] For those living in defiance of God, the details are simply denied.

To illustrate, Thielicke recalls an apologetic detail-debate during the rise of National Socialism in 1930s Germany, which raged around Alfred Rosenberg's *Myth of the Twentieth Century*. The Nazi work provoked "a host of apologetic reactions from the church" including exegetical, ecclesiastical, and historical proofs demonstrating Rosenberg's totally bogus scholarship.[148] Yet the widespread defensive drill "was astonishingly ineffectual," Thielicke remembers, for among the myth's supporters there "were no renegades or converts."[149] Indeed, because of the fervor over the Führer, the Nazi

---

143. *Modern Thought*, 454; *Evangelical Faith*, 3:318.

144. The "New Atheists," as *Wired* magazine has labeled them (Gary Wolf, "The Church of the Non-Believers," http://www.wired.com/wired/archive/14.11/atheism_pr.html/), are a group of scientists and philosophers who have recently launched a public *Bliztkrieg* against Christianity (and Islam). The "four horsemen" of the New Atheism are Dawkins, Hitchens, Daniel Dennett (*Darwin's Dangerous Idea*), and Sam Harris (*Letter to a Christian Nation*).

145. *Modern Thought*, 455; italics added.

146. Ibid., 451, 450; italics added. Such "foolish apologetics . . . focuses on *details* and tries to show that this or that, e.g., Christ's crucifixion, cannot be subsumed under the sum of all longings and is thus contrary to the theory of projection" (*Evangelical Faith*, 3:321; italics added). Van Til also maintains that a detail-debate is ineffectual. The apologist "may be quite proficient in warding off the attack as far as *details* are concerned, but he will forever have to be afraid of new attacks as long as he has never removed the foundation from the enemy's position" (*Theology*, 24; italics added).

147. Regarding the evidence for God, Thielicke claims that "the facts cannot be known by the old self; they are non-existent for its 'mind' and 'heart' (1 Corinthians 2:9)" (*Evangelical Faith*, 1:157).

148. *Modern Thought*, 450. Thielicke focuses on a paper published by the Diocese of Münster entitled "Studies in the Myth of the Twentieth Century" (translation mine).

149. Ibid., 450.

author could boast that what he advocated "in the myth would stand *even if its historical proof could be refuted at every point.*"¹⁵⁰ The reason for this is that the defiant who suppress the truth in unrighteousness and exchange the truth of God for a lie (Rom 1:18, 25) are not disturbed by details. In other words, details do not debunk unbelief.

Traditional apologetics cannot refute Feuerbach, but that does not signal the end of Christian persuasion. The "fiery-brook," rather, is a landmark on the theological map which divides the end of apologetics from its new beginning:

> Feuerbach has done us the unwitting service of radically challenging the traditional apologetics with its mixture of speculations and history. He has thus forced theologians to face the problem of how to conduct a relevant dialogue with those who contest Christian truth. He drives them out of subsidiary theaters, where there is only indecisive skirmishing, to the main front. One might say that he compels theology to abandon matters of *detailed* tactics for strategic considerations.¹⁵¹

To engage effectually with Feuerbach, apologists must abandon the tactical debates over details and initiate a strategic conversation which undermines his "central theme of anthropologizing."¹⁵²

Presuppositionalism

Since there is no neutrality with respect to God, Thielicke states that in conversation with Feuerbach and friends, he must pay "attention to their presuppositions."¹⁵³ As for Thielicke's viewpoint, he shares that "the reality of God as the one who addresses them is always presupposed."¹⁵⁴ Despite the *Anfechtung* contradiction between reality and God, Thielicke "Nevertheless" presupposes God in his methodology because "we are always in relation to God even if the relation is in a negative mode."¹⁵⁵ Since the human race is created in the *imago Dei*, the conversational partners are aware of the existence of God in the core of their being, even though they suppress the knowledge and argue against it. The task of apologetics is to challenge their unbiblical presuppositions and arrest unbelief so that they are without

150. Ibid.; italics added.
151. Ibid., 451; italics added.
152. Ibid., 450.
153. *Evangelical Faith*, 3:375.
154. *Modern Thought*, 456.
155. Ibid.

excuse (Rom 1:20). Thielicke assures, however, "long before we have disentangled . . . false presuppositions, he [Christ] is already present."[156] These statements show that Thielicke obviously accounts for "presuppositions" in his conversational method. For this reason, contemporary apologetic textbooks could categorize him as a presuppositionalist.[157]

Presuppositionalism is a distinct apologetic school that arose in the twentieth century. A helpful apologetics handbook that categorizes such schools explains that in

> Reformed circles, several closely related apologetic systems have been developed as alternative to both the classical and the evidentialist approaches. Most of these systems are known by the label *presuppositionalism*, although the term *Reformed* apologetics is more inclusive of the different systems.[158]

The assorted systems reflect the various personalities associated with the movement and their respective theologies.[159] Although as mentioned in the introduction of this book, Van Til is widely considered as "presuppositionalism's founding father," as described by another critic in yet a different apologetic textbook.[160] To this point, the name of the school seems to have received its name in reference to Van Til's method, which speaks rightly of presuppositions, although it was christened by a critic and not Van Til him-

---

156. *Believe*, 57.

157. Boa and Bowman label Thielicke indirectly as a fideist, one of the four schools of apologetics identified in their handbook. Though *fideism* is a pejorative term for irrational belief, they use the term to refer to a "'responsible' or 'rational' fideism" (*Faith Has Its Reasons*, 338). Their mention of Thielicke is in association with Donald G. Bloesch, a contemporary example of fideism, who places himself in a long tradition which ends with Thielicke. Bloesch states: "My position is much closer to fideism than to rationalism in that I see faith as determining reason and not vice versa. I stand in that tradition which includes Forsyth, Kierkegaard, Pascal, Edwards, Luther, Calvin, Irenaeus and also Paul the Apostle. Some Christian mystics (Bernard of Clairvaux and John of the Cross), as well as luminaries of neo-orthodoxy like Emil Brunner and Karl Barth, evangelical Calvinists such as Martyn Lloyd-Jones, and neo-Lutherans like *Helmut Thielicke*" (*Ground of Certainty*, 187; italics added; see Boa and Bowman, *Faith Has Its Reasons*, 361). Thielicke's association is distant, and the classification does not seem to account for his table-turning style. Nonetheless, he does possess some characteristics that Boa and Bowman associate with the fideistic school; see ch. 6. Thielicke would be satisfied with this classification anomaly since he took some pleasure in being hard to label (*Conversations*, xiv–xv; *Notes*, xvii).

158. Boa and Bowman, *Faith Has Its Reasons*, 221; original emphasis in bold.

159. E.g., Gordon H. Clark, E. J. Carnell, and Francis Schaeffer were all concerned with presuppositions in their apologetic strategies, all of which differ in significant ways.

160. Kelly James Clark, "A Reformed Epistemologist Response," 255.

self.[161] The label stuck and *presuppositionalism* became the name by which the school is most popularly known.

Nonetheless the term *presuppositionalism* might serve to invite misunderstanding of Thielicke's method,[162] for in addition to its various versions, the word *presupposition* conveys different meanings. According to Webster, to presuppose is "to suppose beforehand,"[163] yet the term can also convey primacy. In this sense, the prefix *pre* does not indicate temporality, but eminence, as in *pre*eminence. Van Tilians stress that their system is based this latter notion,[164] and Thielicke certainly employs the term accordingly, as defined in a lecture on *Weltanschauung*: "World views, every one of them, are based upon *faith*, that is, in this case upon a *presupposition which can no longer be proved*."[165] In this sense a presupposition is a first principle, or basic operating assumption about reality, that is not demonstrable. It is a conviction that must be believed. As such, a presupposition is a foundation for one's worldview, whatever that may be, of which one might not even be aware.[166] And herein lies Feuerbach's blind spot which Thielicke exposes in their conversation, where he incidentally employs the term in its temporal sense. Feuerbach "cannot investigate this [projectionism] because to do so would presuppose a prior investigation

---

161. Oliphint notes that J. Oliver Buswell Jr., criticizing Van Til in 1948, "was the first one to coin, in writing, the term 'presuppositionalism,' after it was suggested to him by Allan A. Macrae" (Van Til, *Defense*, 241n10). Van Til went with this designation and dropped his own description of *transcendental* after being accused of succumbing to Kantian philosophy (ibid., x).

162. Oliphint makes a "case for retiring the label *presuppositional* and adopting the label *covenantal*" (*Covenantal Apologetics*, 25). Since there are different meanings of the concept of presupposition, as well as multiple versions of presuppositionalism, he argues that the "label as an approach to apologetics needs once and for all to be laid to rest" (ibid., 39).

163. *Merriam-Webster's Collegiate Dictionary*, 984.

164. Frame, *Apologetics: Justification*, xxxii.

165. *God's World*, 36; second italics added. Bahnsen explains similarly, "It is because of a person's particular presuppositions . . . that he has the kind of worldview he does" (*Van Til's Apologetic*, 465). Although following Van Til, he believes that the Christian presupposition can be proven on rational grounds. Frame claims that Van Til never "defines the term. I define it for him as a 'basic heart-commitment'" (*Apologetics: Justification*, 9). Schaeffer differs and defines as "a belief or theory which is assumed before the next step in logic is developed" (*God Who Is There*, 201). In Schaeffer's sense, a presupposition is a hypothesis to be verified and not an unprovable personal commitment that is one's most basic assumption.

166. Thielicke also uses the term to refer to knowledge or notions in general, outside of God-talk. "With critical vigilance we can take our presuppositions into account, see in them a blind spot (and hence a necessity, not a hermeneutical virtue), and thus keep them under control" (*Modern Thought*, 33).

of this basis, i.e., of the basic state of the human."[167] Feuerbach's presupposition of the basic human situation fails him, which the reader shall see below. Nonetheless, in Thielicke's use of the term *presupposition*, he employs both senses of previous and predominant. His understanding of the word is of a supposition that is first and foremost.

Despite that Van Tilians define *presupposition* as the preeminent interpretive assumption of one's worldview, the term is commonly interpreted in its temporal sense, that is, of supposing beforehand, which has invited much confusion and caricature. William Lane Craig voices a popular objection: "Presuppositionalism is guilty of a logical howler: it commits the informal fallacy of *petitio principii*, or begging the question, for it advocates presupposing the truth of Christian theism in order to prove Christian theism."[168] When one assumes in the premise of an argument what one seeks to prove in the conclusion, the opponent is left begging to have the question repeated since it has been ignored or skipped.

But one wonders whether this criticism of Van Tilianism, which is not shy of proof and is outspoken in its claim to demonstrate God with absolute rational certainty, would apply to Thielicke's version of a *pure* presuppositionalism. If Thielicke never claims to demonstrate God, either by philosophical or evidential proof, is the question ever begged? Clearly, proof has no place in Thielicke's system since in his view it contradicts the biblical nature of faith. "We walk by faith, not by sight" (2 Cor 5:7). Christ reserves the severest condemnation for autonomous empiricism (Matt 12:39) and blesses non-verified belief (John 20:29). Thielicke is further convinced that proof undermines faith and makes it superfluous. It is a false prop that can only fail in *Anfechtung* when the proof in the illusional reality of "what the *senses see* and what *reason recognizes*" contradicts the reality of the hidden God.[169] From the beginning of his reformation, therefore, as seen in chapter 4, Thielicke turns from the characteristic of traditional apologetics which "seeks to *demonstrate* faith . . . and therefore confuses faith with sight and sets itself, not *under* the Word, but rather above it."[170] The proof-providing approach of traditional methods only serves to cater to the idolatrous epistemological standards of fallen humanity, inviting ironically the hearer to judge the truth claims of the Word by the supposedly higher authority of sense-experience and human reason.

167. *Evangelical Faith*, 3:324.

168. Craig, "A Classical Apologist's Response," 232. The Ligonier theologians sympathize, "Feasible as all the presuppositionalist answers sound, do they not beg all the questions?" (Sproul et al., *Classical Apologetics*, 188).

169. *Evangelical Faith*, 2:12; italics added.

170. *God's World*, 216.

In Thielicke's conversation with Feuerbach, he does not seek to prove God; rather, his strategy is to turn the tables on Feuerbach's autonomous presuppositions and confront his atheism. Moreover, the focus on presuppositions in the conversation addresses those of *Feuerbach's* "Where is God?" question, not Thielicke's "Nevertheless" presupposition. Thielicke's strategy is to expose his opponent's presuppositions and ask for an account of their intelligibility, not prove his own. If Feuerbach becomes open to God later, were he still alive, Thielicke would then dare him to take a venture of faith in order to discover whether Jesus exists and who he is, that is, to allow Jesus to prove himself (see chapter 6). Thielicke, however, does not intend to refute projectionism by demonstrating his own presupposition, for "such a refutation, i.e., the *proof* that revelation is not a human projection, would imply the possibility of a *proof* of God."[171] The idea of proving God—impossible for the free and hidden God who is not to be confused with the "god of the philosophers"—is anathema for Thielicke. Thielicke's plan is to disturb Feuerbach's projectionism by counterquestioning his God-question, but he refuses to offer proof to accomplish the task. To the contrary, he draws a line: "I am not prepared to go that far."[172] One thus wonders whether the charge of question-begging lodged against Van Til would apply to Thielicke.[173]

171. *Modern Thought*, 450; italics added. The closest Thielicke comes to acknowledging a proof is the mention of the "history of the impossibility" of modern theology to imprison Christ (ibid., 78). "In spite of his repeated imprisonment in systems, the Holy Spirit constantly raises up new theology to break the systems like earthen vessels. The fact that he does so 'almost' amounts to a proof of God" (ibid.).

172. Ibid., 455. Thielicke's strict counterdemonstrationism could be questioned by an early comment about Paul's argument in 1 Cor 15. The apostle "deals with the resurrection of Christ and with relentless logic faces the question: What would be our situation if Christ did not rise from the dead? Here again, as in Jean Paul's vision, we have a *demonstratio ex contrario*" (*Nihilism*, 131). Later Thielicke seems to tone down the demonstrationism of that statement. Comparing the similarity of Jean Paul's vision to the apostle's strategy, he states, "In this way the positive message of the existence of God is contrasted with its absurd opposite and its credibility is thereby strengthened" (*Evangelical Faith*, 2:425). Elsewhere he refers to Jean Paul's sermon as a "heuristic experiment" (ibid., 1:236), of which the "heuristic point is similar to that of Paul" (ibid.). If the latter statements do not serve to decrease the demonstrationism of the first, then Thielicke's prohibition of direct proof would not apply to an indirect demonstration from the contrary, and he is yet closer to Van Til's proof from the "impossibility of the contrary" (Van Til, *Epistemology*, 205). Nonetheless, for Thielicke, the heuristic purpose of pushing the *Anfechtung* antithesis, as a function of the Law, via an indirect argument from the contrary is categorically distinct from a direct demonstration from autonomous philosophy and evidence.

173. Another criticism of Van Til is that he is a skeptic who responds only with fideism. The charges are invited by difficult statements, e.g., "the only possible way for the Christian to reason with the non-believer is by way of presupposition. He must say to the unbeliever that unless he will accept the presuppositions and with them the

Though Thielicke is a pure presuppositionalist, he never once describes his method as presuppositionalism, for in the German academy, the concept of a presupposition is nothing novel at all, but is rather elementary theology and has been since Kant. Thielicke refers to the apologetic task simply as Christian "witness," "dialogue," "discussion," or "conversation," yet he emphasizes to any would be apologists that "we cannot be completely without presuppositions. We cannot jump over our own shadows."[174]

The Anfechtung Descent into Hell

Christ, in his conversations, meets his critics on their own ground in counterquestioning their false presuppositions.[175] Thielicke engages Feuerbach by following Christ, and meets the missionary of atheism on his own ground of anthropologizing, where arises the possibility of turning the tables.[176] In his "resolution to love others" Thielicke would seek solidarity, and to take "Feuerbach seriously," he states, "I would go so far as temporarily to take down my theological barricade, apparently go over to the enemy, and take a stand on the ground of the projection theory."[177] Since there is no common ground between the reality of God and Feuerbach's contesting of this reality, Thielicke must step over onto enemy territory for the sake of Christian persuasion.[178] This means that Thielicke must hypothetically suspend his belief

---

interpretation of Christianity, there is no coherence in human experience" (*Apologetics*, 197). Frame interprets Van Til in that "when the unbeliever presupposes God in this sense, he is not acknowledging God as his ultimate commitment. Van Til's point here is that in assuming the intelligibility of the world, the unbeliever implicitly concedes the existence of the God that he explicitly denies" (Frame, *Apologetics: Justification*, 9). Nonetheless, critics take statements of this kind to mean that one has to believe in God in order to know anything at all. Thus Gerstner chides that "the presuppositionalist should never get on an airplane with a non-Christian pilot" (Class notes, "Classical Apologetics," Winter 1995, New Geneva Theological Seminary, Colorado Springs, Colorado).

174. *Modern Thought*, 33.

175. Thielicke notices that Schleiermacher follows Christ's method. He "does not demand of his readers that in order to make contact with religion they should discard their presuppositions . . . He tells them instead to be true to themselves." The reason for this is because "he will meet them on *their own ground*." (ibid., 180; italics added).

176. Guinness agrees that "the wilder, the more skeptical or the more hostile the arguments against faith, the wiser and more effective it is to argue against them on their own grounds . . . the principle stands that either we must not argue with a man at all, or we must argue on his ground, and not our own" (*Fool's Talk*, 111).

177. *Modern Thought*, 452. Van Til uses almost identical language, "*we must meet our enemy on their ground*" (*Epistemology*, 205).

178. Critics of presuppositionalism object to it as circular reasoning. "In all systems

in God and assume Feuerbach's premise. "Let it be supposed that I have to accept it. I have to give up the transcendent basis of my faith thus far."[179] This does not mean that Thielicke literally renounces his belief in God. Rather he simply pretends that Feuerbach's position is correct in order to show that the argument, on its own ground, cannot be supported and implodes.[180] On Feuerbach's ground, then, as seen in chapter 2, Thielicke "descends into hell" with him, for, as Althaus teaches, one "cannot possess the heaven of community with God without repeatedly making the descent into hell which takes place when he doubts and even despairs."[181] Likewise Feuerbach must experience the hell of having his cherished worldview incinerated. In other words, Thielicke here pushes the *faith-crisis* antithesis of faith. "He must first be confronted with Nothingness. In theological terms, this means that he must *face* absolute temptation *(Anfechtung)*."[182] For Feuerbach, as one whose mind is closed to the reality of God, this is the only way that

---

of thought except presuppositionalism circular reasoning is considered demonstrative evidence of error. In presuppositionalism, instead of being a vicious circle, it is a sign of intellectual virtue" (Sproul et al., *Classical Apologetics*, 318). Yet the charge implies a misunderstanding of the method and to some extent epistemology. For every worldview uses its own criteria to prove its own conclusions and thus exists in a hermeneutical circle. The empiricist begins with sense-experience, evaluates the evidence in light of empirical standards, and draws a conclusion according to the bar of empiricism. The rationalist considers a philosophy according to the standards of human reason and judges it by human reason with no appeal to any other final authority, i.e., he or she reasons circularly. Thus Van Til contends that, reflective of Thielicke's table-turning style, "the charges made against this type of reasoning we must *turn* upon those who made them" (*Epistemology*, 201; italics added). In following, Oliphint responds cleverly to protestors, "On what basis should I accept your circle over mine?" (*Covenantal Apologetics*, 24).

With hermeneutics clarified, however, the charge of vicious circularity would not apply to Thielicke's (and Van Til's) method. For here he steps over the no-man's land of neutrality and engages Feuerbach on *enemy ground*. If one insists in charging with circular reasoning, then one can only say that Thielicke stands in Feuerbach's circle and reasons within its circularity, or, as Thielicke says, within his atheistic "presupposition that we start with self-enclosed immanence" (*Evangelical Faith*, 2:72).

179. *Modern Thought*, 452.

180. Van Til explains that "the Christian apologist must place himself upon the position of his opponent, assuming the correctness of his method merely for argument's sake (*Apologetics*, 129, see 7).

181. Althaus, *Theology Luther*, 33. Trueman confirms that "this is the logic of the theologian of the cross: God brings to heaven by casting to hell" (*Luther*, 133).

182. *Nihilism*, 168; first italics added. Van Til refers to this as removing "the iron mask" (*Apologetics*, 7). He maintains that Reformed apologetics "tears the mask off the sinner's face and compels him to look at himself and the world for what they really are" (ibid., 196). Schaeffer describes it as "taking the roof off" the shelter, under which people hide from the real world's avalanche of truth (*God Who Is There*, 140).

he will come to reconsider his unbelief. He will never relinquish his position until he faces its implosion. For this reason, as seen in Christ's table-turning method, Jesus "attacks the world with *its* questions and forces it to *face* them."[183] Feuerbach must be forced to face his questions. He must face the negative consequences of his unbelieving presuppositions. The false assumptions of his inverted reality must be pressed until he faces them subverted by true reality. Thielicke emphasizes that "no man will ever come to the truth and thus to a trustworthy bridge over the abyss of Nothingness who has not *faced* doubt, despair and shipwreck . . . In such cases theology speaks of temptation (*Anfechtung*)."[184] Only in *faith-crisis*, when facing the self-contradiction of his belief system and seeing its internal inconsistency, might he be open to rethinking his projectionism.[185]

Feuerbach must be forced to face a consistent atheism. As a "religious" atheist, he wants to live off the inherited capital of Western Christianity and enjoy such ideas as human autonomy, meaning, morality, and rationality,[186] but he cheats on his own worldview. He wants to laugh, but there is nothing at which to laugh. To live consistently with atheism, one must embrace its raw nihilism for what it is; deterministic, meaningless, valueless, and irrational. As we saw with Jean Paul in chapter 1, when facing the abyss of nothingness, he does not stop halfway but pushes the *Anfechtung* antithesis all the way to its logical conclusion, "Alas! If every soul be its own creator and father, why shall it not be its own destroying angel, too?"[187] As Thielicke discussed, "What Jean Paul intimates Nietzsche works out in all its logic. The mad self-creator must also master death. As deicide he must also be suicide."[188] The *Anfechtung* "descent into hell," which Thielicke initiates on

183. *God's World*, 217; second italics added.

184. *Nihilism*, 176; first italics added. Thus in Oliphint's fictional encounter with Dennett, he would attempt to make the latter face the doubt embedded in his own position (*Covenantal Apologetics*, 209n15, 217–20, 222).

185. Van Til's method is to "reason *from the impossibility of the contrary*. The contrary is impossible only if it is self-contradictory when operating on the basis of its own assumptions" (Van Til, *Epistemology*, 205).

186. The analogy of "squandered" or "borrowed capital" is a favorite of both Thielicke (*Waiting*, 23) and Van Til (*Theology*, 152–53).

187. Jean Paul, 198; see *Nihilism*, 130.

188. *Evangelical Faith*, 1:238. Thankfully not all atheists live consistently with atheism. For example, Thielicke indicates, the atheistic doctor does not face its annihilationism. Thus Thielicke turns the tables and asks "the further question: What is the purpose of health? or more precisely: What is the meaning of health in the whole context of being a man?" (*Nihilism*, 67–68). In other words, if the patient's life is meaningless and the doctor's work purposeless, what is the ultimate point of healing the person? Thielicke sharpens the question by quoting Mephistopheles in *Faust*, an epic about the poster boy of nihilism in German culture: "What good of us, this endlessly creating?—What is created then annihilating?" (*Nihilism*, 68; see Goethe, *Faust*, 2:270). Taken to the consistent conclusion of its own worldview, life reduces to absurdity.

Feuerbach's ground, evokes either the "Nevertheless" confession of faith or invites the Netherworld condemnation of absurdity.[189]

Inverting an Inversion

Thielicke asks sociologist Peter L. Berger to join his discussion with Feuerbach in order to help break the ice of a frigid conversation.[190] Guinness also draws Berger into the conversation in his book, *Fool's Talk*.[191] In the way of attempting to persuade Feuerbach, "Peter Berger counsels that the best way to counter such relativists is to 'relativize the relativizers,' and so *turn the tables* on them."[192] Thielicke then turns the tables by countering relativism since Feuerbach's "psychological approach is by nature relativizing."[193]

---

189. This mention of absurdity might initially seem inconsistent with Thielicke's criticism of traditional apologetics for its attempt in "condemning these anti-Christian ideologies and *reducing them to absurdity*" (*God's World*, 216; italics added). The context, however, shows that in this case Thielicke opposes the strategy because it "seeks to *demonstrate* the Christian faith" by placing the opposing ideology "in one common system of co-ordinates" (*God's World*, 216). Herein lies the issue. For the *reductio absurdum* cannot be pressed directly on *common* ground, as there is none, but indirectly on *enemy* ground. As noted above, this is Jesus' style in his conversation with the Sadducees (Mark 12:18–27). They deny the resurrection on the basis of the Pentateuch, so says Thielicke, "Jesus meets them on the basis of the same canon. After dismissing their question and showing how *absurd* it is, he takes them to the Pentateuch . . . and shows them what the resurrection means" (*Evangelical Faith*, 3:404; italics added). Thus Thielicke would press Feuerbach—as the poster boy of "the new form of atheism"—to the unwelcome "*absurdity* of nothingness" (*Evangelical Faith*, 1:232, 244; italics added).

190. *Evangelical Faith*, 3:323n54-55; 324n56; *Modern Thought*, 455–56. Thielicke notes, "For what follows I am especially indebted to P. L. Berger" (*Evangelical Faith*, 3:323n54; see Berger, *Rumor of Angels*). Van Til is critical of Berger for his claim to "proceed with 'methodological atheism'" (*Theology*, 150n36). Berger, in retrospect, recognizes that his theoretical work (*The Sacred Canopy*) "read like a treatise on atheism" (*Rumor*, ix). He regrets the possible effect upon readers and writes *Rumor of Angels* to counter the "value-free" sociological analysis of religion contained in the prior book (ibid., ix, x).

191. Indeed, Guinness dedicates the book to Berger. The sociologist is one of the most influential figures in Guinness' thinking (*Fool's Talk*, 37, 255) and he consults Berger continually (ibid., 71, 76, 78, 113–15, 134, 142, 149, 151–54, 166, 223, 227, 236).

192. Ibid., 113; italics added. When confronting relativism, instead of making assertions, Guinness believes that Berger shows "a better way through *turning the tables*" (ibid., 114; italics added), and Thielicke turns them. He will "not ask Feuerbach to simply to abandon his theory—at any rate as a first step. If he were still alive we should simply ask him to pursue his own anthropological theme in his own field of experimentation" (*Evangelical Faith*, 3:324). In other words, Thielicke would have Feuerbach push the *Anfechtung* antithesis to the end of his own theory. As Berger maintains, one must "see the relativity business through to its very end" (*Rumor*, 50). Van Til argues likewise that one "must seek to understand what the consequences are if one takes this position to the bitter end" (Van Til, *Epistemology*, 211). C. S. Lewis suggests similarly, in English fashion, to follow an idea through to the "absolutely ruddy end" (*Undeceptions*, 213, in Guinness, 118).

193. *Evangelical Faith*, 3:324.

Following Feuerbach, sociology, as the latest scientific disciple to challenge theology, dismisses religion by relativizing it as wish-fulfillment or psychological projection. Belief in God is explained away, or relativized, by historical-social analysis. "Of course, you are a Christian. You are an old, middle class, Republican." On the other hand, the relativist is decidedly a non-Christian. "I do not have the God-gene. I am a millennial. You do not get me." The relativism of the sociological approach relativizes the view of others but has no over-arching standard by which the legitimacy of its own views can be evaluated. Berger thus contends that "sociology is the dismal science par excellence of our time, an intrinsically debunking discipline that should be most congenial to nihilists, cynics," and others opposed to God.[194]

Yet Berger argues that the sociologist's sword cuts both ways, and he wields it to join arms with the theologian. When used against projection theory, he perceives that the view "may be inverted, and that in such an inversion lies a viable theological method in response to the challenge of sociology."[195] At this insight Berger enjoys a good laugh since it becomes "a gigantic joke on Feuerbach."[196] He tells it in a discussion of plausibility structures and other relativizing categories, in which he explains that relativism has a hidden double standard. Relativists relativize the past in terms of social-historical analysis, but the present weirdly escapes relativization. They relativize the biblical writers, but not their writings. They relativize the ideas of others, but not their own. In short, Thielicke states, "relativism relativizes everything except itself."[197] Relativism itself, however, cannot escape relativization, maintains Berger, and "that relativizing analysis, in being pushed to it final consequences, bends back upon itself. The relativizers are relativized, the debunkers are debunked—indeed, relativization itself is somehow liquidated."[198]

Thielicke thus relativizes the relativizers by applying to them the relativism that they apply to others. He sees exactly where to turn the tables. "If Feuerbach has stood his master Hegel on his head, might it not be a theological task to do the same to Feuerbach?"[199] He counterquestions Feuerbach's projectionism and asks "whether projection is not a reflection, a reaction to 'something' which . . . has established affinity between the divine and the human, and which, in biblical terms, has made us the divine

---

194. Berger, *Rumor*, 48.
195. Ibid., 57.
196. Ibid.
197. *Evangelical Faith*, 3:324.
198. Berger, *Rumor*, 52–53.
199. *Modern Thought*, 454.

image?"²⁰⁰ For it is possible that both projection and reflection may coexist, each from a particular point of view. What appears as human projection from the sociological or psychological angle may appear as a reflection of divine reality from the angle of faith.

Thielicke offers an analogy from mathematics to illustrate the point.²⁰¹ For mathematics, if anything at all, it is an intellectual exercise which appears to be a pure projection of the mind. A mathematician can live in a cave, totally isolated from the outside world, and construct mathematical universes which arise in his or her mind as pure products of human intellect. This is especially evident in the laws of planetary motion, which can pre-calculate the movement of the planets, only to have the telescope later confirm the calculations through empirical observation. The geometrical equations that a person projects out of one's own consciousness somehow correspond to a external mathematical reality, which indeed appears to be reflected in one's consciousness. This is so because nature is constructed mathematically, that is, the universe "is permeated by the logos."²⁰² Thielicke contends that "only because there is this analogy between the ontic logos outside and the noetic logos in me can it be true that mathematical projections are not imaginary but reflect an existing logical reality."²⁰³ There is thus an affinity between the structures of human consciousness and the structures of the external world. The mathematical intelligibility of the universe has, as it were, a beachhead in the human mind by means of which it can be reflected in a person.²⁰⁴ Projection and reflection coexist within the same over-all reality.

The illustration accounts for the epistemology of mainstream presuppositionalism. Thielicke adds, "The hermeneutical presupposition of all knowledge of the world is this analogy between the structure of thought and the structure of being."²⁰⁵ This analogy should not at all be confused with the analogy of being. Thielicke's notion of analogical knowledge is not found on common ground as in the *analogia entis*; rather, it is reflective

200. Ibid. Though Barth exposes the "apologetic helplessness" of the theology of Feuerbach's day (*Evangelical Faith*, 3:319), Thielicke does not feel that he "really advanced the debate with Feuerbach. He does not put what seems to me to be the right fundamental question that ought to be put" (ibid., 3:319n47).

201. Ibid.; see Berger, *Rumor*, 58.

202. Ibid., 455.

203. Ibid. Van Til confirms that "the relation of the human mind to objects of its knowledge is founded on the Logos of creation" (*Theology*, 129).

204. Van Til adds that "the laws of mathematics are but modes of the created universe. They are not, as theologians have all too often held, existences that are independent of God. Many theologians have followed Plato in thinking of the laws of mathematics as somehow existing from all eternity alongside of God" (*Theology*, 123).

205. *Evangelical Faith*, 3:323.

knowledge that people possess by virtue of their creation in the *imago Dei*. Human beings think analogically, that is, they think God's thoughts after him. "Might it not be," Thielicke counterquestions, "then that the idea of an alter ego is not a *production* of my own imagination but a *re-production*?"[206] The knowledge that God produces is what people re-produce.[207] For them to know that 3 is the square root of 9 is to re-know something of God's mind, although they will never know the proposition as deeply and meaningfully as God knows it. They can, however, be assured that it is still true knowledge even though it is not exhaustive knowledge. The significance of God's "higher thoughts" (Isa 55:9), seen in chapter 2, resurfaces here. People are to apply their thoughts to God's original thoughts and thus re-interpret his interpretation of reality. This happens whenever individuals know anything. Whether thinking of mathematics, macaroni, or myself, I am thinking God's thoughts after him.

The Fall of humanity introduces the epistemological problem with respect to the knowledge of God. "The *faith-crisis* arises, then," Thielicke states, "out of the fact that our thoughts are not content to be trusting and waiting thoughts but ascribe to themselves normative rank."[208] Fallen people want their thoughts to be normative and not derivative. Not content to be the re-interpreters of the God's interpretation, they choose instead to misinterpret reality and imagine themselves as the original knowers. Thielicke thus insists, "the analogy cannot replace the testimony of the Spirit. Analogies can be appreciated only when the light is kindled in which we see light."[209] To illustrate his point, Thielicke employs a favorite analogy of faith; stained-glass windows.[210] Many ancient sanctuaries have stained-glass windows which retell in pictures the mighty acts of God. The purpose of the windows—at least originally—is not to provide a decorative border for worship space, nor to generate a reverent atmosphere. They are intended to deliver a message. Seen from the outside of the church, however, the windows are lifeless and gray. They are mute and tell nothing. On the inside, however, the windows glow and begin to speak. Everything they have to say is pictured when a person wanders inattentively around outside the sanctuary, while it is not yet for him or her. He or she must be ushered inside, and so Thielicke does so for Feuerbach in their conversation. "The

206. *Modern Thought*, 454.

207. Van Til explains similarly, "All his [man's] knowledge is analogical of God. God is the original knower and man is the derivative re-knower" (*Theology*, 274).

208. *Evangelical Faith*, 2:52; translation mine, cf. *Evangelische Glaube*, 2:62.

209. *Evangelical Faith*, 1:370.

210. *Modern Thought*, 451; see *Meaning*, 53, 57; *Creed*, 218, 228; *Believe*, 201; *Evangelical Faith*, 1:370.

certainty of the reality of God and refutation of Feuerbach can arise only through authoritative proclamation in which the reality comes to light and the theory of projection itself becomes a figment. Only then do I go inside [the sanctuary], and the windows speak."[211]

Thus Thielicke proclaims and persuades, and persuades and proclaims. His attack on Feuerbach's projectionism is resumed the with continual counterquestions:

> Might it not be that the picture of God that supposedly arises by projection has its basis in the affinity of those who project to what is projected? Might it not be that the picture of God that seems to be a mere appearance to empiricists arises in fact as a reflection that God has impressed upon the psyche? How could we arrive at the idea of a heavenly alter ego were it not that we already bear the *imago Dei* within us, that we are created for God, and that there is by creation an affinity between him and us?[212]

The question is so simple and implies such a radical reversal of Feuerbach's theory that there is no need for a futile fight-fact or detail-debate over religious phenomena that somehow manifest themselves as non-projections. For, according to Thielicke, the question effects "the inverting of an inversion!" and undermines the theory in principle.[213] The origin of the alter ego now looks completely different. Yet Thielicke would have us see that he puts the last sentence "as a question not wishing to fall into the assertive style that is customary in apologetics."[214] For his goal is not to provide an answer to a Feuerbach's "Where is God?" question, rather counterquestion projection theory and thereby confront Feuerbach's anti-theism. Yet one could ask in the end whether there is really any difference, whether the answer is contained in the counterquestion, and whether the counterquestion is just an assertion smuggled in through the back door of a question mark. Far from it, Thielicke insists, for Feuerbach has here a choice which keeps open the possibility of offense. He must now choose between projection and reflection, and the counterquestion will not coerce him to go one way or the other. Indeed, herein lies the qualitative difference between an

---

211. *Modern Thought*, 451.

212. Ibid., 454. Thielicke counterquestions until the conversation arrives at Christ: "Might it not be that God has become man, that his word has become flesh, that he has been found in fashion as a man (Phil. 2:7)—and Feuerbach has conceived of the abstruse idea that his affinity between God and us, that the analogy of this condescension, is a reason to see in God a projected alter ego of ourselves?" (ibid.).

213. Ibid., 455.

214. Ibid., 454. He stresses again that this is put "as a question, not an answer" (ibid., 455).

answer and a question, modeled in Christ's own counterquestion style of subverting unbelief. The counterquestion draws Feuerbach out of hiding and unmasks projection theory for what it really is—an excuse for unbelief, without which he is now left (Rom 1:20).

Summary

Thielicke wants to show that "theologians who enter into dialogue with Feuerbach," in this counterquestion style, "may well come across a new transcendence."[215] There lies the issue. Thielicke rejects traditional apologetics because it is unable "to bear witness to transcendence."[216] The philosophical proofs and evidentialism cannot escape the cosmic nexus in order to point to the One in whom the cosmos is held together (Col 1:18). They do not give witness to the realm of reality beyond the immanent that invokes "a Nevertheless which is the basis of the presuppositions of life and thought,"[217] without which there is no standard for meaning and predication. Apologetics traffics in the transcendental.[218] What is

---

215. Ibid., 453.

216. *Evangelical Faith*, 2:68.

217. Ibid., 3:23. Van Til states similarly, "For me the *presupposition* of the possibility of theoretical *thought* and *experience* is the truth of Christ's words . . . " (*Jerusalem and Athens*, 97; italics added).

218. According to Bahnsen, Van Til's transcendental argument is influenced by Kant's epistemological project: "Kant's *particular* recommendation for doing this was philosophically (and religiously) abhorrent to Van Til . . . but the general kind of program (or approach to the proof of fundamental beliefs) that Kant recommended to improve upon rationalism and empiricism was convincing and effective, according to Van Til" (*Van Til's Apologetic*, 498–99). Kant's transcendental analysis investigates the preconditions for the intelligibility of human experience. He calls "all cognition *transcendental* that is occupied not so much with objects but rather with our mode of cognition of objects insofar as this is to be possible *a priori*" (Kant, *Pure Reason*, 149; see Bahnsen, *Van Til's Apologetic*, 499). Kant's concern is not so much with what one knows but *how* one knows what one knows. This type of analysis goes beyond the methods of rationalism and empiricism to find what they assume foremost. He thus maintains that the conclusion of a transcendental argument "has the special property that it first makes possible its ground of proof, namely experience, and must always be presupposed in this" (Kant, *Pure Reason*, 642; see Bahnsen, *Van Til's Apologetic*, 499). Van Til then adopts the method and maintains that his "truly transcendental argument takes any fact of experience which it wishes to investigate, and tries to determine what the presuppositions of such a fact must be, in order to make it what it is" (Van Til, *Epistemology*, 10). This presuppositional approach argues from the "impossibility of the contrary" (ibid., 205) or "possibility of predication" (ibid., *Theology*, 129), i.e., without God there is no basis for the intelligibility of anything: reason, ethics, communication, etc. For Van Til "the only 'proof' of the Christian position is that unless its truth is presupposed there is no possibility of 'proving' anything at all" (*Jerusalem and Athens*, 21).

thus needed is a new apologetic that provides the metaphysical ground to even presuppose the possibility of life experience and theoretical thought, that is, "something which is always on the offensive and, far from giving ready-made answers to the doubtful questions of men, *turns the tables* by putting questions on its own account—aggressive, violent, radical questions—and striking straight to the hearts of men."[219] By striking at the hearts of people, the apologist strikes at the *imago Dei* in the core of their being where the sense of divinity is suppressed, for it is here that the Holy Spirit performs the miracle of conversion. Thielicke's method thus simply focuses on the means by which and the region in which the Spirit does the work of regeneration. The apologist is left then to push the *Anfechtung* antithesis as a function of the Law and pray that the Spirit will use him or her to trigger an awareness of transcendence.

Conclusion

Thielicke's table-turning method attempts to follow the apologetic model of Christ's conversations. With that said, counterquestions do not create faith. Rather they disarm the attacker and arrest him or her cognitively. The person disbelieves whatever it was he or she believed before being counterquestioned, yet for the genuine seeker within whom the longing for transcendence (Eccl 3:14) has been stirred, something more is still needed for effectual Christian persuasion. Guinness agrees, "No one comes to believe in God because of *table turning* or through any purely negative arguments

---

Thielicke speaks of the impossibility of predication without a presuppositional "Nevertheless." In review of the "History of the Idea of the Death of God" (*Evangelical Faith*, 1:232–64), he believes this is where atheism implodes. Since God as a "system of reference is eliminated . . . the whole intellectual world is broken by atheism" (ibid., 1:237–38). Without God, there is no standard for the intelligibility of existence, e.g., meaning and truth, to Thielicke's concern. "Radically meaninglessness cannot be 'thought.' What is thinkable is only mere matter" (ibid., 1:245). So he pushes, "Are those who deny the death of God merely dissemblers when they see transcendence here, i.e., the prior awareness of meaning without which the absurdity of self-engulfing nothingness could not be perceived?" (ibid., 1:246). Even absurdity is unintelligible without an account of meaning which is grasped only in relation to a "Nevertheless," i.e., to transcendence itself. This notion, of course, is completely scandalous to empiricists and moronic to rationalists. Yet Thielicke pushes the apologetic offence of the cross by inverting Descartes' formula, "He is, therefore I think" (*Modern Thought*, 51)—a radical expression of the "Nevertheless which is the basis of the presuppositions of life and thought" (*Evangelical Faith*, 3:23).

The methods of each apologist mirror the other. The fundamental difference is the source, or model, for their methods. Van Til's is rooted in Kantian philosophy, and Thielicke's in Christ's conversations.

219. *Between*, 26; italics added.

... It has to be based on what is positive ... a positive encounter with Jesus himself."[220] To this end, Thielicke encourages his hearers to make a venture of faith, which positive strategy we shall now consider.

---

220. Guinness, *Fool's Talk*, 119; italics added. Guinness, following Berger, looks to trigger the "signals of transcendence," i.e., "phenomena that are to be found within the domain of our 'natural' reality but that appear to point beyond that reality" (ibid., 134; see Berger, *Rumor*, 65–66). These signals, which are pointers and not proofs, point to what would provide a religious interpretation of human experiences such as order, play, hope, judgment, and humor (Berger, *Rumor*, 65–94).

The Apologetic Venture of Faith

THIELICKE'S TABLE-TURNING METHOD ARRESTS unbelief and exposes the hidden presuppositions of the hearer's worldview, of which he or she is often unaware, yet the negative function of the Law-oriented strategy does not implant faith. For effectual Christian persuasion, the positive side of the Law-Gospel dialectic is still needed, which Thielicke describes by the term *venture*.[1] For instance, when dismissing empirical methods of traditional apologetics, he claims that "the impression made on the senses by seeing, however, touches only the periphery of our existence whereas faith *ventures* all and is a reaction of the center of existence, the heart."[2] In addition, spectators who remain removed from Christ "do not want to be committed to discipleship. They are evading the *venture* of faith,"[3] so Thielicke continues to thread the theme of venture through countless examples of preaching and persuasion.[4] In the conclusion to his modern theology, Thielicke predicts that "faith will always be a *venture*. As before, it will involve not a Because but a Nevertheless . . ."[5]

---

1. Van Til's method is also a twofold approach ("Two Step Procedure in Apologetics," Bahnsen, *Van Til's Apologetic*, 495–96) and could be translated into the biblical categories of "Law" and "Gospel." Edgar proceeds in that direction: "These are not meant to be sequential steps, but complementary moves. First, the apologist must get over onto the ground of the unbeliever for argument's sake and show him that his claims cannot succeed" (Van Til, *Apologetics*, 7). As seen above, this *Anfechtung* "descent into hell"—as Thielicke would call it—or pushing the *faith-crisis* antithesis, functions as the Law. "Second," Edgar continues, "the apologist should invite the unbeliever over onto Christian ground, for argument's sake, and show him how meaning and value are established by the biblical worldview . . . In so many ways, this means preaching the gospel" (ibid.).

2. *Evangelical Faith*, 2:36; italics added.

3. Ibid., 2:348–49; italics added.

4. *Between*, 56; *World Began*, 151; *Depths*, 84; *Life Again*, 21, 127, 173, 194; *Kerygma*, 143; *Creed*, xii, 6, 9, 13, 152, 171, 180, 244; *Human*, 21; *Evangelical Faith*, 1:230; 3:362; *Modern Thought*, 38, 511. See also references to the *venture* theme below parsed in the terms of *wager*, *as if*, and *leap*.

5. *Modern Thought*, 563; italics added.

The motif of faith as venture looms large in Thielicke.[6] Perhaps the best way to understand what he means by it is to consider the terms that he uses to gloss his own notion of venture: *wager* associated with Pascal, and *leap* associated with Søren Kierkegaard.

Pascal's Wager

Thielicke treats "The Wager" in an essay that introduces a vital collection of apologetic sermons, *How to Believe Again*.[7] As the title suggests, Thielicke addresses those already inquiring about Christianity. This becomes all the clearer in the first line, "In the following chapters I address myself principally to those of my contemporaries for whom 'God' is an *open* question." As chapter 5 showed, people who are closed to God require a different approach, an apologetic "which is always on the offensive and, far from giving ready-made answers to the doubtful questions of men, *turns the tables* by

---

6. In this regard, Thielicke can claim that faith is an *adventure*, which concept is captured in the title of yet another collection of apologetic sermons, *Faith: The Great Adventure*. Here he puts forth the idea "that we can speak of being a Christian—of setting out into the unknown under this leading and guidance—as an adventure" (*Adventure*, v). In contrast to the nihilist who must ultimately capitulate to mindless fate or chance in an act of *amor fati*, the believer can face the future calmly as "an adventurer of a higher order" who eagerly and expectantly looks "for the surprises God has in store for me" (*Creed*, 6; see 9, 244). Pless too confirms that "Thielicke understood life as an adventure" ("Helmut Thielicke [1908–1986]," 276).

7. "A Word to the Reader," *Believe*, 7–21. "The Wager" is a bold and favorite chapter in Pascal's *Pensées*. Ill health prevented him from finishing the work before a premature death, but the import of its scattered fragments should not be underestimated. The Westminster apologists believe, "Though unfinished, the *Pensées* have become one of the most significant works of apologetics, not only for the seventeenth century but for all time" (Edgar and Oliphint, *Christian Apologetics*, 2:175).

putting questions on its own account."[8] For hearers interested in the message of Christ,[9] Thielicke would persuade them to wager on God.[10]

Gamble on God

"The Wager" is about Pascal's apologetic conversation with an unbeliever, a prominent intellectual and secularist, but one who is not ready to close his mind to faith. Though yet unconvinced of the truth of Christianity, he is equally not convinced by the arguments of atheists, and therefore remains in a state of indecision. Holding the scientist in high regard, he thus approaches Pascal with the God-question. Thielicke imagines that "he thinks, 'This Pascal with his mathematically trained mind must certainly have reasons for believing in God. A man of his intellectual caliber is just incapable of doing things *without* reasons. If only he would share his arguments with me. I'll put myself in his hands.'"[11]

The man wants a rational proof for God. But Pascal denies the request since the hidden God cannot be rationally demonstrated. "If there is a God,

---

8. *Between*, 26; italics added.

9. For positive identification, one should notice Thielicke's description of such a person, a virtual partner photo-shopped from his countless conversations with skeptics and identified throughout his sermons. The man admits that he is like "Faust on Easter eve"—the poster boy of nihilism in German culture—who is just about to commit suicide and "flee into nothingness" (*Believe*, 9). He hears the good news of the God-Man, but "just lacks the faith" (ibid.). Yet he cannot escape the haunting question, "What if I am wrong?" Naturally he does not assume that belief in God would solve "all the riddles of my life and history" since he notices that his friends do not understand the "higher thoughts," yet he concedes that an "absolutely meaningless world without 'higher thoughts' is worse by far" (ibid.). Somewhat reluctantly, he confesses that he remains unconvinced by Camus who tries to wrest some life "theme" out of meaninglessness and sees it for what it is—the absurdity of a joyless existence (ibid.). Rather, he can only understand the words of Jean Paul's "dead Christ" who despairingly shouts into the void and begs chance to obliterate himself into atoms (ibid., 10). The skeptic would like to believe, although he questions whether he would be "giving in to cowardly illusion" and is simply "unable to bear the agony of meaninglessness, and therefore seeks to escape into the never-never land of empty consolation?" (ibid.). So open to faith, he approaches Thielicke to inquire about God (*Believe*, 7).

10. *Believe*, 7; italics added. Frame regrets that "one weakness in Van Til's own writings is the lack of specific arguments" (*Apologetics: Justification*, xxxii). As Van Til devoted most of his attention to developing his methodology, he did not leave many examples of persuasion. Bahnsen offers Van Til's short pamphlet, *Why I am a Christian*, as one of his most effectual models (*Van Til's Apologetic*, 120–43), although it strictly serves as an example of Van Til's negative approach.

11. *Believe*, 11.

He is infinitely incomprehensible."[12] The God in whom "we live and move and have our being" (Acts 17:28) dwells beyond this dimension of reality. He "has neither parts nor limits" that would allow him to be charted among the cosmic constellations.[13] Furthermore, the skeptic should not complain that Pascal does not attempt to provide any proof. "Who then will blame Christians for not being able to give a reason for their belief, since they profess a religion for which they cannot give a reason?"[14] God dwells beyond the limits of human reason; therefore, Christians do not proclaim rational proof (1 Cor 1:21–23). Indeed, for skeptics to ask Christians for proof is then to ask for something that would disprove the message of Christianity. "If they proved it they would not keep their word; it is in lacking proofs that they are not lacking in sense."[15] Although this might excuse Pascal for not offering proof for his message, the friend argues, it would not excuse himself for receiving it without proof. "Reason [however] can decide nothing here," Pascal reminds him.[16] Reason can neither prove God nor disprove him. Basically, the friend is left with a fundamental decision. Pascal then asks surprisingly, "What will you wager?"[17]

Thielicke explains the challenge this way:

> A choice of this sort is made in the form of a decision that is full of risk precisely because it cannot be calculated rationally. To that extent it is like a bet. When you go to a bookmaker to put money on a horse or a football team, you usually follow certain rational leads in determining which way to bet. You may have checked the previous record of the horse or the team; you coolly balance the estimated effect of training and present condition. Yet all of the leads still leave wide latitude for imponderables and unknown factors. No way of calculating can include all the variables. Therefore betting necessarily involves a risk. Instead of taking a rational step, I must do something totally different. I must make a leap.[18]

Pascal's hearer is stunned by this response. It is no more apparent to him than it is to anyone else that the most important decision of one's life is to be decided by a bet. So he resists the suggestion. If it follows that God

12. Pascal, *Pensées*, 233.
13. Ibid.
14. Ibid.
15. Ibid.
16. Ibid.
17. Ibid.
18. *Believe*, 12.

cannot be proven or disproven, he reasons, then "the true course is not to wager at all."[19] Such a course would seem prudent about most things. With respect to God, however, there is no way to reason one's way out of a decision. "Yes; but you must wager," Pascal explains, "It is not optional. You are embarked."[20] In other words, no decision is already a decision. To remain undecided for God is to decide against him.

Either God is or he is not. Since a person cannot help deciding one way or the other, he or she should consider what is in his or her best interest. What is at stake is "your reason and your will, your knowledge and your happiness."[21] Since a decision is inescapable, reason is not harmed in deciding one way rather than the other. What of one's happiness? "Let us weigh the gain and the loss in wagering that God is. Let us estimate these two chances. If you gain, you gain all; if you lose, you lose nothing."[22] What if I "perhaps wager too much," his friend questions.[23] That would be impossible, explains Pascal, even where there is an equal risk of gain and of loss given eternity and an infinity of chances. He does the math. "There is here an infinity of an infinitely happy life to gain, a chance of gain against a finite number of chances of loss, and what you stake is finite."[24] As gain soars to infinity, the finite, in comparison, reduces to null.

Pascal's friend is still not persuaded. He maintains that wagering for God would risk what is certain for what is uncertain. The risk of a finite good for a certain infinite good requires no thought. When it comes to abandoning a certain finite good for an uncertain infinite good, however, then the certainty of loss counters the possibility of gain. It would thus be better to preserve what one actually owns than to forsake it for the possibility of infinite good when one does not know that there is an infinite good to begin with. In reply, Pascal points to the common gambler. "Every player stakes a certainty to gain an uncertainty, and yet he stakes a finite certainty to gain a finite uncertainty, without transgressing against reason."[25] When there is then only the finite at stake to gain the infinite, with equal risk of loss and of gain, one would be imprudent not to gamble. The mathematical probability, then, would urge one to gamble that God is.

19. Pascal, *Pensées*, 233.
20. Ibid.
21. Ibid.
22. Ibid.
23. Ibid.
24. Ibid., 233.
25. Ibid.

Following Pascal, Thielicke thus continually challenges his audience to wager on God and call out, "I don't know who you are, Jesus of Nazareth, but you are different from all the rest of us. I will dare to hold to you."[26]

"As If"

Pascal is convinced that the "Wager" as a proposition is forceful, yet it cannot force conversion, for his friend remains in unbelief. "I am forced to wager, and am not free. I am not released, and am so made that I cannot believe."[27] It seems that the man can take his leave of Pascal, as the mathematician cannot persuade him of God. Above all, the skeptic would remind Pascal of his claim that God must give faith since people cannot muster it. "Faith is different from proof; the one is human, the other is a gift of God."[28]

The conversation has come to a dead-end. Still Pascal wants to lead his friend out. "Endeavor, then, to convince yourself, not by increase of proofs of God, but by the abatement of your passions."[29] The issue of belief and unbelief is far more than intellectual. It also involves the passions. Thielicke explains:

> The word "passions" in this context is used to express the passion of my own self-will—my self-fulfillment, the draining of all

---

26. *Believe*, 76; Thielicke repeats variations of this kind of challenge (*Believe*, 49, 80, 86, 89; *Waiting*, 61–62, 145; *God's World*, 130; *Life Again*, 214; *Sex*, 54; *Creed*, 38, 60, 94, 178).

27. Pascal, *Pensées*, 233.

28. Ibid., 248.

29. Ibid., 233. At this point in Thielicke's essay on Pascal's positive strategy, he cannot resist sidetracking to a table-turning approach in order to deal with his random *reader* who might not be open to God. So he informs of how Pascal deals with his contemporaries that are resistant to belief. "'I would soon have renounced pleasure,' they say, 'had I faith.' For my part I tell you, 'You would soon have faith, if you renounced pleasure'" (*Pensées*, 240; see *Believe*, 13). Thielicke pictures these people as "hedonists who seek the joy of self-fulfillment" (*Believe*, 13). In the midst of their hedonism, however, "there is only one disturbing element that detracts from their interrupted pleasure," i.e., a guilty conscience (ibid.). They consequently want assurance for their unbelief so that they might indulge in their sin undisturbed. They thus shrewdly ask Pascal for proof of God, while convinced that he will pass, which would then excuse their hedonism. "They want Pascal, the mathematical genius and philosophical sage, to turn state's evidence and prove that God is not a reality with whom one needs to deal" (ibid., 14). Pascal, however, sees through the mask and turns the tables against their unbelief. Thielicke narrates, "He *turns their guns back upon them and counterattacks*. 'You've miscalculated,' he informs them. 'It is just not possible to achieve some sort of objective clarity about the existence of God in peace and quiet, and then afterward to draw the practical consequences and change your way of life. It is precisely the other way around. First change your life; then you will discover God!'" (ibid., 15; italics added).

> delights to the dregs, the tasting of all the possibilities that mind and nature can present. Certainly not only the inferior enjoyments, but also the self-embodiment of man in his culture—including the sublimest unfolding of his inner being.[30]

To abate one's passion, then, in order to believe, does not mean that one endeavors to live an even-tempered, emotionally restrained life; rather, the passions are what drives one toward self-will in the quest for one's own undisturbed and autonomous ego. "In this sense," Thielicke continues, "it is not enough for me to stake my *passions* when I bet on God. I must stake myself."[31]

To show how this is done, Pascal points to other skeptics who once took the journey from unbelief to faith. "Follow the way by which they began; by acting *as if* they believed, taking the holy water, having masses said, etc. Even this will naturally make you believe, and deaden your acuteness."[32] Pascal's challenge rings a Roman Catholic note, but Thielicke believes that if the main point is grasped, the details can be overlooked. That is, act "as if" you are a believer, and eventually you will become one.

Here Thielicke modifies the Wager. Pascal has urged his friend to gamble on God since there is nothing for him to lose. "You will at last recognize that you have wagered for something certain and infinite, for which you have given nothing."[33] Thielicke indicates that "according to Pascal, however, these stakes do not involve a great risk. *Either* God wins the game, becoming a certainty to me and subduing my unbelief . . . *or* God loses."[34] Thielicke's modification means that

---

30. *Believe*, 17.

31. Ibid. In contrast to other Enlightenment thinkers, Pascal's method takes into account both the mind and heart. "The heart has its reasons, which reason does not know" (*Pensées*, 277). This does not betray any irrationalism, for here the heart is how one knows unprovable first principles, such as space, time, and the axioms of mathematics, on which reason operates. The heart is "a kind of intellectual instinct" (Copleston, *History Philosophy*, 4:165–66) which provides intuitive, immediate, direct apprehension of a truth which is beyond reason. One knows by "the heart," e.g., that conscious life is not a dream. Pascal employs the term *heart* in multiple ways, but in this context the concept is similar to the biblical use, which signifies the core of human existence directing thought and life (Matt 15:18–19).

Guinness is influenced by Pascal and states that *Fool's Talk* is "also about an 'advocacy of the heart,' an existential approach to sharing our faith that I believe is deeper and more faithful as well as more effective than the common approaches used by many" (18).

32. Pascal, *Pensées*, 233; italics added.

33. Ibid.

34. *Believe*, 17–18.

> I carry out an experiment with God. I act temporarily and tentatively "as if" God existed. To act as if God existed means that I "play" the role of a believer. I behave toward my neighbor "as if" the word of God about loving your neighbor as yourself was really in effect. I deal with my cares "as if" someone were there on whom I could cast them. I forgive my fellow man "as if" God forgave me and I had to hand on the gift I had received. I pray "as if" God were there to hear me.[35]

In Thielicke's "as if" experiment, one does not wait for a mystical revelation exclusively with respect to participating in Roman Catholic ritual, as in Pascal's gesture, and on that evidential basis profess one's willingness to live for God, rather Thielicke argues for the opposite. He expands the "as if" experiment comprehensively, beyond ritual, to include all of life lived *coram Deo* "as if" God were there. To that degree one is placing one's self-will in the balance, and thus one truly become the "stakes" in this game,[36] for one temporarily yields one's claim to them and puts them at the disposal of that Unknown which might possibly come out to be God.

Thielicke believes that in acting like this God will let one know that it was no bogus game or charade when one provisionally played the role of believer and acted "as if" God existed. He will give one the existential certainty that in this way one has not entered a game, but has entered into the truth. "For by this experimental behavior 'as if' he existed, including the necessity of putting my passions on the line, I have 'sought him with all my heart.' I have not tried to get him for nothing."[37] Thielicke's Lutheran view of the Gospel as promise is seen in the proof text for his Wager, for he would simply trust the promise that "You will seek me and find me, when you seek me with all your heart" (Jer 29:13). Those willing to go big or go broke in a high-stake game with God prove that they do not want to keep their lives for themselves. Thielicke argues that "God lets himself be found" by people like this, who put themselves in the balance. Such a radical statement is only intelligible in the context of his commitment to the doctrine of predestination, yet in putting one's life on the line, Thielicke states, "I have made the first move in the wager. Now it is God's turn. In the next moment I will see *if* he is and *who* he is."[38]

---

35. Ibid., 18.

36. Thielicke persuades, "This is a matter of all or nothing. This demands that a person put himself in the balance" (ibid., 166).

37. Ibid., 19.

38. Ibid.

Thielicke's "As If"

Thielicke's "as if" is an apologetic device to which he returns throughout his career. It appears not only in his essay on "The Wager" but is present in his first collection of sermons:

> So I challenge you to start with this working hypothesis—"as if" there were something to this Jesus and "as if" that invitation to come to the table of the King actually existed. And then in the name of this working hypothesis venture for once to be confident and joyful in everything that happens to you today and tomorrow because it is designed for you by a higher hand. Just talk to God—about your sin and that difficulty in your life which you cannot manage—"as if" he existed. Say a good word to that colleague who gets on your nerves or that person in your house who annoys you, but do it in his name and at his behest, "as if" he existed. Just make an experiment with this working hypothesis, Jesus, and see whether you are met with silence or whether he actually shows you that you can count on him.[39]

Thielicke also employs the "as if" device within his systematics. Theologizing about "The Method of Christological Thinking," Thielicke insists that the only proper christological approach incorporates the "as if" experiment:

> We begin with the man Jesus and his solidarity with us. We may put our imagination to work and vividly portray his joys and sorrows, his fulfillments and disappointments. We may read the Gospels *as if* they were biographies among others, taking seriously his solidarity with us and recognizing ourselves in him. Trying to understand him and to see how he touches and affects the questions in our own lives, we may treat him as someone like ourselves, as a man like you and me. Nevertheless, we are always open to the fact that this figure can suddenly transcend all analogies and confront us with the majesty of the Wholly Other. It is then that we know we have reached the real truth.[40]

---

39. *Waiting*, 192. The "as if" experiment is found elsewhere (*Waiting*, 146; *Nihilism*, 124; *God's World*, 119; *Believe*, 17–20, 91, 111–12, 206; *Letters*, 48, 94, 168–70; *Modern Thought*, 74, 75n29). The term "working hypothesis" does not reflect Thielicke's concept of *presupposition* which is instead defined by the "Nevertheless." Rather, as an atheistic buzzword coined by Laplace, Thielicke "baptizes" the phrase to connect with his audience, as noted in ch. 3.

40. *Evangelical Faith*, 2:271; translation mine for the "as if" sentence, cf. *Evangelische Glaube*, 2:333). Bromily provides "as though" for "eben *weil*" and disregards "unter andern." Crow agrees with my translation, cf. the similar passage: "We should concern ourselves now with the man Jesus. Let us compare him with others and read

Thielicke's "as if" venture is an attempt to draw his hearers into a situation in which they might encounter Christ, specifically, in his Word.

Concluding his analogy of the game, Thielicke concedes, "But isn't all that only a poor analogy after all. Are we really the initiators of the game and God merely the reactor?"[41] He insists otherwise. The analogy "is just another mental exercise which we write on the board only to erase again."[42] For God is far more than simply the master player. At this Thielicke pulls back the curtain behind the scenes of existence where the game of life is played in order to show that God is "already at work in me when I become ready to risk the game in the first place."[43]

Summary

As seen for Thielicke, Pascal's "Wager" is not a rational proof nor intended to function as a demonstration. To the contrary, Pascal maintains that human reason cannot prove God. He employs the positive strategy in a conversation with a skeptic open to the truth of Christianity, yet who remains uncommitted and indifferent.[44] So the mathematician reviews risk and chance,

---

his biography just *as if* he were only one among many" (*Letters*, 94; italics added); and "Read the gospels *as if* they were his biography" (ibid.,168; italics added).

41. *Believe*, 20.

42. Ibid.. The other is the "point of contact," as seen in ch. 5 (*Ethics*, 1:324; *Evangelical Faith*, 1:146).

43. Ibid., 21. Elsewhere Thielicke uses the analogy from the pulpit, "Learning the faith is so human that it can be presented in the form of a game. God will follow if only I am ready to open. We live on this promise. And if the game then goes further, I begin to notice that God was already at work while I was sitting down to make the first move. The Holy Spirit is always on the scene before my decisions. But if those who play and wager can count on God's cooperation and his carrying through the game to the end, what about those who are in dead earnest?" (*Creed*, 94).

44. Dawkins pokes fun at Pascal's Wager (*God Delusion*, 103–5) since some have tried to persuade him using it, although it is designed for only those open to God. As seen in ch. 5, those closed to faith like Dawkins and his New Atheist ancestor Feuerbach require a table-turning strategy. Dawkins mocks rightly "the ludicrous idea that believing is something you can *decide* to do," about which he parades his inability (ibid., 104). Yet Pascal never makes such a claim and states clearly that faith is a gift of God. Dawkins criticizes Pascal for "cowardly bet-hedging" which only results in "dishonestly faked belief" (ibid.), but Pascal challenges his conversation partner—who like Dawkins confesses his inability to believe—daringly to stake his own passions, i.e., himself, and act "as if" God existed in the earnest hope that God would freely bestow genuine faith in Christ. Dawkins also expresses confusion about which God to wager on, "Mightn't Pascal have been better off wagering on no god at all rather than on the wrong god?" (ibid.). Yet Pascal, as a committed Christian, is addressing a person inquiring specifically about Christianity. The Wager is not intended for those interested in comparative

that is, probability theory.[45] Then he challenges his hearer to gamble on God and practice ritual "as if" he existed. Thielicke expands the "as if" challenge to include all of life and thus urges his hearers boldly to stake themselves in faith and live *coram Deo* "as if" God were there. In other words, Thielicke's version of the Wager is an extremely clever way to confront the indecisive with the exhortation, "Repent and believe the gospel" (Mark 1:15).[46]

Kierkegaard's Leap

Thielicke's venture is influenced by another apologetic challenge akin to Pascal's "Wager," the leap of faith advocated by Søren Kierkegaard (1813–55). The Dane was the son of a wealthy merchant, whose inheritance allowed him to live independently as a free-lance writer, yet more than money was passed on to the heir, specifically, the father's melancholy. The patriarch had imagined that his moral lapses invited the curse of God upon his family, and the younger inherited the gloomy outlook. Thielicke believes that "the profound melancholy that overshadowed his life, and that had some psychopathic features, was a legacy from his father."[47] Kierkegaard thus did not live a normal life and excluded himself from the common order of society. He took neither position nor post and even broke off the engagement to his fiancée, whom he loved until death. He envisaged himself as a man with a mission that office and marriage would only hinder. Kierkegaard was to wage an apologetic war on two fronts: Hegel's Idealism in one theater and the dead state Church of Denmark in the other. The two problems were not unrelated in Kierkegaard's view, however. Hegelianism fed the spiritual sickness of Danish Christianity to imagine that the totality

---

religions since they are not prepared for it. Instead, Pascal would direct them to other kinds of evidence which distinguishes Christianity from its competitors, e.g., Islam, Judaism, paganism (*Pensées*, 589–641), so that they might become open to wager on the God of Abraham, Isaac, and Jacob, who is the Father of Jesus Christ. Hodge, however, reconsiders the Wager and argues for its value with assertive atheists such as Dawkins ("Pascal's Wager Today," 698–710).

45. Van Til rejects all arguments for Christianity based on probability since, in his view, they deny the objective certainty of God's revelation. In defense of Pascal, Frame notes correctly "that Pascal did not intend the Wager to influence people who think that Christianity is absurd or highly improbable. Rather, the Wager is for those who . . . agree that Christianity has a high probability of being true, but are unwilling to make a final commitment" (Frame, *History of Western Philosophy and Theology*, 228n20).

46. Boa and Bowman list Pascal as a forerunner of fideism in their apologetic handbook (*Faith Has Its Reasons*, 342–45). Though they do not apply the derogatory label to him, the mastermind mathematician could hardly be charged with any irrationalism.

47. *Modern Thought*, 491.

of religion was contained in true doctrine, and the sickness of the church weakened its witness to the sanctity of the existing individual over against Hegel's philosophy. Kierkegaard attacked both out of the melancholy and heartbreak of his own spiritual journey.

Apologetic Authorship

During his lifetime, the Dane was little known outside of his own country, yet in the twentieth century he became a powerful influence in Western philosophy and theology.[48] Like many complex thinkers, he is both often quoted and misunderstood. Thielicke argues that the hermeneutical key to Kierkegaard is in his complicated authorship, for he writes under various pseudonyms like Johannes de Silentio, Vigilius Haufniensis, and Johannes Climacus, to name but a few. The pen names, however, did not confuse the citizens of Copenhagen about the true identity of the writer. Yet his pseudonymous and indirect approach, as well as other features of Kierkegaard's style such as irony and the combination of alternative viewpoints, have resulted in divergent interpretations of his work.[49] Thielicke's understanding of Kierkegaard is taken directly from the writer's own description of his authorship. He operates as "God's spy" in a special service,[50] that is, to undermine "the monstrous illusion of Christendom, i.e., that all those who live in a particular country are Christians."[51]

In using different disguises, the undercover author is not trying to deceive the reader about his real self or escape responsibility for what is written pseudonymously. Instead, the various costumes serve to represent different lifestyles or existential stages. Kierkegaard states, "There are thus

---

48. Kierkegaard has a significant influence on Barth, Bultmann, and Brunner, the latter referring to him as "incomparably the greatest Apologist or 'eristic' thinker of the Christian faith within the sphere of Protestantism" (*Christian Doctrine of God*, 100; see *Natural Theology*, 50). Guinness lists Kierkegaard as one of the most creative persuaders of Christendom and laments that more attention has not been given him (*Fool's Talk*, 107, 178).

49. The philosopher Karl Jaspers, e.g., whom Thielicke debated on the subject while they both taught at Heidelberg, argues that Kierkegaard's Christianity is "merely a cipher for a general philosophy of existence" (*Modern Thought*, 512n63; see *Notes*, 100–102). In this vein, many Kierkegaardian themes reappear in the existentialism of atheists like Sartre and Camus. Another interpretation is that Kierkegaard evolved as a writer; "his successive publications mark the development of his thought from the aesthetic to the religious and soon to the definitely Christian point of view" (*Oxford Dictionary*, 779).

50. *Modern Thought*, 511; see Kierkegaard, *Point of View*, 87.

51. *Modern Thought*, 512; see Kierkegaard, *Point of View*, 22.

three spheres of existence: the aesthetic, the ethical, the religious."[52] Under the guise of each, he writes as himself, a Christian author. "He himself both is and is not these various writers," Thielicke explains.[53] For he writes indirectly, in a way that anticipates Thielicke's *Anfechtung* approach. In other words, Kierkegaard assumes the perspectives of his pseudonyms. He adopts their points of view and stands on their own ground.[54] So unlike his archenemy, Hegel, Kierkegaard does not write from an aloof vantage point of intellectual superiority which assumes it has an entire view of the world spirit; rather, Kierkegaard writes from the readers' chair and is prepared to "descend into hell" with them. He thus invites them to identify with the characters, like Abraham facing *faith-crisis* when called to sacrifice his son Isaac,[55] and challenges them to decide whether to accept or reject this association. In this aspect Kierkegaard's indirect approach previews Thielicke's own table-turning strategy. By donning the various masks, the latter argues that Kierkegaard

> is making a Socratic appeal to his readers, not with a view to maieutically releasing their own possibilities, but with a view to *questioning these, throwing doubt upon them*, for even as he ironically adopts an aesthetic or a Socratic position he is a religious author, and he understands these positions better than those who hold them.[56]

Kierkegaard's readers cannot think their way to being in truth (John 18:37). If, however, he were to push the *Anfechtung* antithesis—in its negative function as the Law—until they experience cognitive dissonance, then perhaps he can help them to think their way out of their former positions so as to become open to truth.

---

52. Kierkegaard, *Concluding Unscientific Postscript*, 448.

53. *Modern Thought*, 491. Perhaps for this reason, as Roberts notes, "Thielicke never does Kierkegaard the favor of citing his pseudonymous authors" as he had requested ("Helmut Thielicke," 322). For the most part, we shall follow Thielicke's practice in this analysis and use "Kierkegaard" as a reference for all the authors and ideas contained in the works under his name whether pseudonymous or not.

54. Kierkegaard explains that "if it is an illusion that all are Christians—and if there is anything to be done about it, it must be done indirectly, not by one who vociferously proclaims himself an extraordinary Christian, but by one who, better instructed is ready to declare that he is not a Christian at all . . . A direct attack only strengthens a person in his illusion, and at the same time embitters him" (*Point of View*, 24–25).

55. The term *Anfechtung* is found in parentheses (*Fear and Trembling*, 42, 65–67, 71, 79, 88–89, 91, 127, 267n47).

56. *Modern Thought*, 511; italics added.

In the end, Kierkegaard accomplishes his clandestine mission as an author. He takes off his masks and aborts his indirect approach. Thielicke believes he changes his style because "the communication of the Christian element must conclude with witness and hence with direct statement,"[57] that is, the positive side of the Law-Gospel antithesis. The Socratic method is useful in subverting cultural Christianity, but finally the covert author must declare his allegiance and become a direct witness of the Gospel. Kierkegaard is well aware of the cost of discipleship when he retires from his secret service as God's spy, abandons his pseudonyms, and publicly acknowledges his belief. He hears the disillusioned critics who question whether he perceives what he has lost in the eyes of the world. He admits:

> I lose the interesting distinction of being an enigma, seeing it is impossible to know whether this thorough-going defence of Christianity is not a covert attack most cunningly conceived. This interesting distinction I lose, and for it is substituted, at the farthest remove from the interesting, the *direct communication* that the problem was, and is, how to become a Christian.[58]

As an author, Kierkegaard dedicates himself from the beginning to the problems of religious existence, specifically to *how* one becomes a Christian in Christendom.[59]

True Christianity

Kierkegaard writes against Hegelianism, the reigning theology in Denmark, which posits the idea of the absolute spirit coming into being via the dialectic of thesis, antithesis, and synthesis. To engage Hegel, Kierkegaard meets him with a dialectic of his own, but unlike the former's rational dialectic, Kierkegaard's is existential. It is not concerned with the all-encompassing universal, but with the individual facing the possibilities of existence. The dialectic thus moves within the three existential spheres of the aesthetic, the ethical, and the religious. A simple explanation of the three stages is that

---

57. Ibid., 512.
58. Kierkegaard, *Point of View*, 93.
59. As seen in ch. 5, Thielicke is very interested in the *how*—though not to the point of attempting to objectify the work of the Holy Spirit. So he explains Kierkegaard, "Not *what* we think is essential, but *how*, the extent to which we are existentially involved, whether we are 'existing thinkers'" (*Modern Thought*, 492). The "existing thinker" accounts for subjectivity and thinks about existence as an actor rather than a disinterested spectator. In contrast, the "abstract thinker" focuses on timeless objectivity and attempts to conceive of existence without historical movement. Thielicke believes that the former concept is "the term which brings out Kierkegaard's singularity" (ibid., 495).

they function "very much like a Hegelian triad: the aesthetic as the thesis, the ethical as the antithesis, the religious as the synthesis."[60] Each new stage raises selfhood to a higher level of existence (*aufgehoben*), but the transition to the religious stage does not mean that the existential movement from the aesthetic to the religious is forever past. Instead, all three are continual possibilities, and the movement from one stage to the next does not occur by thinking as in Hegelianism, but by choice, an assertion of the will,[61] that is, a "leap."[62] Nonetheless, it is Kierkegaard's treatment of the religious sphere that influences the positive side of Thielicke's apologetic approach.

Infinite Passion of Inwardness

For the leap into the religious stage, a person needs infinite passion in order to distinguish between false and true religion. The former for Kierkegaard is the syncretic mixture of Christianity and Hegelianism of the Danish State Church (Religion A), and the latter is pure and true religion of Jesus Christ (Religion B). Since the propositions of the official church are supported by objective proofs including Hegelian philosophy, Kierkegaard provides a corrective to its dead objectivity by emphasizing the subjective role of the knower in the recognition and appropriation of the religious truth, coined by Thielicke as "true truth." He explains, "A truth that may be fixed apart from the subject is not true truth."[63] True truth does not consist of a "what" regarding its content, but a "how," that is, the manner of its appropriation. Thielicke arrives at this explanation from Kierkegaard's own "definition of truth: *An objective uncertainty held fast in an appropriation-process of the most passionate inwardness is the truth*, the highest truth attainable for an *existing* individual."[64] This is not to suggest that there is no such thing as objective empirical truth like mathematical theorems, but one usually just accepts them as personally irrelevant and remains indifferent. Thielicke adds, "Once I have understood objective truths I lose interest in them. They do not affect my existence. They call for no commitment."[65] On the other hand, when I realize that my eternal destiny hangs in the balance of

---

60. Frame, *Philosophy*, 317.

61. Kierkegaard, however, insists "that Faith is not an act of the will" (*Philosophical Fragments*, 77), but the result of one's condition or spiritual state, i.e., a new creature who has transitioned from non-being to being by new birth.

62. Kierkegaard asserts, "No reflection can bring a movement about. This is the continual leap in existence which explains the movement" (*Fear and Trembling*, 53n).

63. *Modern Thought*, 496.

64. Kierkegaard, *Postscript*, 182; see *Modern Thought*, 510.

65. *Evangelical Faith*, 1:306.

a truth that is not objectifiable, "the infinite passion of my inwardness is unleashed."[66] True truth is that on which one stakes one's whole being, yet it is not something which cannot be denied without logical contradiction. It is something which can be doubted, but which is so significant that if accepted, it is done with the passionate commitment of one's entire being. Kierkegaard elaborates:

> The truth is precisely the venture which chooses an objective uncertainty with the passion of the infinite. I contemplate the order of nature in the hope of finding God, and I see the omnipotence and wisdom; but I also see much else that disturbs my mind and excites anxiety. The sum of all this is an objective uncertainty. But it is for this very reason that the inwardness becomes as intense as it is, for it embraces this objective uncertainty with the entire passion of the infinite.[67]

This description of true truth is exactly what Kierkegaard means by faith. "Without risk there is no faith. Faith is precisely the contradiction between the infinite passion of the individual's inwardness and the objective uncertainty."[68] Faith involves the risk of God's non-objectifiability. If we could grasp God objectively, then we would not "believe" but "see" (2 Cor 5:7), and whatever could be seen would be shown not to be God. Precisely because we cannot see God, however, we must believe, and in order not to undermine faith, hold fast to the objective uncertainty. Kierkegaard likens this to being out on the deep ocean, over seventy thousand fathoms. Those in Thielicke's space age might update the image with an astronaut risking the adventure of extra-vehicular activity, floating over deep darkness. True truth exists in passionately appropriating the objectively uncertain.

To illustrate how the infinite passion of inwardness is unleashed, Thielicke is happy to relate Kierkegaard's metaphor of lovers, a favorite paradigm of the involvement of one's entire being. Even erotic love can conflict with objective uncertainty. A lover, for example, assures his beloved of his affection by constantly expressing it to the point of idolatry. Then he comes up with the idea of testing whether she really believes that he loves her. He feigns indifference, withdraws, deceives and mistreats her terribly, to the point that he is unrecognizable by his actions. In this scenario, despite all appearances to the contrary, he then asks: "Do you believe that I love you?" Now she must choose what to believe about him.[69] Thielicke continues,

66. Ibid.
67. Kierkegaard, *Postscript*, 182.
68. Ibid.
69. *Modern Thought*, 510. Here Thielicke draws from Kierkegaard (*Training in*

"She has lost the certainty of objective knowledge. This loss poses a demand for the Nevertheless of faith, the venture of her existence."[70] The objectively uncertain unleashes the full potential for extreme passion—expressed in the "Nevertheless."[71] This passionate venture is exactly what Thielicke persuades his listeners to undertake:

> God's grace is not cheap; it is not handed out for a mere song. God loves those who take the kingdom of heaven by force (Matt 11:12). They are the only ones who then have their experiences with God and know what they have in having him. This is what Kierkegaard meant when he said that God is always entering incognito; he makes himself uncertain and even ambiguous to us, in order that we may be plunged into a concern for him, into an agitated and searching uncertainty and thus there be aroused in us the "infinite passion of inwardness."[72]

Here Kierkegaard convinces Thielicke to consider another obstacle to faith which triggers extreme subjective passion: God's incognito.

God's Incognito

In Hegel's dialectic, Christ is deindividualized and reduced to a representation of the idea of reconciliation, which avoids the head-on collision with the incarnation. Thielicke explains that "for Kierkegaard, however, the eternal God does not merge into a suprapersonal idea through which he might become the object of our thinking. He becomes 'an individual man.' This 'is the greatest possible, the infinitely qualitative, remove from being God, and therefore the profoundest incognito.'"[73]

Christianity, 141). Thielicke also relates how "Kierkegaard can venture the bold metaphor that God practices the art of love. He is like a girl who leaves her lover uncertain whether she loves him in return and who thus stirs him to the most ardent passion" (*Evangelical Faith*, 1:306).

70. *Modern Thought*, 510–11.

71. Thielicke repeats from the pulpit, "In just this sense Kierkegaard says that precisely when I have no objective certainty, when I have no certainty that comes from touching, feeling, and seeing, the 'infinite passion of inwardness' awakens . . . we learn to say in such times of disquiet, 'Nevertheless I shall remain with thee'" (*World Began*, 246).

72. *Meaning*, 92; see *Human*, 266; *Ethics*, 2:241n11; *Believe*, 147, 164.

73. *Modern Thought*, 499, cited in Kierkegaard, *Training*, 127. Thielicke explains that "Kierkegaard was protesting against this Hegelianism when he found the paradox of the incarnation, the supreme condescension of God, precisely in the fact that God does not stop at an idea but becomes a man, lavishing his fullness on one example, accepting an extreme incognito, the scandalous opposite of what reason has always

The God-Man is a paradox with which objective thought, not tolerating contradictions, cannot cope, for it combines that which is irreconcilable like divinity and humanity, the infinite and the finite, eternity and time. The incarnation transcends the competence of objective thinking and cannot be made one of its objects, and it is thus categorized as "absurd" by those outside of faith.[74] In other words, the Logos incarnate has the trait of unrecognizability. Although an undercover detective is similarly unrecognizable, "for God to be an individual man," Thielicke argues, "involves absolute unrecognizability, and therefore the most profound incognito."[75] This unrecognizability is a mark of the God-Man and not the result of secondary causes such as historical or cultural distance. The Man was and is very God of very God and therefore was unrecognizable, so that it was not the rational power of flesh and blood or empirical proximity that allowed Peter to perceive him directly (Matt 16:17). Thielicke explains that for Kierkegaard the God-Man's incognito "is constitutive of his divine-human existence, and we blaspheme and desecrate this if we try to make him directly apprehensible."[76] By stressing the incognito of Christ then, in his view, "Kierkegaard rejects a theology of glory and espouses a theology of the cross."[77]

The God-Man's incognito raises the question concerning his messianic secret. If Christ's unrecognizability makes it impossible for anyone to perceive him, one would ask why he conceals himself as a despised outcaste, why he forbids those who learn his secret to inform others (Mark 1:44), and why he intentionally remains mysterious instead of revealing his identity publicly. Thielicke believes that "Kierkegaard has given us a profound answer to that very basic question: He was disguised in misery and lowliness so that only those could find him who search with infinite passion."[78]

Christ's incognito arouses the extreme subjective passion of the spiritual seeker, which evokes the "Nevertheless" of faith. Yet Thielicke will not leave these three themes, for they are vital to the positive side of his own apologetic approach. In the sermon referenced in the last quotation, he

---

understood by God" (*Evangelical Faith*, 1:81).

74. Kierkegaard, *Postscript*, 183–84.
75. *Modern Thought*, 500.
76. Ibid., 501.
77. Ibid.
78. *Believe*, 164. Elsewhere Thielicke preaches, "He wanted to remain ambiguous. He wanted to stay in the picture-puzzle so that we would have to search for him with all our powers of mind and heart fully engaged and totally committed. He didn't want to be cheaply bought when he himself paid the highest price. He wanted, as Kierkegaard put it, to release 'the infinite passion of inwardness.'" (*Creed*, 66).

breathlessly joins them to the proof text for his modified Pascalian Wager in order further to expound the meaning of a whole-hearted search:

> He who does not give up but keeps at it has learned in precisely such dark times to seek God with every fiber of his being. He has ultimately found God, has discovered his hand waving to him and graciously grasping him, and has then burst out, "Nevertheless I am continually with thee" (Ps 73:23). "When you seek me with all your heart, I will be found by you, says the Lord" (Jer 29:13–14). How else could I put my whole heart into my seeking except by knowing that he dwells in darkness and is not lying about on the street.[79]

Thielicke would persuade a genuine seeker to make a whole-hearted, passionate, "Nevertheless" leap in order to discover the unrecognizable God-Man. For the one who takes such a leap, Jesus miraculously emerges from the incognito of the despised and crucified and suddenly stands before him or her as "My Lord and my God!" (John 20:28).

Historical Uncertainty

The infinite passion of inwardness is also necessary for a leap into the religious sphere because genuine faith in Christ, Kierkegaard stresses, cannot be established on historical evidence. He asserts, "It is true of all historical knowledge and learning that it is only an approximation, even at its maximum."[80] Regarding his view about the uncertainty of history, Kierkegaard acknowledges the influence of the Enlightenment thinker, G. E. Lessing, to whom the Dane devotes a considerable amount of attention. He treats at length the thesis that Lessing puts to Christianity: "Accidental truths of history can never become proof of necessary truths of reason."[81] Writing from a deistic worldview, Lessing argues that the historical events of the life of Jesus could not prove religious truth because religious truth itself has the character of the necessary truth of universal reason. In this he does not claim that the historical record of the miracles and prophecies found in Scripture

---

79. *Believe*, 165; see *God's World*, 128–30, *Creed*, 66–67.

80. Kierkegaard, *Postscript*, 509.

81. Kierkegaard engages Lessing's thesis in the motto on the title page of *Fragments* (Lessing, *Theological Writings*, 53, in *Fragments*, xlix). Kierkegaard asks, "Is an historical point of departure possible for an eternal consciousness; how can such a point of departure have any other than a merely historical interest; is it possible to base an eternal happiness upon historical knowledge?" Kierkegaard raises Lessing's thesis again in *Postscript* (18, 86) which he treats from a subjective approach. He asks, "How may I, Johannes Climacus, participate in the happiness promised by Christianity?" (ibid., 20).

are any less reliable than other historical testimony, for example, the record of Alexander the Great; however, argues Lessing, to base an eternal decision on uncertain evidence is incommensurable with the course of reason. He sighs, "That, that is the wide ugly ditch, over which I cannot cross, as often and earnestly I have attempted to make the leap."[82] For Lessing, the leap is the transition in thought, or decision, regarding eternal salvation, which Kierkegaard in turn baptizes as the "leap of faith."[83] The leap is vital since the phenomenon of Christ cannot be based on the uncertainty of historical means. Kierkegaard thus concludes, "Conceding that the historical account of Christianity is true—then, though all the historians of the world were to unite investigating for the sake of attaining certainty—it would be impossible nevertheless to attain more than an approximation."[84]

Thielicke criticizes Kierkegaard for throwing "out the baby with the bathwater" in his rejection of historical-critical investigation of Scripture.[85] For in his view, historical-critical methodologies serve a significant function in evaluating the material content of Christology. As he states, "To eliminate historical data altogether involves the danger of reducing the material definitions of Christology to the mere assertion that in Christ we have the presence of God in an individual," which reduction he believes happens in Kierkegaard.[86]

---

82. Kierkegaard quotes the German text without citation (*Postscript*, 90; translation mine). According to him, Lessing himself attributes the concept to Aristotle, and excuses his inability to make the leap to weak legs and a heavy head (ibid., 94).

83. Ibid., 15. He defines it as "the qualitative transition from non-belief to belief" (ibid.).

84. Ibid., 511.

85. *Modern Thought*, 502.

86. Ibid. E.g., Kierkegaard concludes that "if the contemporary generation had left nothing behind them but these words: 'We have believed that in such and such a year the God appeared among us in the humble figure of a servant, that he lived and taught in our community, and finally died,' it would be more than enough" (*Fragments*, 130). Thielicke thus believes Kierkegaard has an unbalanced tip-toe theology that stands on a single point, "The *content* of Christ's appearance and message retreats behind the *fact* of it, the fact that paradoxically this individual is God" (*Modern Thought*, 515). Consequently, Kierkegaard can never develop the Gospel in its entirety. Thielicke harbors other concerns about Kierkegaard's apologetic program which he expresses in a fair but "Critical Evaluation" (ibid., 514–19). Though appreciative of Kierkegaard's emphasis on subjectivity, he realizes that its one-sidedness costs a hefty price and questions, "Can there or should there ever be any Kierkegaardians?" (ibid., 518).

Van Til is severely critical of Kierkegaard, to whom he reacts through a critic of his own, James Daane, who wrote a doctoral thesis on "Kierkegaard's Concept of the Moment," 209–15. In the controversy, Van Til asserts that "Kierkegaard does not believe in the God of Scripture" (*Defense*, 209) and against Kierkegaard asserts "that taking the God of Scripture as the presupposition of our thought gives us a sound, and the

Convinced of Kierkegaard's point, Thielicke resists the notion that since Christ was an individual in history, he belongs to the sphere of objective historical research, for in Christ there is the union of the individual and historical dimension with the universal and cosmological dimension. Thielicke thus reminds the reader that "time is in his hands (Psalm 31:15) but he is also in the hands of time."[87] From the individual historical aspect, Christ is David's Son, and, from the universal cosmological aspect he is also David's Lord (Matt 22:41–46). One cannot separate these two aspects of Christ, the human and divine elements, from his person in order to make one element the object of research according to the modern methods of historical inquiry. Thielicke insists that "the universal and historical or divine and human elements cannot be discursively sundered from one another, that one cannot say where one begins and the other ends, or that the one can be grasped objectively while the other is not objectifiable."[88]

Indeed, the trouble in attempting to separate the historical and suprahistorical can be seen in the repeated failures of all exploration in this direction, most popularly epitomized by Albert Schweitzer's *Quest of the Historical Jesus*.[89] All such attempts, however, are bound to fail because there is no neutrality about God, and consequently no one remains neutral about the incarnation of his Son. For this reason, a double bias is embedded in both historical research and record. On the one hand, researchers on a quest for the historical Jesus presuppose that he "is a normal if outstanding figure of history whose depiction demands the elimination of anything supernatural, suprahistorical, transcendent, or divine."[90] This elimination is based on the assumption that the early Christian community added supernatural color to the plain portrait of the historical Jesus, and since that which transcends history has to be mythological, it would warrant any such depiction to be

---

only sound, argument for the existence of God" (ibid., 214). Thielicke believes that it is unquestionable whether Kierkegaard argues for the God of the Bible, whom the latter actually presupposes in his method, as he explains through the pseudonymous author and unbeliever, Johannes Climacus: "For if the God does not exist it would of course be impossible to prove it; and if he does exist it would be folly to attempt it. For at the very outset, in beginning my proof, I would have presupposed it, not as doubtful but as certain (a presupposition is never doubtful, for the very reason that it is a presupposition), since otherwise I would not begin, readily understanding that the whole would be impossible if he did not exist" (*Fragments*, 49). Climacus justifies his approach by Socrates' example who "always presupposed the God's existence" (ibid., 54). Kierkegaard treats presuppositions elsewhere (*Dread*, 73; *Postscript*, 18).

87. *Evangelical Faith*, 2:297.
88. Ibid., 2:302.
89. Schweitzer, *Quest of the Historical Jesus*.
90. *Evangelical Faith*, 2:302–3.

discarded. On the other hand, the quest of the historical Jesus is bound to fail because of the bias found in the actual texts used as the historical record of the quest, namely, the Gospels. This does not at all imply that the Gospels are inaccurate or falsified reports, rather as the evangelists happily admit, the Gospels are written to persuade the reader to believe (John 20:31). The reporters do not write as detached, disinterested archivists, but with intense subjective passion. Like pardoned prisoners, they can only write in stunned amazement at the mighty acts of God they have witnessed in the life of Christ. For them the Nazarene is "the receptacle of the Logos, the universal pantocrator, whom the universe cannot contain."[91] Since the Gospel writers are most definitely not neutral about Christ, their biased accounts "slam the door on any possibility of objectivity" according to the modern standards of historical research, as Thielicke preaches.[92] So he returns to the Dane to express his belief, "That God became an individual man is the *absolute paradox*, as Kierkegaard would say,"[93] which one can only appropriate in a leap of faith.[94] The unsurprising upshot, in Thielicke's view of Kierkegaard, is that dependence on historical research "means trying with the help of history . . . to arrive at a Therefore. Therefore he was God."[95] Faith, however, grasps the God-Man with a "Nevertheless," with the infinite passion of inwardness.

Summary

For Kierkegaard, the incarnation pushes human reason beyond its limits. It remains the Absolute Paradox, the Absurd, the Miracle. In this way, Thielicke would persuade genuine seekers to make a "Nevertheless" leap into faith. For example, when preaching on Nicodemus' encounter with the Nazarene, Thielicke ends his sermon by appealing to such inquisitive listeners: "Leap into the sun, Nicodemus, leap into the wind, for the sun shines and the wind of God roars; for Jesus Christ is standing before you!"[96]

---

91. Ibid., 2:304.
92. *How Modern?* 38.
93. *Evangelical Faith*, 2:304; italics added.
94. "Thus," Thielicke explains, "immediacy to God cannot arise in the static state of a timeless relation, but only momentarily in a leap. The 'moment' replaces mediation. Faith as the subjective side of immediacy to God is an event of the moment when the leaps takes place" (*Modern Thought*, 506).
95. Ibid., 503.
96. *Depths*, 70. Thielicke takes the imagery of wind from Jesus' conversation with Nicodemus about the Holy Spirit generating new birth (John 3:8). He borrows the imagery of the sun from Luther whom he quotes to explain the idea of leaping into the wind, "A Christian is a man who leaps out of a dark house into the sun" (*Depths*, 69). Thielicke also persuades his hearers to make a leap in other places (*Waiting*, 148; *Between*, 56; *Depths*, 77; *Life Again*, 92, 166; *Creed*, x).

Thielicke's Venture

As seen above, the positive side of Thielicke's apologetic method incorporates features of Pascal's "Wager" and Kierkegaard's leap of faith. Thielicke persuades those open to truth to gamble on God or leap into belief, that is, venture faith in order to see if God is and who he is. The theme of venture, however, is not just apologetic theory or sentimental platitude for Thielicke. Rather, it is an existential example of an all-or-nothing gamble that he made literally to save his own life.

During his university years, Thielicke underwent an elective surgery to treat swelling in his thyroid gland, but the operation ended in disaster. While on the table, Thielicke suffered a pulmonary embolism which forced the surgeon to remove a rib in order to keep him alive. After the surgery, Thielicke contracted a postoperative tetany. The illness threw him into terrible fits of tetanic paralysis that seized the respiratory system and brought him to the brink of suffocation. He remembers one such attack, "The convulsion had already agonizingly paralyzed all my muscles and I was gasping for breath in struggle against asphyxia."[97] Calcium injections provided temporary relief until the veins in his arms became so inflamed that it was impossible to continue them. He rotated through university hospitals from one to another—Marburg, Erlangen, and Bonn—but no relief could be found. Doctors made numerous attempts to replace the epithelial cells destroyed in the operation. These cells control the level of acidity in the body. While Thielicke eked out an existence in a wheelchair, doctors tried implanting the glands obtained from sheep, cadavers, and the rare stillborn from the gynecological ward—but to no avail. Thielicke finally received a newly developed, though untested formula, as an experimental treatment. The "Poison" label on the bottle warned the reason why the doctors dared to prescribe only the smallest dose to him. After years of torment, Thielicke confesses, "I drank the whole bottle in despair, I wanted to force a decision: either this maximum dose of the medicine would help me or the 'poison' would kill me."[98] That night he bid his life farewell and stared at the crucifix on the wall in front of him. Upon awakening the next morning, Thielicke was totally astonished to discover that he was not only alive, but cured. The risky gamble for his life became a paradigmatic event that helped shape the positive side of his apologetic approach. "I now knew what *faith* meant"— the "Nevertheless" venture for one's existence.[99]

---

97. *Notes*, 64.

98. *Notes*, 65.

99. Ibid., 66; italics added. A year after his recovery Thielicke lettered in sports. Though restored to health, for the rest of his life he was dependent upon his "daily bread" of Collipian Para-T-Hormone.

7

The Advance of Christian Apologetics

As mentioned in the introduction of this book, the presentation of Thielicke's apologetic reformation is undertaken with the subsidiary purpose of comparing and contrasting him to Cornelius Van Til. For the latter is popularly acclaimed as the pioneer of presuppositionalism, to the extent that even his critics concede "Van Tillianism [sic] is almost a synonym for presuppositionalism."[1] Many Van Tilians, however, realize that the father's reformation of apologetics is itself in need of reformation. Indeed, the heir to his chair, Scott Oliphint, is not shy about the necessity and boldly attempts "to translate much of what is *meant* in Van Til's writings from their often philosophical and technical contexts to a more basic biblical and theological context."[2] A Reformed apologetic requires a "biblical" and "theological" translation of Van Til. We raise the question of whether the unique idiom of Thielicke's apologetic reformation—unrelenting in its biblical and theological form and force—could assist the task particularly along the lines for which Oliphint calls, in order to "take a Reformed apologetic and move it forward."[3]

Footnotes have addressed this question extensively over the course of six chapters. Clearly, Thielicke and Van Til are fellow travelers heading in the same direction toward the renewal of apologetics. Space will not allow a lengthy rehearsal of the parallels and analysis, so we offer a brief review of what could be the most substantial advancements according to Thielicke's own description of his project.

---

1. Sproul et al., *Classical Apologetics*, 183.

2. Oliphint, *Covenantal Apologetics*, 26; see 28–30, 38, 139, 198, 222. Frame agrees that Van Til's work is "in need of translation" (*Apologetics to the Glory*, xii), yet he realizes that some Van Tilians consider his work a revision (ibid., xi, xii).

3. Oliphint, *Covenantal Apologetics*, 26.

Rational Certainty

The agenda of Thielicke's reformation is set by the three problematic features of traditional apologetics that warrant its rejection, which in the scope of his entire corpus he treats exhaustively. The first issue, as seen in chapters 1 and 2, is that it does not hold the conversation from the genuine position of *faith-crisis*. Instead, Thielicke complains, it "speaks from a position of certainty and from its secure position addresses others who have gone astray. The apologist is sure that he possesses the truth and is confident that error is abroad somewhere fairly far from his gates."[4] Herein lies the most significant contrast between Thielicke's presuppositionalism and that of Van Til—the *Anfechtunglos* position of rational certainty. In fact, the exact image of the gated fortress which Thielicke employs to symbolize the unrealistic approach of traditional apologetics is what Van Til coincidentally envisages as his standpoint, "the figure of a fortress or citadel,"[5] that is, "the fortress of Christian theism."[6] To be fair, Van Til would "guard against a misuse that might be made of the figure of the fortress,"[7] which he would not wish to propagate. Nonetheless, we shall capture the common image for the sake of illustrating a fine distinction between Thielicke and Van Til. In addition, to utilize the fortress image in this manner would be hermeneutically safe, for Van Til's concern over a misuse of the analogy is associated with the wrong impression that it might give of a defensive role for apologetics rather than an offensive one. He is not at all concerned that the image could give the impression that the Christian apologist speaks from a secure position within a citadel of certainty, for that is exactly his idea.

Cross versus Glory

Van Til insists that "there is absolutely certain proof for the existence of God and the truth of Christian theism."[8] He teaches that "we as Christians alone have a position that is philosophically defensible" and is "certain . . . that Christianity is objectively valid and that it is the only rational position for man to hold."[9] Oliphint follows closely and claims that this rational

---

4. *God's World*, 217–18.
5. Van Til, *Apologetics*, 22.
6. Ibid., 23.
7. Ibid.
8. Ibid., 133–34.
9. *Common Grace*, 8, 82, in Bahnsen, *Van Til's Apologetic*, 74. Van Til's notion of certainty seems to leave no room for doubt, at least as his use of the term "certainty" is

"certainty should inform part of our apologetic approach."[10] The Van Tilian emphasis on rational certainty, which is indeed *philosophically* unassailable, would cause Thielicke to question whether the Reformed approach is still engaged in activities for which he rejected traditional apologetics. Is the anti-philosophical position still philosophical? It claims to have escaped rationalism, but is it rationalistic? Is the break that it made from natural theology sufficiently radical?

Thielicke's complaint about apologists who operate from a citadel of certainty does not imply that he rejects the notion of certainty altogether, for Thielicke also initiates Christian conversation from a position of certainty. He insists, however, that it is a *"certainty* of the reality of God" achieved through *Anfechtung* and confessed in the "Nevertheless."[11] In other words, it is an existential *"certainty* about God . . . which I cannot establish *rationally."*[12] Existential certainty, that is, the testimony of the Spirit through faith (Rom 8:15–16; Heb 11:1) is categorically distinct from rational certainty which drinks from the well of rationalism.[13] In short, the former is associated with an apologetic of the cross, the latter an apologetic of glory, as it were.

Solidarity

Thielicke would raze a citadel of certainty to its foundation for another reason. For speaking down to unbelievers from an unrealistic position simply cannot foster the solidarity needed to connect with them and win

---

defined by Bahnsen: "The claim that a basis for doubt is inconceivable is justified whenever a denial of the claim would violate the conditions or presuppositions of rational inquiry" (*Van Til's Apologetic*, 78–79n98).

10. Oliphint, *Covenantal Apologetics*, 217n25. Oliphint also fervently holds to an existential certainty: "The testimony of the Spirit gives us an assurance, a *certainty*, that can only come from above" (ibid., 202).

11. *Modern Thought*, 451; italics added.

12. Ibid., 56; italics added. Guinness agrees that certainty cannot be established rationally: "Faith's certainty lies elsewhere than in the rapier sharp logic or the sledgehammer power of the apologist. At the end of the day, full certainty comes from the conviction of the Holy Spirit" (*Fool's Talk*, 58).

13. Van Til bases his rational certainty on the perspicuity of general revelation: "The Reformed apologist maintains that there is an absolutely valid argument for the existence of God and for the truth of Christian theism. He cannot do less without virtually admitting that God's revelation to man is not clear (Van Til, *Apologetics*, 134–35), yet his proof from "the impossibility of the contrary," i.e., transcendental argument, is taken from the Kantian-Hegelian model. "Van Til held that something akin to the transcendental argument of absolute idealism represents the lone valid method of theistic proof" (Bosserman, *Trinity and Vindication*, 79).

them over, rather such a position can often lead to belittling and adversarial conversation. Oliphint himself illustrates the concern in his fictional encounter with Daniel Dennett. He retorts, "Unless you've had your naturalistic head in the ground, you will recognize that . . ."[14] Granted, this is a virtual conversation offered as an example of an apologetic encounter, which for the most part is quite helpful. In reality, such conversations can take a myriad of paths and continue for hours. Perhaps Oliphint is simply trying to keep the reader's attention or inject humor. Maybe he and Dennett are actually acquaintances and routinely jest with one another. Yet in a real encounter with most morally-minded atheists, one would ask if such condescension usually encourages the conversation or completes it. A vulnerable attitude of *Anfechtung*—antithetical to rational certainty—does not lend to antagonism. The doctrine of justification teaches the apologist that the unbelief of a naturalist also dwells within oneself and is a condition from which one has been saved by an act of grace, over which one has no control. For this reason, Thielicke insists, solidarity-oriented conversation with unbelievers should flow out of the radical conversation that one has with oneself about one's own indwelling unbelief, which "is carried on, not in certainty and security, but in *Anfechtung*, in faith assailed and tempted by doubt and despair."[15]

Granted, Oliphint's Christian convictions would prevent him from engaging in a real apologetic encounter antagonistically. He realizes, and moreover, teaches, the importance of identifying with one's hearers in order to win them,[16] but, within a citadel of certainty, an apologist would find a basis to seek solidarity with one's hearers from the philosophers. Oliphint turns to the classical categories of persuasion, particularly to Aristotle's *Rhetoric*.[17] Using the philosopher's category, *pathos*, Oliphint explains, "we are interested in a proper and personal understanding of those to whom we speak."[18] Of course, the question is not about common grace, specifically, whether believers can or should learn from unbelievers. Rather, the

---

14. Oliphint, *Covenantal Apologetics*, 213.

15. *God's World*, 218.

16. "Walk in Wisdom toward Outsiders" (Oliphint, *Covenantal Apologetics*, 193–224).

17. Oliphint, *Covenantal Apologetics*, 136–58. After a discussion of common grace, Oliphint helps the reader "to see them in their proper biblical and theological categories" (139).

18. *Covenantal Apologetics*, 146; see 193, 196–98, 228, 235. On the other hand, an apologist of the cross, e.g., Guinness, abandons the criteria of classical rhetoric since "*Christian persuasion is a matter of cross talk, not of clever talk*" (*Fool's Talk*, 39).

question is whether Aristotle's categories serve to translate Van Til from philosophical and technical contexts or leave him there.

Thielicke, on the other hand, locates the need of solidarity by recourse to biblical and theological categories. One is in the doctrine of justification, as just mentioned. The second is in the doctrine of the incarnation. As seen in chapter 2, the solidarity that the God-Man displays with humanity does not end at the cradle, but at the cross in his descent into hell. In Christian persuasion, then, one shows solidarity with one's hearer by stepping over onto his or her ground for the sake of conversation. Here the apologist "descends into hell" with the nonbeliever as they together face *Anfechtung*, being exposed to the despair of nothingness. Van Til refers to this descent in the language of quicksand. He states that the apologist must argue on his opponent's ground to "show him that on his view of man and the cosmos he and the whole culture is based upon, will sink into quicksand," which sinks of its own weight.[19] Oliphint translates Van Til's notion as the "Quicksand Quotient."[20] In applying it, the apologist shows that "the 'ground' chosen by the position is insufficient to support its own principles."[21] The illustration is useful, but again, the question is, which comparison translates the discussion into a biblical and theological form—the descent into hell or the Quicksand Quotient? Which has greater theological force?

Language

Thielicke is not opposed to engaging with the philosophers or other leaders of competing world religions. To the contrary, in apologetic conversation, he even uses their own language to meet them on their own ground in order to relate to and with them. This tactic, to "baptize" or redefine their vocabulary,[22] is a favorite of Thielicke's. Van Til also advocates using "the language of the philosophers" and forewarns that we must "be on our guard to put Christian content into this language that we borrow."[23] Oliphint translates Van Til's practice into the terms of "co-opted," "adopted," and "surgically removes . . . and transplants."[24] Which term best translates the

19. Van Til, *Jerusalem and Athens*, 91. Van Til also refers to this as removing "the iron mask" (*Apologetics*, 7). He maintains that Reformed apologetics "tears the mask off the sinner's face and compels him to look at himself and the world for what they really are" (ibid., 196).

20. Oliphint, *Covenantal Apologetics*, 76, 85, 115, 165, 221, 224, 228.

21. Ibid., 77.

22. *Evangelical Faith*, 1:80, 100, 104, 125, 202; 2:27, 98, 356; *Trouble*, 35.

23. Van Til, *Defense*, 46; see 60n23, 242.

24. Oliphint, *Covenantal Apologetics*, 53, 148, 149.

notion into a biblical and theological form—baptize or co-opt? Which has greater theological force?

"Nevertheless" versus "Therefore"

Thielicke argues that rational certainty is like the "Q.E.D." (*quod erat demonstrandum*) at the end of a mathematical proof. It is a postsuppositional, "Therefore." It confesses, "Because there is rational certainty, Therefore, we hold God exists." But, in the end, the position of rational certainty does not square with the abnormal reality of a fallen world. Faith exists in the countercausative. It makes a radical "Nevertheless" confession of God's existence against the empirical and intuitive which seem to contradict his being and providence.

Oliphint recognizes that life in the citadel of certainty is inconsistent with life in the real outside world, and, to his credit, he tries to address it. In his endeavor to translate Van Til into more biblical and theological categories, he searches for a basis for a radical confession of faith in God against all appearances to the contrary. Turning to the mandate for apologetics (1 Pet 3:15), he points to Peter's first century readers, suffering believers scattered throughout the Roman Empire, who are persecuted by those hostile to the faith (1:6; 3:13–17; 4:12–19; 5:9–10). In this context, Oliphint focuses on Peter's preliminary command to "sanctify Christ as Lord in your hearts" (NASB) in order to do apologetics. The Lordship of Christ, as a conviction of one's heart, means that "we are to think about and live in the world according to what it really is, not according to how it might at times *appear* to us."[25] Peter issues the command, explains Oliphint, because he "recognizes that one of their paramount temptations is to interpret their circumstances in such a way that would not acknowledge Christ as Lord."[26] Oliphint thus concludes that "instead of looking at the overwhelming suffering around them and declaring that there is no God, they are rather to declare, 'Jesus is Lord.'"[27] Thielicke would enthusiastically support Oliphint's exposition since it reflects Asaph's *Anfechtung* in Psalm 73. Yet, is it an inadvertent concession that the citadel of certainty has a crack in its wall? Would the urgency for such a radical confession of faith indicate the necessity for yet another translation? Does the postsuppositional "Therefore" of rational certainty need to be translated into a presuppositional "Nevertheless"? Or is

---

25. Oliphint, *Covenantal Apologetics*, 35.
26. Ibid.
27. Ibid., 34.

the temptation to believe that reality is as it might *appear*, that is, to live by sight instead of faith, actually not that serious?

Demonstration

A second fault of traditional apologetics, to which Thielicke sets his agenda, is that it removes the scandal and folly of the cross "because it seeks to *demonstrate* the Christian faith . . . and therefore confuses faith with sight and sets itself, not *under* the Word, but rather above it."[28] For this reason, as seen in chapter 4, Thielicke rejects the epistemological methodologies of supposedly neutral empiricism and rationalism which purport to judge the data, and hence God's existence, according to the bar of autonomous science and philosophy.

Van Til's program in apologetics also tacks against the demonstrationism of traditional apologetics. With Thielicke, he sides against the idea of demonstration as the "exhaustive penetration by the mind of man, pure deduction of one conclusion after another from an original premise that is obvious," and therefore insists that "such a notion of demonstration does not comport with the Christian system."[29] For this reason, Van Til rails against traditional apologetics in its attempt to meet the empiricist or rationalist on alleged common ground. With respect to the evidence which the former requires, Van Til fervently preaches that it must be interpreted,—using Thielicke's favorite proof text—"In thy light shall we see light" (Ps 36:9; KJV).[30] Against the latter, Van Til explains that unregenerate human reason is like a wrongly set buzz-saw which can only cut boards "slantwise"[31] (Thielicke expresses the same idea in the radical and offensive terms of "Devil's whore" [Rev 17:5]). With respect to the latter, we must ask again, which better translates the idea into a biblical and theological form—buzz saw or Devil's whore? Which communicates the theological problem with more radical force?[32]

---

28. *God's World*, 216.
29. Van Til, *Defense*, 198.
30. Ibid., *Apologetics*, 65, 140–41.
31. Ibid., 93–94.
32. It should be noted that Oliphint seeks a translation suitable to "a *radical* (from *radix*, 'root') approach" which strikes at "the root of the problematic position" (Oliphint, *Covenantal Apologetics*, 47).

Role of Proof

In the context, though, of both apologists' resistance to neutral demonstrationism, the methods of the two presuppositionalists diverge with respect to role of proof. The difference is subtle but significant, for it raises the question of the actual purpose of apologetics. Thielicke categorically rejects the idea of proof. For that matter, the closest Thielicke ever admits to any proof of God at all—and closely approaching Van Til—is his view of the "history of the impossibility" of modern theology to imprison Christ: "In spite of his repeated imprisonment in systems, the Holy Spirit constantly raises up new theology to break the systems like earthen vessels. The fact that he does so 'almost' amounts to a proof of God."[33] Though the miracle is marvelous in Thielicke's eyes, he will still not concede that it is "proof," for the thought of even trying to prove the hidden God who dwells outside the cosmic nexus is unbearable to Thielicke. Van Til, on the other hand, a champion of certainty who speaks securely from within his citadel, triumphs at the thought. He insists that "there is absolutely certain proof for the existence of God and the truth of Christian theism."[34] He then adds that the Reformed apologist cannot maintain anything less "without virtually admitting that God's revelation to man is not clear."[35] So he offers irrefutable proof of God, his transcendental argument by which he reasons from the "impossibility of the contrary,"[36] a method virtually identical to that of Thielicke's, yet one which the latter refuses to call "proof."

The difference is slight, but serious, for it brings into focus the purpose of apologetics: Just what is its task? Is the goal of apologetics to "prove" God? Van Til answers in the affirmative.[37] Thielicke, in the negative. The difference in their views is a product of two factors: the emphasis that each apologist places on either the objectivity or subjectivity of natural revelation; and, the definition of proof.

Van Til stresses the objectivity of general revelation and maintains that "it is fatal for the Reformed apologist to admit that man has done justice to

---

33. *Modern Thought*, 78.
34. Van Til, *Apologetics*, 133–34.
35. Ibid., 135.
36. Van Til, *Epistemology*, 205. For Van Til, the "'proof' of the Christian position is that unless its truth is presupposed there is no possibility of 'proving' anything at all" (*Jerusalem and Athens*, 21). According to Bosserman, "Van Til clearly indicates that his transcendental method is slated to supply the definitive sort of proof after which Kant had unsuccessfully striven" (*Trinity and Vindication*, 95n30).
37. Bahnsen explains Van Til's view in the section, "The Goal of Objective, Absolutely Certain Proof" (*Van Til's Apologetic*, 78–82).

the objective evidence [of God's revelation] if he comes to any other conclusion than that of the truth of Christian theism."[38] Thielicke also holds to the perspicuity of general revelation. The heavens, the earth, and the sea, and all that is in them are evidence of the Creator. The issue for Thielicke, though, is that the unregenerate person is spiritually blind to the evidence and lives in denial of it. Thielicke therefore stresses the subjectivity of natural revelation which results in such descriptions as "ambiguous," "ambivalent," and "parabolic."[39] For this reason, he believes it is pointless for the apologist to appeal to the proof of God in creation. Calvin balances the two positions when commenting on the evidence of God in creation. He says, "Let this difference be remembered, that the manifestation of God, by which he makes his glory known in his creation, is, with regard to the light itself, sufficiently clear; but that on account of our blindness it is not found to be sufficient."[40] The proof is both objectively sufficient, yet, subjectively insufficient. Both apologists totally agree with the reformer, yet each in his own right stresses either the objective or subjective aspect.

Not surprisingly, the apologists' respective emphases on objectivity and subjectivity informs their conceptions of proof. Thielicke insists that the evidence of God in creation does not convert anyone, and consequently it is not proof in his mind. For Thielicke, proof trades in rational certainty and compels the confession of a Therefore, as in mathematics. "Proof, Therefore: God." Van Til's takes the opposite position, his idea of proof does not equate "objective validity with subjective acceptability to the natural man."[41] Proof, then, for Van Til is "that which *ought* to persuade, rather than as something that actually persuades."[42] So it would seem that the two apologists are at an impasse.

Proclamation versus Proof

Thielicke still challenges Van Til's notion of the role of his proof. To be clear, Thielicke has no complaint about Van Til's tactic of reasoning "from the impossibility of the contrary," for he persuades in virtually the same manner. He pushes the *Anfechtung* antithesis, in application of the Law, steps

38. Van Til, *Apologetics*, 135.

39. *Evangelical Faith*, 1:150; 3:99; *Waiting*, 11.

40. Calvin, *Romans*, 71.

41. Van Til, *Apologetics*, 133–34. Oliphint follows closely, "One's subjective acceptance or rejection of an *argument* is not a criterion of its validity" (Van Til, *Defense*, 126n13).

42. Frame, *Apologetics: Justification*, 58. Van Til stresses that, from natural revelation, "men *ought* to see that God is the creator of the world" (*Theology*, 140).

over onto the ground of his hearer, and "descends into hell" with him or her in order to show the unintelligibility of the position and its absurd unlivability. Just so, Thielicke refuses to call this tactic "proof," for his radical theology of the cross constrains him otherwise. Indeed, a theology of the cross dictates that the apologist's task is not proof, but proclamation! "For Jews demand signs and Greeks seek wisdom, but we preach Christ crucified, a stumbling block to Jews and folly to Gentiles" (1 Cor 1:22–23). For this reason, Thielicke insists that "theological statements cannot have the character of proof or demonstration. They will always be proclamation, address, and appeal."[43] Proof, strictly speaking, is the task of the Holy Spirit. Preaching, or proclamation, is the task of the apologist.

Putting Thielicke in conversation with Van Til, the Lutheran therefore would suggest that the Calvinist drop the rhetoric of "proof" and simply "proclaim" the impossibility of the contrary. In other words, the apologist should "push," that is, "preach" the *faith-crisis* antithesis without announcing, "Now, I am going to employ the transcendental proof of God,"[44] for faith comes by hearing and not seeing (Rom 10:17). Perhaps, then, in order to advance a Reformed apologetic, the idea and rhetoric of *proof* is better translated into the biblical and theological form of *proclamation*.

Counterquestion

The final flaw of traditional apologetics is that it operates in a defensive mode which "proposes to give Christian answers to human questions"—the complete opposite of the offensive counterquestion role of Christian conversation which rightly "attacks the world with *its* questions and forces it to face them."[45] Van Til agrees with the aggressive task of apologetics which is to "*attack* him [the unbeliever] in his philosophy of fact, as well as on the question of the actuality of the facts themselves."[46] Both therefore pursue an offensive method that confronts the hearer's unbelief by challenging his or her interpretive paradigm. So both apologists take a stand on the unbeliever's ground for the sake of conversation, and press the consistency of the person's worldview until he or she can sense the hellish absurdity of his or her own position.

---

43. *Evangelical Faith*, 1:211; *Conversations*, 43.

44. Bahnsen announces his use of the transcendental proof in the legendary debate with atheist Gordon Stein. (*The Great Debate: Does God Exist?* http://www.credo-courses.com/blog/2015/does-god-exist-bahnsen-vs-stein-debate-transcript/).

45. *God's World*, 217.

46. Van Til, *Theology*, 242; italics added.

Model of Method

There yet remains a significant distinction with respect to the primary rationale for the respective methods of each apologist. According to Bahnsen, Van Til's transcendental argument is influenced by Kant's epistemological project: "Kant's *particular* recommendation for doing this was philosophically (and religiously) abhorrent to Van Til . . . but the general kind of program (or approach to the proof of fundamental beliefs) that Kant recommended to improve upon rationalism and empiricism was convincing and effective, according to Van Til."[47] Kant's transcendental analysis investigates the preconditions for the intelligibility of human experience. He calls "all cognition transcendental that is occupied not so much with objects but rather with our mode of cognition of objects insofar as this is to be possible *a priori*."[48] Kant's concern is not so much with what one knows but *how* one knows what one knows. This type of analysis goes beyond the methods of rationalism and empiricism to question what they assume foremost. He thus maintains that the conclusion of a transcendental argument "has the special property that it first makes possible its ground of proof, namely experience, and must always be presupposed in this."[49] Van Til, adopting the method, maintains that "a truly transcendental argument takes any fact of experience which it wishes to investigate, and tries to determine what the presuppositions of such a fact must be, in order to make it what it is."[50] His presuppositional approach argues from the "impossibility of the contrary,"[51] or "possibility of predication,"[52] that is, that without God there is no basis for the intelligibility of anything: reason, ethics, communication, and so on. For Van Til, "the only 'proof' of the Christian position is that unless its truth is presupposed there is no possibility of 'proving' anything at all."[53]

In a parallel fashion, Thielicke focuses on the impossibility of predication without a presuppositional "Nevertheless." In review of the "History of the Idea of the Death of God,"[54] he believes this is where the atheistic worldview self-destructs. Since God as a "system of reference is eliminated

---

47. Bahnsen, *Van Til's Apologetic*, 498–99.
48. Kant, *Pure Reason*, 149; see Bahnsen, *Van Til's Apologetic*, 499.
49. Kant, *Pure Reason*, 642; see Bahnsen, *Van Til's Apologetic*, 499.
50. Van Til, *Epistemology*, 10.
51. Ibid., 205.
52. Ibid., *Theology*, 129.
53. Ibid., *Jerusalem and Athens*, 21.
54. *Evangelical Faith*, 1:232–64.

... the whole intellectual world is broken by atheism."[55] Without God, there is no standard for the intelligibility of existence, for example, meaning and truth. "Radically meaninglessness cannot be 'thought.' What is thinkable is only mere matter," Thielicke explains.[56] So he counterquestions, "Are those who deny the death of God merely dissemblers when they see transcendence here, i.e., the prior awareness of meaning without which the absurdity of self-engulfing nothingness could not be perceived?"[57] Even absurdity is unintelligible without an account of meaning, which is grasped only in relation to a "Nevertheless," that is, to transcendence itself. This notion, of course, is completely scandalous to empiricists and folly to rationalists (1 Cor 1:23). Yet Thielicke pushes the apologetic offence of the cross by inverting Descartes' formula, "He is, therefore I think"[58]—a radical expression of that "Nevertheless which is the basis of the presuppositions of life and thought."[59]

The methods of each apologist mirror the other. The fundamental difference is the original source, or model, for their methods. Which model translates the method into a biblical and theological form? Which has greater force—Kant's philosophy or Christ's conversations?

Conclusion

A comparison of Thielicke and Van Til displays that they are fellow pilgrims traveling the same road enroute to the reformation of apologetics. Further shown is that the unique idiom of Thielicke's venture can serve to supplement the task for which Oliphint calls, that is, to translate what is intended in Van Til from more philosophical and technical contexts into biblical and theological categories (see table 1 below).

With this task in view, Oliphint himself makes the largest leap of all, specifically, to change the name by which Van Til's school is known. Since there are different meanings of the concept of presupposition, as well as multiple versions of presuppositionalism, he argues that the "label as an approach to apologetics needs once and for all to be laid to rest."[60] So in order to move a Reformed apologetic forward, he makes a "case for retiring

---

55. Ibid., 1:237–38.
56. Ibid., 1:245.
57. Ibid., 1:246.
58. *Modern Thought*, 51.
59. *Evangelical Faith*, 3:23.
60. Oliphint, *Covenantal Apologetics*, 39.

the label *presuppositional* and adopting the label *covenantal*."[61] The modifier reflects Oliphint's distinct Calvinistic tradition articulated in the Westminster Confession of Faith. He specifically has in mind chapter 7.1, "Of God's Covenant with Man."[62]

What would Thielicke think of Oliphint's new label? This is not at all a rhetorical question, but it lies at the heart of Thielicke's reformation. Thielicke avoids the term *apologetics* because of its epistemological baggage in natural theology,[63] so he refers to the task of persuasion as Christian "conversation," "discussion," or "dialogue."[64] These descriptors, too, include a broad range of methods and are subject to misunderstanding. Thielicke's new way of executing the task of apologetics correspondingly requires a new name. If he were alive today and forced to christen his approach, could he adopt Oliphint's label of *covenantal* apologetics?

Thielicke would not be averse to using the modifier, reflective of a strict Calvinistic heritage, just for the sake of protecting the ecclesiastical territory of his own tradition. For as already learned, he uses Calvin to supplement his Lutheran theology.[65] Furthermore, the pioneer sees that a presuppositional apologetic is indeed based upon the covenant. In describing the starting point for apologetics in the doctrine of the Holy Spirit, Thielicke states that "faith is simply a ratification of the *covenant* for me. This ratification today, however, is grounded in the existing *covenant*. If I today die and rise again with Christ (2 Corinthians 4:11; 2 Timothy 2:11), this *presupposes* that Christ has already died and risen again."[66] Thielicke agrees that a "covenantal" apologetic "presupposes" that Christ is Lord (1 Pet 3:15), as per Oliphint's exposition—a New Testament formula of the ancient confession, "Nevertheless." Thielicke would thus undoubtedly appreciate Oliphint's new label. Since the confession for apologetics, however, is and always shall be a "Nevertheless," he might simply label his *method* as an "apologetic of the cross,"[67] the *message* of the cross itself putting the

61. Ibid., 25.

62. Ibid., 39.

63. Thielicke cautions, "Here, if we are not afraid of an overloaded term, is the *apologetic* task of theology" (*Modern Thought*, 9).

64. *God's World*, 217–18.

65. Thielicke integrates into his Lutheran theology both Calvin's view of Christ's descent into hell (*Creed*, 130, *Evangelical Faith*, 2:420), seen in ch. 2, and the *extra Calvinisticum* which "is kind of a safety valve when Luther presses the condescension of God to finitude so insistently" (*Evangelical Faith*, 1:374, see 292–94, 345, 375, 377).

66. *Evangelical Faith*, 1:129; italics added.

67. This echoes Thielicke's description of himself as a theologian, i.e., apologist. "We are theologians of the cross and not of glory" (ibid., 2:33; see *Theologie Anfechtung*, iv).

ultimate counterquestion to the world's "Where is God?" question, that is, "Man, where art thou?" With the label of the method translated into this radical biblical and theological form, perhaps then there is reason even for the most committed Van Tilians to look to a Lutheran in order to advance a Reformed apologetic.

Thielicke's Translation of Van Til

Terms / Concepts	From Van Til / Oliphint	To Thielicke
Antithesis	Antithesis	Faith-Crisis (*Anfechtung*)
Presupposition	Presupposition	"Nevertheless" of Faith
Certainty / Certainty's Confession	Rational "Therefore"	Existential "Nevertheless"
Stand / Argue on Hearer's Ground	Quicksand Quotient	Descent into Hell
Use of Philosopher's Language	Co-opt, etc.	Baptize
Unregenerate Reason	Misadjusted Buzz-saw	Devil's Whore
Type of Method	2 Step	Law / Gospel
Task of Apologetics	Prove / Proof	Proclaim / Proclamation
Model for Method	Kant's Philosophy	Christ's Conversations
New Label	Presuppositional / Covenantal	Apologetic of the Cross

---

An obvious benefit of this label is that it is actually indicative of the method; which counterdemonstrational, counterquestion approach can be explained in a few sentences, whereas the label *covenantal* requires more effort (Oliphint, *Covenantal Apologetics*, 38–47).

8

Conclusion

THE INTRODUCTION OF THIS book ventured the hypothesis that all of Thielicke's theology is a participant in reformation of apologetics. Thielicke himself confesses that

> this may even be the particular goal that hovers before the author and his work—that it must take over the task of previous apologetics in a *new way* and perhaps contribute in a small way to transplanting the task of Christian discussion to a different and *theologically genuine level*."[1]

We showed that Thielicke's reformation is mapped against three problematic features of traditional apologetics, specifically, that it speaks from a citadel of certainty instead of *faith-crisis*; seeks to demonstrate the faith according to epistemological paradigms of unbelief; and operates in a defensive answer-giving mode rather than an offensive counterquestion role.[2] The research traced the course that Thielicke navigates away from these destructive features where he discovers, or rather rediscovers, a "new way" of persuasion, that is, a table-turning method modeled after Christ's conversations. This new apologetic operates on the "theologically genuine level" of a *faith-crisis* theology of the cross. The counterquestion approach integrates the counterdemonstrationism of the cross which repudiates the allegedly unbiased systems of empiricism and rationalism. Simply put, the method is true to its own message, which is the gospel of *sola gratia*.

We argued that Thielicke's self-description of his goal to reclaim the task of apologetics holds and provides the interpretive paradigm for his theological enterprise as a whole. This case pivoted around the above characteristics of traditional apologetics which he sees as troublesome, each of which has been addressed specifically in particular chapters. Thielicke responds to the first matter with his *faith-crisis* theology and its corresponding confession of "Nevertheless," covered in chapters 1 and 2; he treats the

1. *God's World*, 217; italics added.
2. Ibid., 216–18.

second issue with an apologetic of the cross, covered in chapter 4; and he responds to the third concern by highlighting apologetics' offensive role to counterquestion unbelief, examined in chapter 5. The remaining chapters of the book served to the supplement the triadic lay-out. Chapter 3 reviewed his accent on the history of apologetics and its failure. Chapter 6 featured the positive side of the Law-Gospel dialectic, embedded within Thielicke's apologetic, which balances his negative table-turning strategy. Chapter 7 answered the relevant question whether the unique idiom of Thielicke's apologetic could connect with and be used to translate Van Til's project in order to advance a Reformed apologetic in a welcome direction. A concise review of each chapter is presented below.

Review of Chapter 1

Chapter 1 introduced Thielicke's theology for apologetics, between which two fields he never distinguishes. For him, apologetics is theology and theology is apologetics. This particular form of theology which Thielicke describes as his own destiny is a "theology of *Anfechtung*," elemental to a theology of the cross. After a survey of Thielicke's corpus, I translated Luther's loan word as *faith-crisis*, the antithesis of faith. We next saw that on a superficial level, a theology of *faith-crisis* seems similar to a modern philosophy of doubt in that both utilize doubt as a heuristic tool. They are categorically distinct, however, for the former is egocentric and the latter theocentric. Indeed, the theocentric focus of a theology of *faith-crisis* makes it vital to apologetics since, according to Luther, *faith-crisis* is what makes the apologist. For it is not until one is in the hell of *faith-crisis* that one can see what is really genuine and come to the truth. At this point, its vital relevance for the task of apologetics was unveiled. In Christian conversation, the apologist must push the *faith-crisis* antithesis through the borderline of nihilism, that is, a complete and unlivable absurdity.

Review of Chapter 2

Chapter 2 articulated a confession for apologetics, the "Nevertheless." This confession is what overcomes *faith-crisis* and emerges as the fundamental presupposition of all knowledge and experience, and thus the presupposition for the task of apologetics. We then considered its source in the paradigmatic example of *faith-crisis*, Psalm 73, which is echoed in a more radical expression in Christ's "Nevertheless" cry of dereliction on the cross (Mark 15:34). The "Nevertheless" confesses the certainty of God's existence, but one that cannot be proven rationally, and hence repudiates a causative "Therefore." Closer examination of the "Nevertheless" showed that it reflects an absolute antithesis, that is, faith *in* God and faith *against* the idolatrous appearance of reality which contradicts his existence. Here we saw the origin of the *faith-crisis* antithesis, the collision between human thoughts and God's higher thoughts. In theological reflection, one realizes that the "Nevertheless" which triumphs over *faith-crisis* is only uttered because of the grace of God that predestines one to salvation. Finally, it was shown that the *faith-crisis* antithesis is expressed in an inner and outer conversation between the natural and spiritual sides of one's personality. This doubt-laden conversation with oneself is what qualifies the apologist to initiate a genuine, solidarity-driven conversation with the world.

Review of Chapter 3

Chapter 3 reviewed the history and failure of traditional apologetics which, according to Thielicke, warrant its rejection. The survey began with those to whom he frequently returns, the early Logos Apologists, the archetypical examples of its bankrupt features. We then rehearsed the philosophical proofs of classical apologetics and their repudiation by Pascal and Kant, both of whom Thielicke believes brought their use to an end. This review progressed to a consideration of evidentialism, specifically its scientific approaches geared toward responding to the modern age. Here it was argued that despite the achievements of stopgap apologetics or even the impressive research of the Intelligent Design movement, Thielicke would say that both fail simply because they do not rise above the level of empirical science and bear witness to transcendence.

Review of Chapter 4

Chapter 4 applied Thielicke's *faith-crisis* theology to develop a "Nevertheless" apologetic of the cross—the polar opposite of an unrealistic apologetic of glory. The latter exults in the supposed demonstrability of God, the former triumphs in the reality of his hiddenness. Thus we showed that a cross-centered apologetic is committed to and controlled by the counterdemonstrationism of its own message. In this way, the offensiveness of Christ crucified is retained in that the method is both counterempirical and counterintuitive. The epistemological paradigms of unbelief interpret this as scandalous and foolish, which fundamentally means that there is no neutrality to the proof of God whatsoever. In this light, we reviewed specific cases of Thielicke's counterdemonstrationism with respect to general revelation, miracles, resurrection appearances, eyewitness reports, and the role of human reason. Throughout the exposition of this material, we saw repeatedly that the ability to perceive God, over and against the empirical and rational which contradicts his existence, is a function of faith.

Review of Chapter 5

Chapter 5 treated the feature of Thielicke's apologetic modeled after the counterquestion style of Christ's conversations, that is, his negative table-turning approach which turns the tables on traditional apologetics. Initially, we explained that Thielicke previews Christ's method in light of its foreshadow in God's first conversation with fallen humanity. In this context, the study displayed that whenever Jesus is questioned he responds with a counterquestion, and thus the conversation rewinds to God's postlapsarian encounter with Adam. The person's "Where is God?" type of question is replaced by the original Law-like question: "Man, where art thou?" For penetrating analysis of Christ's approach, we examined his encounter with the rich young ruler which Thielicke upholds as the classic example of Jesus' style of conversation. Next was a review of the popular issue in apologetic theory regarding the so-called "point of contact," which addresses the issue of how to apply the counterquestion, that is, where to turn the tables in Christian conversation. Thielicke considers consciousness of the moral law and the *imago Dei*. This showed that in both his preaching and persuasion, Thielicke appeals to that "something" which is below the radar of his hearer's consciousness, in the sense of deity that one seeks to suppress and deny. Finally, we analyzed Thielicke's "how to" conversation with Feuerbach, where he models the table-turning method of his new apologetic. Here the study reemphasized that the presuppositional approach, which pushes the *faith-crisis* antithesis of the hearer's worldview, simply focuses on the means by which, and the region in which, the Holy Spirit does the work of regeneration.

Review of Chapter 6

Chapter 6 displayed the positive side of the Law-Gospel dialectic of Thielicke's apologetic, his venture of faith which incorporates features of Pascal's "Wager" and Kierkegaard's leap of faith. Thielicke persuades those open to truth to gamble on God or leap into belief in order to see if God is and who he is. We thus reviewed "The Wager" which Pascal employs in a conversation with a skeptic already interested in Christianity, yet who remains uncommitted and indifferent. Following this, consideration was given to Kierkegaard's influence on Thielicke. The study showed the complex author to be on an apologetic mission that employs an indirect method which previews Thielicke's table-turning strategy. With this task in view, the chapter considered how Kierkegaard persuades his audience to subjectively appropriate religious truth in the context of a dead cultural, or objective, Christianity. Finally, we showed that this risky leap and the above wager, that is, venture, is not just apologetic theory for Thielicke. Rather, it is an existential example of the most significant moment of his life, when he intentionally over-dosed on experimental medication in order to force a live or die decision with respect to a terminal illness.

Review of Chapter 7

Chapter 7 fulfilled the subsidiary promise to compare and contrast Thielicke with Van Til. We executed this in view of Oliphint's call to translate Van Til from his philosophical and technical contexts into more biblical and theological forms. Since prior footnotes provided the extensive parallels and analysis, they were not included in the text. Instead, we briefly reviewed the most substantial advancements according to Thielicke's agenda to reform the three faulty features of traditional apologetics. A helpful translation table summarized these.

The Future of Apologetics

Helmut Thielicke was a wayfaring star—to borrow from the title of his own autobiography—in the brilliant constellation of twentieth century theologians. It is not surprising, then, that critical scholarship has been devoted to his theology in general, specifically to his Christology, soteriology, anthropology, pneumatology, and eschatology; as well as to his ethics and homiletics. There is, however, no substantive treatment in the English language that addresses his apologetic. This void is magnified all the more, given that the scope of his theological enterprise fundamentally was directed to the task of apologetics, that is, initiating a counterquestion conversation with the secular world.

Perhaps this analytical account of Thielicke's reformation of apologetics, and his theology as a whole, could be used in a small way to help reinvigorate Christian conversation and advance a Reformed apologetic. Thus believers in the Lord Jesus Christ can always be ready (1 Pet 3:15) to turn the tables on the world's unbelief.

Bibliography

Aland, Barbara, Kurt Aland, Johannes Karavidopoulos, Carlo M. Martini, and Bruce M. Metzger, eds. *The Greek New Testament*. 4th rev. ed. Stuttgart: Deutsche Bibelgesellschaft, 1994.
Althaus, Paul. *The Theology of Martin Luther*. Translated by Robert C. Schultz. Philadelphia: Fortress, 1975.
Anaxagoras. *Fragment 12*. Quoted in Frederick Copleston, SJ. *A History of Philosophy*. 9 vols. Mahwah, NJ: Paulist, 1946–75.
Anselm, *Proslogium*. Quoted in William Edgar and K. Scott Oliphant, eds. *Christian Apologetics: Past and Present*. 2 vols. Wheaton, IL: Crossway, 2009–2011.
Aquinas, Thomas. *Summa Theologica*. 5 vols. Notre Dame: Ava Maria, 1948.
Aristotle. *Metaphysics*. Quoted in Frederick Copleston, SJ, *A History of Philosophy*. 9 vols. Mahwah, NJ: Paulist, 1946–75.
Augustine. *The City of God*. In vol. 2 of *The Nicene and Post-Nicene Fathers*, Series 1. Edited by Philip Schaff. 1886–89. 14 vols. Repr., Peabody, MA: Hendrickson, 1995.
———. *De libero arbitrio*. Quoted in Frederick Copleston, SJ, *A History of Philosophy*. 9 vols. Mahwah: Paulist, 1946–75.
Bahnsen. Greg L. *Van Til's Apologetic: Readings and Analysis*. Phillipsburg: P & R, 1998.
Barth, Karl. *Church Dogmatics*. 5 vols. Edited by G. W. Bromiley and T. F. Torrance. 1936–77. Reprint, Peabody: Hendrickson, 2010.
Bauer, W., W. F. Arndt, F. W. Gingrich, and F. W. Danker. *A Greek-English Lexicon of the New Testament and Other Early Christian Literature*. 2nd ed. Chicago: University of Chicago Press, 1979.
Bayer, Oswald. *Theology the Lutheran Way*. Translated by Jeffrey G. Silcock and Mark C. Mattes. Grand Rapids: Eerdmans, 2007.
Behe, Michael J. *Darwin's Black Box: The Biochemical Challenge to Evolution*. New York: Free, 1996.
Berger, Peter L. *A Rumor of Angels: Modern Society and the Rediscovery of the Supernatural*. Garden City: Doubleday, 1969.
———. *The Sacred Canopy—Elements of a Sociological Theory of Religion*. Garden City: Doubleday, 1967.
Berlinski, David. *The Devil's Delusion: Atheism and Its Scientific Pretensions*. New York: Crown, 2008.
Bloesch, Donald. *The Ground of Certainty*. Grand Rapids: Eerdmans, 1971.
Boa, Kenneth D., and Robert M. Bowman, Jr. *Faith Has Its Reasons: An Integrative Approach to Defending Christianity*. Waynesboro, GA: Paternoster, 2006.

Bonhoeffer, Dietrich. *Dietrich Bonhoeffer Works*. Edited by Victoria J. Barnett and Barbara Wojhoski. Vol. 8, *Letters and Papers from Prison*, edited by John W. De Gruchy. Minneapolis: Fortress, 2010.

Bosserman, B. A. *The Trinity and the Vindication of Christian Paradox: An Interpretation and Refinement of the Theological Apologetic of Cornelius Van Til*. Foreword by K. Scott Oliphint. Eugene: Pickwick Publications, 2014.

Bromiley, Geoffrey W. "Thielicke, Helmut." In *New Dictionary of Theology*. Downers Grove, IL: InterVarsity, 1988.

Brunner, Emil. *The Christian Doctrine of God*. Translated by Olive Wyon. Philadelphia: Westminster, 1950.

Brunner, Emil and Karl Barth. *Natural Theology: Comprising "Nature and Grace" by Professor Dr. Emil Brunner and the reply "No!" by Dr. Karl Barth*. Translated by Peter Fraenkel. 1946. Reprint, Eugene: Wipf & Stock, 2002.

Butler, Joseph. *The Analogy of Religion*. 1736. Reprint, New York: Ungar, 1961.

Calvin, John. *The Epistles of Paul the Apostle to the Corinthians*. 2 vols. Calvin's Commentaries. Translated by Rev. William Pringle. Grand Rapids: Eerdmans, 1948.

———. *The Epistle of Paul the Apostle to The Romans*. Calvin's Commentaries. Translated by Rev. John Owen. Grand Rapids: Eerdmans, 1955.

———. *Gospel according to John*. 2 vols. Calvin's Commentaries. Translated by Rev. William Pringle. Grand Rapids: Eerdmans, 1956.

———. *Harmony of the Evangelist: Matthew, Mark, and Luke*. 3 vols. Calvin's Commentaries. Translated by Rev. William Pringle. Grand Rapids: Eerdmans, 1957.

———. *Institutes of the Christian Religion*. 2 vols. Edited by John T. McNeill. Translated by Ford Lewis Battles. Philadelphia: Westminster, 1960.

Clark, Kelly James. "A Reformed Epistemologist's Response." In *Five Views on Apologetics*, edited by Steven B. Cowan, 255–63. Grand Rapids: Zondervan, 2000.

Collins, Francis. *The Language of God: A Scientist Presents Evidence for Belief*. New York: Free, 2006.

Copleston, Frederick, S. J. *A History of Philosophy*. 9 vols. Mahwah, NJ: Paulist, 1946–75.

Cosmic Evidences for Christ. Produced by Reasons to Believe. DVD.

Cowan, Steven B., ed. *Five Views on Apologetics*. Grand Rapids: Zondervan, 2000.

Craig, William Lane. "Classical Apologetics." In *Five Views on Apologetics*, edited by Steven B. Cowan, 26–55. Grand Rapids: Zondervan, 2000.

———. *Reasonable Faith: Christian Truth and Apologetics*. Rev. ed. Wheaton, IL: Crossway, 1994.

Craig, William Lane, and John Dominic Crossan. *Will the Real Jesus Please Stand Up A Debate between William Lane Craig and John Dominic Crossan*. Edited by Paul Copan. Grand Rapids: Baker, 1998.

Crick, Francis. *Life Itself: Its Origin and Nature*. New York: Simon & Schuster, 1982.

Cross, F. L. and E. A. Livingstone, eds. *The Oxford Dictionary of the Christian Church*. 2nd ed. Oxford: Oxford University Press, 1993.

Daane, James. "Kierkegaard's Concept of the Moment." PhD diss., Princeton Theological Seminary, 1947.

Darwin, Charles. *The Descent of Man, and Selection in Relation to Sex*. Introduction by James Moore and Adrian Desmond. 1871. Reprint, London: Penguin, 2004.

---. *The Life and Letters of Charles Darwin, including an autobiographical chapter.* Edited by Francis Darwin. London: John Murray, 1887. Accessed May 22, 2015. http://darwin-online.org.uk/online.org.uk/content/frameset?viewtype=side&itemID=F1452.1&pageseq=327/.

---. *The Origin of Species: by Means of Natural Selection or the Preservation of Favored Races in the Struggle of Life.* 6th ed. 1872. Reprint, New York: Random House, 1993.

Dawkins, Richard. *The God Delusion.* New York: Houghton Mifflin, 2006.

---. *River Out of Eden: A Darwinian View of Life.* New York: Basic, 1995.

DeMar, Gary. *Pushing the Antithesis: The Apologetic Methodology of Greg L. Bahnsen.* Edited by Gary Demar. Powder Springs, GA: American Vision, 2007.

Dembski, William A. *The Design Revolution: Answering the Toughest Questions about Intelligent Design.* Downers Grove, IL: InterVarsity, 2004.

---. ed. *Uncommon Dissent: Intellectuals Who Find Darwinism Unconvincing.* Wilmington, DE: Intercollegiate Studies Institute, 2006.

Dennett, Daniel. *Darwin's Dangerous Idea: Evolution and the Meanings of Life.* New York: Touchstone, 1996.

Denton, Michael. *Evolution: A Theory in Crisis.* Chevy Chase, MD: Adler & Adler, 1985.

Descartes, René. *Discourse on Method.* Quoted in Frederick Copleston, SJ, *A History of Philosophy.* 9 vols. Mahwah, NJ: Paulist, 1946–75.

Descartes, René. *Principles of Philosophy.* Quoted in Frederick Copleston, SJ, *A History of Philosophy.* 9 vols. Mahwah, NJ: Paulist, 1946–75.

Diocese of Münster. "Studien zum Mythus des 20. Jahrhunderts." 1934.

Edgar, William. "Two Christian Warriors: Cornelius Van Til and Francis A. Schaeffer Compared." *Westminster Theological Journal* 57 (1995) 57–80.

Edgar, William and K. Scott Oliphant, eds. *Christian Apologetics: Past and Present.* 2 vols. Wheaton, IL: Crossway, 2009–11.

Expelled: No Intelligence Allowed. Featuring Ben Stein. Directed by Nathan Frankowski. Premise Media Corporation. DVD. Rampart Films, 2008.

Fant, Clyde. *20 Centuries of Great Christian Preaching.* Waco, TX: Word, 1971.

Fee, Gordon D. *The First Epistle to the Corinthians.* The New International Commentary on the New Testament. Grand Rapids: Eerdmans, 1987.

Feuerbach, Ludwig. *Essence of Christianity.* Translated by George Eliot. New York, 1959. Quoted in James C. Livingston, *Modern Christian Thought.* 2 vols. 2nd. ed. Minneapolis: Fortress, 2006.

---. *Kleine Philosophische Schriften.* Edited by Max Gustav Lange. Leipzig, 1950. Quoted in James C. Livingston, *Modern Christian Thought.* 2 vols. 2nd. ed. Minneapolis: Fortress, 2006.

---. *Works.* Edited by Freidrich Hodl. Stuttgart, 1959-1960. Quoted in Frederick Copleston, SJ, *A History of Philosophy.* 9 vols. Mahwah, NJ: Paulist, 1946–75.

Flew, Antony, with Roy Abraham Varghese. *There Is a God: How the World's Most Notorious Atheist Changed His Mind.* New York: HarperOne, 2007.

Frame, John M. *Apologetics to the Glory of God: An Introduction.* Phillipsburg, NJ: P & R, 1994.

---. *Apologetics: A Justification of Christian Belief.* Edited by Joseph E. Torres. 2d ed. Philipsburg: P & R, 2015.

---. *Cornelius Van Til: An Analysis of His Thought.* Phillipsburg, NJ: P & R, 1995.

---. *A History of Western Philosophy and Theology.* Phillipsburg, NJ: P & R, 2015.

Fry, C. George. "Helmut Thielicke." Logos Library System. http://biblecentre.net/theology/books/het/het200.html/.

Giberson, Karl. *Saving Darwin: How to Be a Christian and Believe in Evolution*. New York: HarperOne, 2008.

The God Delusion Debate. Produced by Larry Taunton. DVD. Fixed Point Foundation, 2007.

Goethe, J. W. *Faust*. Translated by Philip Wayne. 2 vols. Baltimore: Penguin, 1949–1959.

The Great Debate: Does God Exist? Credo Courses. http://www.credocourses.com/blog/2015/does-god-exist-bahnsen-vs-stein-debate-transcript/.

Guinness, Os. *Fool's Talk: Recovering the Art of Christian Persuasion*. Downers Grove, IL: InterVarsity, 2015.

Hamilton, Victor P. *The Book of Genesis*. 2 vols. New International Commentary on the Old Testament. Grand Rapids: Eerdmans, 1990–95.

Hamm, Jeffery L. "*Descendit*: Delete or Declare? A Defense against the Neo-Deletionists." *Westminster Theological Journal* 78 (2016) 93–116.

Harris, Sam. *Letter to a Christian Nation*. New York: Knopf, 2006.

Has Science Buried God? Produced by Larry Taunton. DVD. Fixed Point Foundation, 2009.

Heidegger, Martin. *Being and Time*. Translated by John Macquarrie & Edward Robinson. San Francisco: Harper, 1962.

Hendriksen, William. *Mark*. New Testament Commentary. Grand Rapids: Baker, 2002.

Hitchens, Christopher. *God Is not Great: How Religion Poisons Everything*. New York: Twelve, 2007.

Hodge, Charles. *Systematic Theology*. 3 vols. 1871–73. Reprint. Grand Rapids: Eerdmans, 1997.

———. *What is Darwinism?* New York: Scribner, Armstrong, 1874.

Hodge, Joel. "Pascal's Wager Today: Belief and the Gift of Existence." *New Blackfriars* 95 (2014) 698–710.

Horton, Michael. *The Christian Faith: A Systematic Theology for Pilgrims on the Way*. Grand Rapids: Zondervan, 2011.

Hunter, Cornelius G. *Darwin's God: Evolution and the Problem of Evil*. Grand Rapids: Brazos, 2001.

Janz, Denis R. "Whore or Handmaid." In *The Devil's Whore: Reason and Philosophy in the Lutheran Tradition*, edited by Jennifer Hockenbery Dragseth, 47–52. Fortress: Minneapolis, 2011.

Johnson, Phillip E. *Darwin on Trial*, 2d ed. Downers Grove, IL: InterVarsity, 1993.

Kant, Immanuel. *Critique of Pure Reason*. Translated by Paul Guyer and Allen W. Wood. Cambridge: Cambridge University Press, 1998.

———. *Critique of Practical Reason*. Translated by Mary Gregor. Cambridge: Cambridge University Press, 2015.

"Kanzel und Katheder." *Der Spiegel*, December 21, 1955.

Keil, C. F., and F. Delitzsch. *Commentary on the Old Testament*. Translated by Rev. Francis Bolton. 10 vols. 1866–91. Reprint, Peabody: Hendrickson, 1996.

Kierkegaard, Søren. *Concluding Unscientific Postscript*. Translated by David F. Swenson and Walter Lowrie. 1941. Reprint, Princeton: Princeton University Press, 1968.

———. *Fear and Trembling and The Sickness unto Death*. Translated by Walter Lowrie. 1941. Reprint, Princeton: Princeton University Press, 1973.

———. *Journals and Papers*. Edited by Howard V. Hong and Edna H. Hong. 7 vols. Bloomington: Indiana University Press, 1967-1978.
———. *Philosophical Fragments*. Translated by David Swenson and Howard V. Hong. 1936. Reprint, Princeton: Princeton University Press, 1974.
———. *The Point of View for My Work as an Author*. Translated by Walter Lowrie. 1939. Reprint, New York: Harper, 1962.
———. *Training in Christianity*. Translated by Walter Lowrie. 1944. Reprint, Princeton: Princeton University Press, 1972.
Klann, Richard. "Helmut Thielicke Appraised." *Concordia Journal* 6:4 (1980) 155–63.
Kuyper, Abraham. *Principles of Sacred Theology*. Translated by J. Hendrik De Vries. 1898. Reprint, Grand Rapids: Baker, 1980.
Lane, William A. *The Gospel of Mark*. The New International Commentary on the New Testament. Grand Rapids: Eerdmans, 1974.
Lennox, John C. *God's Undertaker: Has Science Buried God?* Oxford: Lion, 2007.
Lenski, R. C. H. *The Interpretation of St. Mark's Gospel*. 1946. Reprint, Minneapolis: Augsburg, 1964.
Lessing, G. E. *Theological Writings*. Translated by Henry Chadwick. Stanford: Stanford Press, 1957. Quoted in Søren Kierkegaard, *Philosophical Fragments*. Translated by David Swenson and Howard V. Hong. 1936. Reprint, Princeton: Princeton University Press, 1974.
Lewis, C. S. *Miracles: A Preliminary Study*. 1947. Reprint, New York: HarperCollins, 2001.
———. *Mere Christianity*. 1952. Reprint, San Francisco: Harper Collins, 2001.
———. *The Problem of Pain*. 1962. Reprint, New York: Touchstone, 1996.
———. *Undeceptions*. London: Geoffrey Bles, 1971. Quoted in Os Guinness, *Fool's Talk: Recovering the Art of Christian Persuasion*. Downers Grove, IL: InterVarsity, 2015.
Livingston, James C. *Modern Christian Thought*. 2 vols. 2nd. ed. Minneapolis: Fortress, 2006.
Luther, Martin. *Luthers Werke: Kritische Gesamtausgabe* (*Weimarer Ausgabe; Schriften*). 65 vols. Weimar: H. Böhlau, 1883–93.
———. *Luther's Works*. 55 vols. Edited by Jaroslav Pelikan and Helmut T. Lehmann. St. Louis and Philadelphia: Concordia and Fortress, 1958–86.
———. *Martin Luther's Basic Theological Writings*. Edited by Timothy F. Lull. Fortress: Minneapolis, 1989.
Martyr, Justin. *The Second Apology*. In vol. 1 of *Ante-Nicene Fathers*. Edited by Alexander Roberts and James Donaldson. 1885–87. 10 vols. Repr., Peabody, MA: Hendrickson, 1995.
Marx, Karl, and Friedrich Engels. *Historische-Kritische Gesamtausgabe, erste Abteilung*. Quoted in James C. Livingston, *Modern Christian Thought*. 2 vols. 2nd. ed. Minneapolis: Fortress, 2006.
Merriam-Webster's Collegiate Dictionary. 11th ed. Springfield: Merriam-Webster, 2009.
Meyer, Stephen C. *Signature in the Cell: DNA and the Evidence for Intelligent Design*. San Francisco: HarperOne, 2009.
Miller, Kenneth. *Finding Darwin's God: A Scientist's Search for Common Ground Between God and Evolution*. New York: HarperCollins, 1999.

Montgomery, John W. "Once upon an A Priori." In *Jerusalem and Athens: Critical Discussions on the Theology and Apologetics of Cornelius Van Til*, edited by E. R. Geehan, 380–403. Philadelphia: Presbyterian and Reformed, 1971.

———. "Thielicke on Trial." *Christianity Today* 22, no. 12 (March 24, 1978) 57.

Morris, Leon. *The Gospel according to John*. The New International Commentary on the New Testament. Grand Rapids: Eerdmans, 1995.

Nietzsche, Friedrich. *The Gay Science*. Translated by J. Nauckhoff. Cambridge: Cambridge University Press, 2001.

———. *Thus Spoke Zarathustra*. Translated by Walter Kaufmann. 1954. Reprint, New York: Modern, 1995.

Oliphint, K. Scott. *Covenantal Apologetics: Principles & Practice in Defense of Our Faith*. Foreword by William Edgar. Wheaton, IL: Crossway, 2013.

Othmer, Ekkehard. *Deutschland—Demokratie oder Vaterland: Die Rede an die Deutschen von Helmut Thielicke und eine Analyse ihrer Wirkung*. Tübingen: Wunderlich, 1964.

The Oxford Dictionary of the Christian Church. Edited by F. L. Cross and E. A. Livingstone. 2nd ed. Oxford: Oxford University Press, 1993.

Paley, William. *Natural Theology; Or, Evidences of the Existence and Attributes of the Deity, Collected From Nature*. Boston: Guild & Lincoln, 1857.

Pascal, Blaise. "Memorial." Christian Classics Ethereal Library. http://www.ccel.org/ccel/pascal/memorial.i.html/

———. *Pensées: Thoughts*. Translated by W. F. Trotter. 1958. Reprint, Lexington: n.p., 2015.

Paul, John. *Wit, Wisdom, and Philosophy of Jean Paul Fred. Richter*. Edited by Giles P. Hawley. New York: Funk & Wagnalls, 1884.

Penner, Myron Bradley. *The End of Apologetics: Christian Witness in a Postmodern Context*. Grand Rapids: Baker, 2013.

Pless, John T. "Helmut Thielicke (1908-1986)." *Refo500 Academic Studies*. Edited by Herman J. Selderhuis. Vol. 10, *Twentieth-Century Lutheran Theologians*, edited by Mark C. Mattes. Göttingen: Vandenhoeck & Ruprecht, 2013.

Roberts, Kyle A. "Helmut Thielicke: Kierkegaard's Subjectivity for a Theology of Being." *Kierkegaard Research: Sources, Reception and Resources*. Edited by Jon Stewart. Vol. 10, *Kierkegaard's Influence on Theology, Tome I: German Protestant Theology*. Farnham: Ashgate, 2012.

Rueger, Matthew. "Individualism in the Christology of Helmut Thielicke's Sermons: Analysis and Response." PhD diss., University of Durham, 2003.

Sartre, Jean-Paul. *Existentialism*. Translated by Bernard Frechtman. New York: Philosophical Library, 1947. Quoted in Thielicke, *Nihilism*.

———. *No Exit and Three Other Plays*. Translated by Stuart Gilbert. New York: Random, 1948.

Scaer, David P. "The Concept of *Anfechtung* in Luther's Thought." *Concordia Theological Quarterly* 47 (1983) 15–30.

Schaeffer, Francis A. *The Francis A. Schaeffer Trilogy*. Wheaton, IL: Crossway, 1990.

Schaff, Philip. *The Creeds of Christendom*. 3 vols. Edited by Philip Schaff. Revised by David S. Schaff. Reprint, Grand Rapids: Baker, 2007.

Schweitzer, Albert. *The Quest of the Historical Jesus: A Critical Study of Its Progress from Reimarus to Wrede*. Translated by W. Montgomery. 1910. Reprint, New Orleans: Cornerstone, 2014.

Sire, James W. *The Universe Next Door: A Basic Worldview Catalog*. 3rd ed. Downers Grove, IL: InterVarsity, 1997.
Speier, Holger. *Gott als Initiator des Fragens: Helmut Thielickes Apologetik im theologie- und zeitgeschichtlichen Kontext*. Marburg: Tectum, 2009.
Spencer, Archie J. *The Analogy of Faith: The Quest for God's Speakability*. Downers Grove, IL: InterVarsity, 2015.
Sproul, R. C., et al. *Classical Apologetics: A Rational Defense of the Christian Faith and a Critique of Presuppositional Apologetics*. Grand Rapids: Academie, 1984.
Tatian. *Address of Tatian to the Greeks*. In vol. 2 of *Ante-Nicene Fathers*. Edited by Alexander Roberts and James Donaldson. 1885-1887. 10 vols. Repr., Peabody, MA: Hendrickson, 1995.
Taylor, Charles. *A Secular Age*. Cambridge: Harvard University Press, 2007.
Temptation: Confessions of a Marriage Counselor. Written and directed by Tyler Perry. DVD. Tyler Perry Studios, 2013.
Thielicke, Helmut. *African Diary*. Translated by Word. Waco, TX: Word, 1974.
———. *Being a Christian When the Chips Are Down*. Translated by H. George Anderson. Philadelphia: Fortress, 1979.
———. *Being Human . . . Becoming Human: An Essay in Christian Anthropology*. Translated by Geoffrey W. Bromiley. Garden City, NY: Doubleday, 1984.
———. *Between God and Satan*. Translated by C. C. Barber. Grand Rapids: Eerdmans, 1961.
———. *Between Heaven and Earth: Conversations with American Christians*. Translated by John W. Doberstein. New York: Harper & Row, 1965.
———. *Christ and the Meaning of Life: Book of Sermons and Meditations*. Translated by John W. Doberstein. New York: Harper & Brothers, 1962.
———. *Christus oder Antichristus*. Barmen: Emil Müller, 1935.
———. *Death and Life*. Translated by Edward H. Schroeder. Philadelphia: Fortress, 1970.
———. *The Doctor as Judge of Who Shall Live and Who Shall Die*. Translated by Edward A. Cooperrider. Philadelphia: Fortress, 1976.
———. *Encounter with Spurgeon*. Translated by John W. Doberstein. Philadelphia: Fortress, 1963.
———. *The Ethics of Sex*. Translated by John W. Doberstein. New York: Harper & Row, 1964.
———. *The Evangelical Faith*. 3 vols. Translated and edited by Geoffrey W. Bromiley. 1974-82. Reprint, Macon, GA: Smyth & Helwys, 1997.
———. *Der evangelische Glaube*. 3 vols. Tübingen: Mohr/Siebeck, 1968-1978.
———. *Faith: The Great Adventure*. Translated by David L. Scheidt. Philadelphia: Fortress, 1985.
———. *The Faith Letters*. Translated by Douglas Crow. Waco: Word, 1978.
———. *Fragen des Christentums an die moderne Welt*. Tübingen: Mohr/Siebeck, 1948.
———. *The Freedom of the Christian Man: A Christian Confrontation with Secular Gods*. Translated by John W. Doberstein. New York: Harper & Row, 1963.
———. *Geschichte und Existenz: Grundlegung einer evangelischen Theologie der Geschichte*. Gütersloh: Bertelsmann, 1935.
———. *Glauben und Denken in der Neuzeit*. Tübingen: Mohr/Siebeck, 1988.
———. *Goethe und das Christentum*. Munich: Piper, 1982.

———. *The Hidden Question of God*. Translated by Geoffrey W. Bromiley. Grand Rapids: Eerdmans, 1977.
———. *How Modern Should Theology Be?* Translated by H. George Anderson. Philadelphia: Fortress, 1969.
———. *How the World Began: Man in the First Chapters of the Bible*. Translated with introduction by John W. Doberstein. Philadelphia: Fortress, 1961.
———. *How to Believe Again*. Translated by H. George Anderson. London: Collins, 1973.
———. *I Believe. The Christian Creed*. Translated by John W. Doberstein and H. George Anderson. Philadelphia: Fortress, 1968.
———. *In der Stunde Null*. Tübingen: Mohr/Siebeck, 1979.
———. *Jesus Christus am Scheidewege*. Berlin: Furche, 1938.
———. *Life Can Begin Again: Sermons on the Sermon on the Mount*. Translated by John W. Doberstein. Philadelphia: Fortress, 1963.
———. *A Little Exercise for Young Theologians*. Translated by Charles L. Taylor. Grand Rapids: Eerdmans, 1962.
———. *Living with Death*. Translated by Geoffrey W. Bromiley. Grand Rapids: Eerdmans, 1983.
———. *Man in God's World*. Translated by John W. Doberstein. New York: Harper & Row, 1963.
———. *Modern Faith and Thought*. Translated by Geoffrey W. Bromiley. Grand Rapids: Eerdmans, 1990.
———. *Nihilism: Its Origin and Nature—With a Christian Answer*. Translated by John W. Doberstein. New York: Harper & Row, 1961.
———. *Notes from a Wayfarer*. Translated by David R. Law. New York: Paragon, 1995.
———. *Out of the Depths*. Translated by Geoffrey W. Bromiley. Grand Rapids: Eerdmans, 1962.
———. *The Prayer that Spans the World: Sermons on the Lord's Prayer*. Translated by John W. Doberstein. 1965. Reprint, Cambridge: Lutterworth, 1978.
———. "The Restatement of New Testament Mythology." In *Kerygma and Myth*, by Rudolf Bultmann and Five Critics, edited by Hans Werner Bartsch, 138–74. New York: Harper & Row, 1961.
———. "The Resurrection Kerygma." In *The Easter Message Today: Three Essays*, translated by Salvator Attanasio and Darrell Likens Guder, 59–116. New York: Nelson, 1964.
———. *Schuld und Schicksal: Gedanken eines Christen* über *das Tragische*. Berlin: Furche, 1937.
———. *The Silence of God*. Translated by Geoffrey W. Bromiley. 1962. Reprint, Farmington Hills: Oil Lamp, 2010.
———. "Temptation." *Encyclopedia of the Lutheran Church* III (1965) 2327–29.
———. *Theological Ethics*. 2 vols. Edited by William H. Lazareth. Philadelphia: Fortress, 1966–69.
———. *Theologie der Anfechtung*. Tübingen: Mohr/Siebeck, 1949.
———. *The Trouble with the Church*. Translated and edited by John W. Doberstein. New York: Harper & Row, 1965.
———. *Das Verhältnis Zwischen dem Ethischen und Ästhetischen: Eine systematische Untersuchung*. Leipzig: Meiner, 1932.

———. *Vernunft und Offenbarung: Eine Studie über die Religionsphilosophie Lessings*. Gütersloh: Bertelsmann, 1936.

———. *Voyage to the Far East*. Translated by John W. Doberstein. Philadelphia: Muhlenberg, 1962.

———. *The Waiting Father: Sermons on the Parables of Jesus*. Translated with introduction by John W. Doberstein. New York: Harper & Row, 1959.

———. *Wo ist Gott? Aus einem Briefwechsel*. Göttingen: Vandenhoeck & Ruprecht, 1940.

———. *Zwischen Gott und Satan: Die Versuchung Jesu und die Versuchlickkeit des Menschen*. 1938. Reprint, Hamburg: Furche, 1955.

Trueman, Carl R. *Luther on the Christian Life*. Wheaton, IL: Crossway, 2015.

Van Til, Cornelius. *Christian Apologetics*. Edited by William Edgar. 2nd ed. Phillipsburg, NJ: P & R, 2003.

Van Til, Cornelius. *Christian-Theistic Evidences*. Philadelphia: Westminster Theological Seminary, 1961. Quoted in Greg L. Bahnsen, *Van Til's Apologetic: Readings and Analysis*. Phillipsburg, NJ: P & R, 1998.

Van Til, Cornelius. *Christianity in Conflict*. 3 vols. Philadelphia: Westminster Theological Seminary, 1962–64. Quoted in Greg L. Bahnsen, *Van Til's Apologetic: Readings and Analysis*. Phillipsburg, NJ: P & R, 1998.

———. *Common Grace*. Philadelphia: Presbyterian and Reformed, 1947. Quoted in Greg L. Bahnsen, *Van Til's Apologetic: Readings and Analysis*. Phillipsburg, NJ: P & R, 1998.

———. *The Defense of the Faith*. Edited by K. Scott Oliphint. 4th ed. Phillipsburg, NJ: P & R, 2008.

———. *An Introduction to Systematic Theology*. Edited by William Edgar. 2nd ed. Phillipsburg, NJ: P & R, 2007.

———. *Jerusalem and Athens: Critical Discussions on the Theology and Apologetics of Cornelius Van Til*, edited by E. R. Geehan. Philadelphia: Presbyterian & Reformed, 1971.

———. *Reformed Pastor and Modern Thought*. Philadelphia: P & R, 1971. Quoted in Greg L. Bahnsen, *Van Til's Apologetic: Readings and Analysis*. Phillipsburg, NJ: P & R, 1998.

———. *A Survey of Christian Epistemology*. In Defense of the Faith, vol. 2. Philadelphia: Presbyterian & Reformed, 1969.

Warfield, B. B. *The Works of Benjamin B. Warfield*. 10 vols. 1932. Reprint, Grand Rapids: Baker, 2003.

———. *B. B. Warfield: Evolution, Science and Scripture, Selected Writings*. Edited by Mark A. Noll and David N. Livingstone. Grand Rapids: Baker, 2000.

Wells, Jonathan. "Darwin of the Gaps." In *God and Evolution*, edited by Jay W. Richards, 117–28. Seattle: Discovery Institute, 2010.

———. *Icons of Evolution: Science or Myth? Why Much of What We Teach About Evolution is Wrong*. Washington, DC: Regnery, 2000.

Wolf, Gary. "The Church of the Non-Believers." *Wired Magazine*. November 2006. http://www.wired.com/wired/archive/14.11/atheism_pr.html/.

Yandell, Keith E. "Thielicke, Helmut." *Routledge Encyclopedia of Philosophy*. Edited by Edward Craig. Vol. 9. New York: Routledge, 1998.

www.ingramcontent.com/pod-product-compliance
Lightning Source LLC
Chambersburg PA
CBHW051639230426
43669CB00013B/2363